CASEBOOK SERIES

PUBLISHED

Wilde

Comedies

Lady Windermere's Fan
A Woman of No Importance
An Ideal Husband
The Importance of Being Earnest

A CASEBOOK

EDITED BY

WILLIAM TYDEMAN

First published 1982 by
THE MACMILLAN PRESS LTD
London and Basingstoke
Companies and representatives throughout the world

ISBN 0 333 27322 2 (hc)
ISBN 0 333 27323 0 (pbk)

Printed in Hong Kong

CONTENTS

Part Three: *Critical Comment, 1900–1967*

Part Four: *Modern Critical Studies*

ACKNOWLEDGEMENTS

The editor wishes to express his gratitude to Miss Madeleine Bingham (Lady Clanmorris), Dr Frank Bradbrook, Messrs Christies Ltd (Major William Spowers and Miss Susan Mayor), Professor Leon Edel, and Dr Russell Jackson, for their advice or co-operation in compiling this Casebook; and also Mr Donald Sinden (for permission to print an unpublished Wilde letter in his possession), and the Library Staff of the University College of North Wales, especially those administering the Inter-Library Loan service.

The editor and publishers wish to thank the following who have given permission for the use of copyright material:

Max Beerbohm, extracts from articles in *Saturday Review*, reprinted in *More Theatres 1898–1903* (1969) and *Last Theatres, 1904–10* (1970) by permission of Granada Publishing Ltd; Eric Bentley, extract from *The Playwright as Thinker* (1946) by permission of Harcourt Brace Jovanovich, Inc.; Ashley Dukes, extract from *The Youngest Drama: Studies of Fifty Dramatists* (1923) by permission of Ernest Benn Ltd; A E Dyson, extract from *The Crazy Fabric* (1965) by permission of the author; Richard Foster, essay 'Wilde as Parodist: A Second Look at *The Importance of Being Ernest*', from *College English*, vol. 18 (October 1956) by permission of the author and the National Council of Teachers of English; Arthur Ganz, essay, 'The Divided Self in the Society Comedies of Oscar Wilde' in *Modern Drama*, III (1960) by permission of the Editor; Ian Gregor, essay 'Comedy and Oscar Wilde', in *Sewanee Review*, 74, 2 (Spring 1966) copyright © 1966 by the University of the South, reprinted by permission of the Editor; Christopher Nassaar, extracts from *Into the Demon Universe* (1974) by permission of Yale University Press; Vincent O'Sullivan, extract from *Aspects of Wilde* (1936) by permission of Constable Publishers; David Parker, essay 'Oscar Wilde's Great Farce: *The Importance of Being Ernest*', *MLQ*, 35 (1974) by permission of the author and the editor, *Modern Language Quarterly*; Hesketh Pearson, extracts from *Beerbohm Tree: His life and Laughter* (1956) and *Life of Oscar Wilde* (1954) by permission of the Trustees of the Estate of Hesketh Pearson; Arthur Ransome, extract from *Oscar Wilde: A Critical Study*, by permission of Methuen & Co. Ltd; Otto Reinert, essay 'Satiric Strategy in *The Importance of Being Ernest*' from *College English*, vol. 18 (October 1956) by permission of the author and the National Council of Teachers of English; Bernard

Shaw, extract from *My Memories of Oscar Wilde* (1918) by permission of The Society of Authors on behalf of the Bernard Shaw Estate; Rodney Shewan, extract from *Oscar Wilde: Art and Egotism* (1977) by permission of A D Peters & Co. Ltd; John Russell Taylor, extract from *The Rise and Fall of the Well-Made Play* (1967) by permission of the author; Oscar Wilde, extract from letter to Fred Terry, January 1894, by permission of Mr Donald Sinden; Oscar Wilde, extracts from *The Letters of Oscar Wilde*, editor Rupert Hart-Davis (1962) by permission of the Trustee of the Estate of Vyvyan Holland.

Every effort has been made to trace all the copyright holders but if any have been inadvertently overlooked the publishers will be pleased to make the necessary arrangement at the first opportunity.

To

JOSEPHINE and ROSALIND

who have taught their father
the importance of not being too earnest

GENERAL EDITOR'S PREFACE

The Casebook series, launched in 1968, has become a well-regarded library of critical studies. The central concern of the series remains the 'single-author' volume, but suggestions from the academic community have led to an extension of the original plan, to include occasional volumes on such general themes as literary 'schools' and genres.

Each volume in the central category deals either with one well-known and influential work by an individual author, or with closely related works by one writer. The main section consists of critical readings, mostly modern, collected from books and journals. A selection of reviews and comments by the author's contemporaries is also included, and sometimes comment from the author himself. The Editor's introduction charts the reputation of the work or works from the first appearance to the present time.

Volumes in the 'general themes' category are variable in structure but follow the basic purpose of the series in presenting an integrated selection of readings, with an Introduction which explores the theme and discusses the literary and critical issues involved.

A single volume can represent no more than a small selection of critical opinions. Some critics are excluded for reasons of space, and it is hoped that readers will pursue the suggestions for further reading in the Select Bibliography. Other contributions are severed from their original context, to which some readers may wish to turn. Indeed, if they take a hint from the critics represented here, they certainly will.

A.E. DYSON

INTRODUCTION

The reception accorded to Oscar Wilde's earliest plays could scarcely have been regarded as auspicious, even by their youthfully sanguine creator. The first, 'a drama on modern Russia' entitled *Vera; or, The Nihilists*, its London *première* abandoned in 1881 because of English officialdom's sensitivity to the play's 'avowedly republican sentiments', reached the New York stage on 20 August 1883, but the critics were generally unimpressed with Wilde's attempt 'to express within the limits of art that Titan cry of the peoples for liberty'. The *New York Daily Tribune* found *Vera* 'a fanciful, foolish, highly peppered story of love, intrigue and politics, invested with the Russian accessories of fur and dark-lanterns, and overlaid with bantam gabble about freedom and the people'; the *New York Times* pronounced it 'unreal, longwinded, and wearisome', while the *New York Herald* curtly dismissed the piece as 'long-drawn, dramatic rot, a series of disconnected essays and sickening rant'. *Vera* closed after a week.

Its successor, the inevitable five-act tragedy in Jacobean blank verse, written for the twenty-three-year-old American actress Mary Anderson, fared little better. *The Duchess of Padua*, completed in Paris on 15 March 1883, was forwarded to Miss Anderson with Wilde's assurance that it was 'the masterpiece of all my literary work, the *chef d'oeuvre* of my youth' (*Letters*, pp. 135–42). However, the actress was less impressed than the author, and it was not until January 1891 that the play achieved twenty-one performances in New York, under the title *Guido Ferranti* and initially without Wilde's name on the bills. This time the journals were at least charitable, the *New York Times* concluding that if the poet was not inspired, 'he at least tried very hard to be, and certainly thought he was'. Although *Guido Ferranti* only ran two weeks, Wilde hoped to persuade Henry Irving into giving it a single trial performance at London's Lyceum Theatre, but the great actor was not to be drawn, remarking that the writer had no doubt read *The Merchant of Venice*, and evidently thought little of it.[1]

However, by 1891, Wilde's theatrical ambitions were more shrewdly pragmatic than in 1883, and he now turned his attention back to the theatre ostensibly though not exclusively from financial motives; he had freely admitted to the prospective manager of the Globe Theatre in the summer of 1890:

. . . I could not afford to let my work be quite speculative. If you want a play from me I would require £100 down on the scenario being drawn out and approved of, and £100 on completion of the manuscript. Then royalties of course to follow. If not, I fear I could not give up paying work for speculative. I am always in need of money, and have to work for certainties.   (*Letters*,* pp. 275–6)

It was doubtless an agreement of this kind which was reached, probably during the middle part of 1890, between Wilde and George Alexander, a rising West End actor-manager in his early thirties, who in November 1890 embarked on a highly successful tenancy of the St James's Theatre in King Street. There is an unproven tradition that, fascinated by his effervescent conversation at a dinner-party, Alexander commissioned a play from him on the spot. Certainly, a few days after Alexander opened at the St James's, Wilde wrote with news of his abortive progress on what was to be *Lady Windermere's Fan*, and offered to return an advance of £50 (see Part One: 1 below). But the actor kept faith, despite Wilde's provoking evasions, and the comedy was written during the summer of 1891, eventually reaching Alexander accompanied by the blasé remark that it was 'one of those modern drawing-room plays with pink lampshades'.

Lady Windermere's Fan was first presented at Alexander's now-fashionable playhouse on 20 February 1892. With the public it was an instant success, the apparent authenticity of its intimate picture of high society vouched for by the playwright's familiarity with the dinner-tables of the affluent and influential, and its psychological improbabilities and the antiquated nature of its incidents compensated for by the provocative wit and worldly cynicism of its scintillating dialogue. However, the professional critics were less unanimous in their applause: many viewed Wilde as a mixture of charlatan and clown, an image his brash curtain-speech congratulating the spectators on their perspicuity in recognising his genius did nothing to dispel. If the dramatist's skill in transferring to the stage his own conversational brilliance and personal style of paradoxical humour was acknowledged, some reviewers found the relentless verbal fencing and incessant striving after epigram wearisome, being reluctant to accept the convention by which all the characters were miraculously endowed with their author's flair for coining apt felicities at every breath. Nor were they as prepared as the average playgoer to tolerate an over-familiar story-line and contrived situations, or stock figures whose behaviour was governed less by considerations of credibility

* Rupert Hart-Davis (ed.), *The Letters of Oscar Wilde* (London, 1962): hereafter the abbreviation *Letters* is observed.

than by a need to engineer the requisite quota of tense dramatic moments. The extensive use of soliloquy in the part of Lady Windermere was condemned as outmoded, but the fiercest debating-point centred on Wilde's decision to hold back until late in the action the revelation of Lady Windermere's parentage. Many commentators, like Alexander himself, felt that the audience's ignorance hampered its full appreciation of Acts II and III, only William Archer and A.B. Walkley[2]* apparently preferring perplexity to foreknowledge. Wilde capitulated on the question without rancour, inserting the essential information into Lord Windermere's final speech in Act I (see Part One: 1 below), but the wisdom of the alteration is still debatable.

During the latter part of 1891 he had embarked on a drama as superficially unlike *Lady Windermere's Fan* as it is possible to imagine. *Salome* – originally composed in flamboyant (if not always accurate) French in the hope that it might be staged at the Comédie Française – was rapidly completed during November and December while he was staying in Paris, where his friends scrutinised and improved the draft manuscript. This tragedy of 'blood and ferocity' with its virtuoso central role appealed sufficiently to the eminent French *tragèdienne* Sarah Bernhardt for her to consent to play the part in London in June 1892, but once again rehearsals for a Wilde *première* had to be hastily cancelled, at the insistence of the Lord Chamberlain who refused to sanction the presentation of a biblical subject on stage. 'The whole affair is a great triumph for the Philistine', wrote Wilde to Archer, 'but only a momentary one' (*Letters*, p. 319). *Salome* had to await its first performance until February 1896 when it was rather inadequately produced at the Théâtre de l'Oeuvre in Paris. Informed in Reading Gaol of its performance, Wilde remarked in a letter: '. . . it is something that at a time of disgrace and shame I should still be regarded as an artist' (*Letters*, p. 399).

His chagrin at the ban on *Salome* and his threat to settle permanently in France where an artist was properly appreciated were of short duration, and during the summer of 1892 he was at work on his second society comedy, *A Woman of No Importance,* written principally at a rented house near Cromer, Norfolk. The recipient on this occasion was Herbert Beerbohm Tree, manager of the Theatre Royal, Haymarket, later celebrated for his powerful character acting and for the most lavishly spectacular Shakespearean productions of the Edwardian era. Wilde's piece, which the author later referred to as 'a

---

* A numbered source-reference for a critical writer on Wilde's comedies referred to in this Introduction indicates that this particular written matter is not included in the Casebook selection; details will be found in the Notes at the end of the Introduction.

woman's play', was to have been ready by the end of September 1892, but discussions between Tree and the author seem to have necessitated Wilde's working further on the text at Babbacombe in South Devon where he and his family spent most of the winter of 1892-3. Eventually *A Woman of No Importance* with Tree as the caddish Lord Illingworth opened at the Haymarket on 19 April 1893, and ran for 113 performances.

The critical reaction was again a mixture of guarded praise and solemn reproach: once more the keenness of Wilde's intelligence, the smartness of his repartee, and the polish of his stage conversations were given due credit, but reviewers were still inclined to find the constant cut-and-thrust of the speeches tiring, the 'clever' characters 'too clever by half', and the epigrams too strained and frequent, Wilde often being detected borrowing from his own printed works. 'Epigram, my dear Duke', parodied *Punch*,[3] 'is the refuge of the dullard, who imagines he obtains truth by inverting a truism'; however, others complained that the dialogue was more memorable and creditable than the often derivative conventions of plot and situation it adorned. In addition, there was now felt to be a dangerous division between episodes which made thoughtful statements about the injustices of the Victorian sexual code, and others which many regarded as irrelevant comic digressions where the action was held in abeyance in order for Oscar to indulge his talent as the master of the *bon mot*. For some, not only had he allowed his reputation and facility as a jester to distract him from his graver task, but even in those portions of the comedy where he had given rein to his 'real' subject, there was something spurious about his portraits of aristocratic wickedness and feminine resentment. Nonetheless, although the general view was that Wilde had failed to capitalise on his initial success, a suspicion was growing that, in the words of one critic reported by Walkley, 'hang it all, one can't help feeling that there is more in the fellow than in all the other beggars put together'.[4]

Before *A Woman of No Importance* completed its first run, he was at work on *An Ideal Husband*, planning to entrust its presentation to John Hare, who had made his name as a young character actor in the plays of Tom Robertson in the 1860s and whose abilities Wilde greatly admired. He began to construct his next offering at The Cottage, Goring-on-Thames, which he had rented for the summer; but he was to claim in *De Profundis* that the presence of Lord Alfred Douglas so distracted him that he was later forced to rent rooms in St James's Place in order to complete the work. By the end of the year he had some misgivings about Hare's reaction to his unfinished piece, telling Douglas 'I am going to make an effort to induce him to see that my new play is a masterpiece, but I have grave doubts' (*Letters*, p. 348). When Hare declined the comedy on the grounds that its last act involved too many exits and entrances, it was the romantic actor Lewis Waller who agreed to take it for performance at the Haymarket during the absence of Beerbohm Tree.

An Ideal Husband was finished during the first fortnight of February 1894, and casting was probably in progress by July or August, Wilde writing during this period to an actor friend: '. . . I should like to have you in my play, but I question whether there is a part to suit you. Of the two big parts, Waller plays one [Sir Robert Chiltern], and the other [Lord Goring] has been offered already – and accepted, if the actor [Charles Hawtrey?] can cancel another engagement. . .' (*Letters*, p. 359). At about this time he was preparing to depart for Worthing, on whose Esplanade he had taken a house for the summer – 'very small, and I have no writing room', he complained to Douglas – to which he could escape from the pressures of London life which now included importunate creditors and Lord Alfred's father, the Marquess of Queensberry. In intervals between bathing, sailing, building sandcastles for his sons, entertaining stray boys, and worrying over the state of his finances, Wilde composed the greater part of his dramatic masterpiece, *The Importance of Being Earnest*.

According to Hesketh Pearson's *Life*, the play was originally set in the time of Sheridan and had a more complicated plot, but once freed from these incumbrances and fortified from a stock of his own witticisms supplied by Robert Ross (see Part One: 4 below), Wilde produced the work with some alacrity, concluding the first version in four acts while still at Worthing. On about 25 October 1894 he sent George Alexander the first copy of his 'somewhat farcical comedy' which bore the designation *Lady Lancing* to prevent the proposed title being noised abroad. Wilde was at pains to emphasise that the piece was not suited to Alexander's style of playing or to the artistic policy of the St James's, but this may have been a subtle attempt to stimulate the interest of an actor whose air of 'earnestness' had already been commended by the *Sunday Times* (see Part Two: 4 below). Charles Hawtrey later alleged that had he possessed £50 when Wilde returned from Worthing with the manuscript, the play would have been his, but in any event it is significant that the playwright did not initially submit *The Importance of Being Earnest* to either Hawtrey or Charles Wyndham, the light comedy actors whom he named to Alexander as 'the people it wants', but rather to a manager whose professional standards and concern for detail and finish he clearly respected.

However, despite Wilde's assertion that 'I would like to have my play done by you', it was only as a result of an accident that Alexander came to stage it. The comedy did find its way to Wyndham, possibly through Alexander's reluctance to take a creation which he may genuinely have believed at first was not suitable for his *clientèle*. Wyndham no doubt intended to present the work at some later date, his main preoccupation during the autumn of 1894 being the staging of Henry Arthur Jones's *The Case of Rebellious Susan*. However, the failure of Henry James's historical drama *Guy Domville* at the St James's early in the new year led Wilde to approach Wyndham with a plea that he should release *The Importance of Being Earnest* to Alexander for immediate production, to retrieve the disaster of *Guy Domville* and to enable the impecunious dramatist to realise more speedily the financial fruits of his labours. Wyndham generously complied, and the play was put into immediate rehearsal.

At what precise point in this sequence of events the dramatist was persuaded to convert *Earnest* from four acts to three remains uncertain, but his son Vyvyan Holland has claimed that it was at Alexander's request that Wilde shortened the original text by the removal of two minor characters and some twenty per cent of the dialogue.[5] The principal changes were to conflate the action of the original Acts II and III to form a new second act, and to adapt the final act to harmonise with the earlier revisions. His other comedies have four acts, as do most of the society plays of Jones and A.W. Pinero, and it is unclear whether Alexander considered four acts too expansive for a work of a 'somewhat farcical' nature, or merely wished to make room for an inoffensive curtain-raiser entitled *In the Season*. At all events, no expressions of authorial reluctance, no references to any expenditure of energy or ingenuity which the adaptation involved, survive in Wilde's extant correspondence or in the reminiscences of others.

While *The Importance of Being Earnest* was laboriously being brought to theatrical birth, Waller and his co-manager H.H. Morell were proceeding with *An Ideal Husband*, which opened on 3 January 1895, the Prince of Wales occupying a box at the Haymarket for the occasion. Many reviewers, including William Archer and H.G. Wells, had reservations about the piece, the former noting 'a disproportionate profusion of inferior chatter'; some renewed the charge that the celebrated paradoxes were little more than purely mechanical inversions of clichés. It was again objected that what the *dramatis personae* said possessed greater interest and originality than what they were and what they did in the hackneyed situations supplied to them. Nevertheless, others pointed out that *An Ideal Husband* was a new departure for Wilde in that a strong narrative interest was now present, whose handling testified to the dramatist's ability and adroitness in keeping audiences intrigued and satisfied by more than the exercise of wit. It was also felt that the epigrams no longer conflicted with his more sober purposes, but had been happily subordinated to the legitimate interests of plot and character. However, Bernard Shaw,[6] the recently appointed critic of the *Saturday Review*, was more inclined to praise 'the subtle and pervading levity', boldly claiming that 'In a certain sense Mr Wilde is to me our only thorough playwright. He plays with everything . . .'.

The Importance of Being Earnest opened on 14 February 1895. It is alleged that Wilde's interventions during rehearsals became so importunate that Alexander had to ban him from attending them; but for roughly three weeks of preparation Wilde was in Algiers with Douglas, and his subsequent remark to Mrs Bernard Beere (the first Mrs Arbuthnot) that 'I am hard at work rehearsing' (*Letters*, p. 382) does not suggest that he was absolutely debarred from the theatre. The opening at least proved a total success. A hostile demonstration by the Marquess of Queensberry was averted, and the play voted a minor triumph even by formerly censorious papers such as the *Daily Telegraph* which remarked that the quality of Wilde's work was 'in many respects, brilliant' – even if its critic could not resist the gibe that the dramatist 'refrained from making any comment on the evening's proceedings, and his reception was none the less cordial on that account'. A few reviewers dismissed the play as merely a routine farce in smart clothing, declaring the story preposterous and the tone frivolous, disliking the outrageous extravagance of its personages, and grumbling that Act II was repetitious and Act III too hastily concluded. But only Shaw[7] complained that the humour was mechanical and lacking in humanity: many of his contemporaries found the exuberant gaiety fresh and delightful, 'excellent fooling' in which Wilde's stylistic *brio* and elegance were at last matched with appropriately exaggerated attitudes and an abundance of absurd situations. Linguistic paradox seemed perfectly wedded to nonsensical behaviour, and numerous publications now accepted Wilde as the indubitable successor to W.S. Gilbert. Moreover, the more discriminating recognised that, by his implied ridicule of stale theatrical conventions and threadbare situations, the dramatist had shown himself refreshingly capable of self-criticism. Though many regarded the work as only a temporary escape into 'a world that is real yet fantastic', Wilde's ingenuity and inventiveness were generally as widely praised as they had formerly been denigrated.

Neither *The Importance of Being Earnest* nor *An Ideal Husband* survived long following their author's arrest on 6 April 1895. Alexander's conduct in blanking out Wilde's name from the posters outside the St James's has been excused on the ground that Wilde's desperate need for ready cash made it imperative to keep *The Importance of Being Earnest* running as long as possible, but the policy appears to have continued at least until the London revival of 1914. Wilde, however, bore Alexander no subsequent grudge, and the actor not only made him voluntary payments after his release from gaol, but bequeathed his rights after his death in 1917 to Wilde's surviving son. Waller and Morell also deleted the playwright's name for the last Haymarket performances of *An Ideal Husband*, but to his credit Charles Wyndham, to whose Criterion Theatre the production was to transfer, refused to permit the move unless Wilde still featured on all publicity material. But it is doubtful whether his disappearance from one set of playbills and his continued presence on another influenced attendances: one may note that *An Ideal Husband* only ran until 13 April and *The Importance of Being Earnest* closed on 8 May. However, this is more likely to reflect the popular view of the relative merits of Wilde's last two plays than public response to the fact that his name had, in one case, been decorously dissociated from his work.

'I thought he might get rid of his tomfoolery and affectation and do something really fine', lamented William Archer just prior to the close of Wilde's first trial.[8] Even today this blend of reproof and regret continues to colour evaluations of the comedies, and it certainly infused many assessments of his achievements made at the time of his death on 30 November 1900. Typical was the *Pall Mall Gazette's* remark that Wilde's pieces 'were full of bright moments, but devoid of consideration as drama. . . . He was content, for the most part, that his characters should sit about and talk paradoxes'; while the *New York Times* spoke of him as 'hampered by his utter lack of sincerity and his inability to master the technical side of playwriting'. Since then there have always been those who feel they detect in Wilde a lack of proper respect for dramatic art. Uneasy misgivings that he frittered his talent away through irresponsible indifference to the niceties of his craft have died hard, despite abundant demonstrations of his skill as a theatrical technician. Even two appreciative early critics – Archibald Henderson and St John Hankin – accuse him respectively of failure to sublimate his essentially egotistical individuality to the needs of the theatre, and of manifesting a fundamental contempt for the stage; while, for Edouard Roditi in 1947, prodigality seduced Wilde into deliberately catering for 'the bad dramatic tastes and habits of his own times'.[9] Others have argued that the bad taste evident in the plays (most notably in the sentimental fustian of evidently seriously intended 'purple passages') arose less from carelessness or cupidity than from a deficiency in artistic sensitivity.

To these and other charges the earliest critical accusations that Wilde was pouring the excellent new wine of his satirical intelligence from cracked bottles of antiquated design have always lent credence. Re-formulated by numerous commentators, these attacks perhaps achieved their maximum destructive capacity during the late 'forties and early 'fifties, with such assaults as James Agate's in 1947[10] ('Wilde's plays are, apart from their wit, the purest fudge, put together without any kind of artistic conscience, and using all the stalest devices of the theatre . . .'), St John Ervine's savagely iconoclastic 'present time appraisal' of 1951,[11] or Louis Kronenberger's devastating description of *A Woman of No Importance* as 'a misalliance of trash and wit' in 1952.[12] Indeed, there have been those prepared to deny the plays even the mitigating merit of wit: in July 1918 Upton Sinclair fiercely informed Frank Harris that, far from being imperishable masterpieces, Wilde's comedies were an unmitigated bore, and that anyone could learn 'the trick of taking the simple commonsense of mankind, the moral heritage of the race for countless ages, and making epigrams by proclaiming the opposite. . . . If I had nothing else to do, I could go round jotting down "epigrams" of that sort on my cuff, and very soon have enough to fill four acts of a "society" play.'[13] Even those whose instinctive response to Sinclair would be Shaw's sally ('As far as I can ascertain, I am the only person in London who cannot sit down and write an Oscar Wilde play at will') might confess to sometimes having quitted a Wilde comedy wondering if they had not been merely the bemused victims of some striking but meretricious verbal conjuring-trick.

However, whenever his abilities as a playwright have been called in question, it has traditionally been to Wilde's elegantly phrased dialogue that his supporters have firmly pointed. While early defenders of his reputation such as Max Beerbohm and J.T. Grein commended his instinctive theatrical sense, his nimble intellect, his cynical but playful irreverence, and his capacity for achieving 'the right mean between literary style and ordinary talk', it was above all upon the timeless quality of his finely pointed witty exchanges that they based their case that a stage writer of genius had been among them. Beerbohm was the first of a long line of critics disposed to dismiss as unharmful to Wilde's essential status the often gimcrack nature of his trite plots and contrived situations, the windy rhetoric and unlikely conduct of his leading figures: his linguistic ingenuity and verve remained the key to his mastery of the theatre. Hence for Beerbohm the dialogue of *Lady Windermere's Fan* was 'incomparable in the musical elegance and the swiftness of its wit', *The Importance of Being Earnest* 'a horse-play among words and ideas, conducted with poetic dignity'. Certainly revivals of the latter during the 1900s emphasised how seriously most of its first reviewers had underestimated its durability and potential stature as a comic classic. While the shortcomings of the other society comedies were generally felt to be even more pronounced in revival — 'really the play as a whole is *vieux jeu*', said the *Illustrated London News* of *An Ideal Husband* in May 1914, while praising the neatness and felicity of its conversations — *Earnest* continued to retain its hold over the public for the perennial freshness and *joie de vivre* of what John Drinkwater labelled 'a comedy of pure fun'. And 'pure fun' it has thankfully remained for the grateful thousands who watch it each year.

However, as early as the 1900s, critics (especially on the Continent) were developing the view that Wilde's stylish wit, even in *The Importance of Being Earnest,* had a more central function than the mere provision of 'fun', 'light relief', or even aesthetic satisfaction. The familiar charges that Oscar had been shallow and flippant, that his work lacked 'sincerity', and that he had always been willing to sacrifice consistency of attitude or character for a well-turned epigram, come to be subsumed in the discovery that even his devotees have often seen only the glitter, not the gold. A suspicion has grown that his studied *insouciance* and 'triviality', like his evident fondness for derivative incidents and implausible psychology, may distract us from the true content of his dramas; that the sprightly mockery of his banter has for too long diverted attention from the sustained comedic commentary on the foibles of man and society. Wilde's awareness of the inconsistencies and absurdities of human behaviour, and his veiled but perceptive criticism of the socio-ethical values of his day, were touched on by pioneering writers such as Henderson and Hankin; but more recent commentators have inferred that in the comedies the apparently casual badinage is actually a shimmering patina in which far more significant preoccupations than the paternity of Lady Windermere or Gerald Arbuthnot are reflected. A fresh importance thus attaches to Wilde's far from incidental satiric observations, so that it has even become plausible for George Woodcock[14] to discuss him as a clear-sighted assailant of the upper-class code, or for Eric Bentley to treat him as a kind of secret Shaw, probing the moral and social inadequacies of English society and disclosing his contempt for its hypocrisy and priggishness through a barbed running commentary of only seeming inconsequence.

Others would reply that Wilde's gestures of disapproval are too lethargic and fitful to be truly effective, and that he himself would have dismissed all attempts to credit him with such critical tendencies. Indeed, it might be objected that it is precisely their enviable freedom from the naturalistic obsession with social relevance and 'lifelikeness' which gives his comedies their distinction. As a festive counterbalance to the sombre topicality and raw argumentativeness of more portentous playwrights, his apparent lack of deeply felt concern or commitment takes on major significance, so that in 1914 Harris Merton Lyon[15] can upbraid those dramatists who dutifully concentrate on the drably ephemeral and polemical as the true stuff of drama, and praise Wilde for being 'above the life of his time' rather than of it. The implication is that, although Wilde's men and women behave more freely and mint more striking phrases than do people 'in real life', yet these are only heinous crimes if the sole function of art is to copy nature slavishly rather than to transcend it. Wilde's glittering talk may be irrelevant to his plots or fail to illuminate his characters, but it delights and satisfies the ear as twentieth-century colloquial speech rarely does. Regarded in this light, his 'artificiality', his 'lack of sincerity', his highly stylised manner, become positive aspects of the playwright's rightful prerogative in a theatre no longer committed to the objective presentation of 'reality'. From this point of departure, much fruitful discussion of the formal and dandiacal elements in Wilde's plays has proceeded, and appreciation of his faith in the supremacy of the aesthetic imagination has taken the edge off some of the sharper early criticisms of his work.

Yet it remains difficult to demolish entirely the view that his was a flawed talent. Unfortunately Wilde did not always remain contentedly within the realms of pure art: he felt the need to preach and convert too, and in his first three comedies the stumbling-block to this aim remains his failure to complement wit, keen powers of observation and a gift for cutting comment with a talent for freshly conceived theatrical invention. Some have made light of this: Ingleby urges that to demand original plots and situations of a commercial dramatist of the 1890s is unreasonable; Montague maintains that on the accumulated heaps of stale loans 'Wilde sheds wit and mischief till the old stuff gleams and sparkles'; recently John Russell Taylor has enthused over the bare-faced effrontery with which Wilde shamelessly used worn-out structures on which to exhibit 'a glittering display of epigrams'. Yet Geoffrey Stone[16] has pointed out the clash between the demands of 'Strong Society Drama' and Wilde's deeper purposes, and Arthur Ransome's stricture that too many of his plays consist of a time-worn story carelessly narrated, accompanied by a 'quite separate verbal entertainment' cannot be completely dismissed. Moreover, it is not quite true that, as J.W. Marriott claimed in 1934, 'we don't care what happens if only the characters will keep talking'.[17] It is not only evident that Wilde made it impossible for audiences to remain careless about 'what happens', but that he intended not merely to create a 'strong' theatrical impact but to advance a responsible sociological, psychological, or moral argument which too often appears blatantly tawdry. What Ashley Dukes refers to as the strain of the second-rate in Wilde's talent too often undermines his intentions: scenes, as Alan Harris observes,[18] 'give the impression of coming straight from something in Wilde which resisted all sophistication and went on responding to stock situations with the heart-felt clichés that make the whole world kin'. Nor is the impression of disharmony in his plays simply attributable to the contrast between original mortar and substandard bricks: there is a distinct conflict of tone between the tautly sprung verbal combats which give Wilde his unique advantage over his dramatic contemporaries, and the slack cadences and banal terminology of those pretentiously impassioned passages in which he sinks far below them. Under scrutiny all Wilde's comedies except the last reveal a dangerous tendency to disintegrate.

Nonetheless it is plainly misguided to treat the predecessors of *The Importance of Being Earnest* as a set of unsuccessful attempts to discover a formula which ultimately produced 'the finest as well as the funniest farce in the English language' and 'the only purely verbal opera in English'.[19] Though most critics would regard *Earnest* as superior to Wilde's earlier comedies – still believing that, as Ransome observes, 'the lambent laughter . . . is due to the radio-activity of the thing itself, and not to glow-worms stuck incongruously over its surface' – it is obviously unjust to dismiss the previous achievements as no more than 'trash and wit'. Theatregoers at least still respond to even the stagey clichés they contain, and stricter judges have restored them to something closer to parity of esteem by stressing the presence of those paradoxical inversions which anticipate Wilde's masterpiece. Thus, one of the goals modern critics have been forced to set themselves has been to comprehend Wilde's dramatic output as a totality, and by emphasising the essential unity of the plays rescue his greatest theatrical success from total isolation.

It cannot be truthfully claimed that recent assessments of the comedies have resolved all the critical dilemmas which their many facets pose. Wilde's stature as a playwright remains ambiguous, and his plays continue to provoke controversy as to their true merits, dividing opinions in a manner which one suspects would have proved greatly to his taste. Certainly one of the most helpful approaches to the plays since c. 1945 has been by way of the dramatist's covert presence in his own dramas: a route first sketched out by André Gide in a comment on Ransome's study in his *Journal* for 29 June 1913:

> Perhaps he over-admires to some extent the ornamentations with which Wilde loved to mask his thoughts, and which still appear to me rather artificial – and by contrast he does not bring out to what extent the plays *An Ideal Husband* and *A Woman of No Importance* are revelatory – and I was going to say, confidential – in spite of their apparent objectivity.   (Editor's translation)

On 1 October 1927 comes Gide's remark that 'Wilde's plays disclose, alongside the verbal display which scintillates like fake jewellery, a number of strangely revealing phrases of powerful psychological interest', and these suggestions have been developed by a range of commentators – among them A.H. Nethercot,[20] A.G. Woodward,[21] E.H. Mikhail,[22] and Arthur Ganz – who have variously differentiated the autobiographical traits in such figures as Mrs Erlynne, Mrs Arbuthnot, Lord Illingworth, Sir Robert Chiltern, and even the joint heroes of *The Importance of Being Earnest:* possessors of guilty secrets which involve them like their creator in living double lives from which the author seeks to release them.

This notion has been further developed by Richard Ellmann,[23] Christopher Nassaar, Rodney Shewan and others, who suggest that Wilde views such a sense of guilt as a universal experience, and employs his art partly to make a plea for wider tolerance of those whom the 'respectable' and conventionally minded members of society seek to ostracise. Thus, it may be more fundamental to Wilde's creative stance that he should expose Lady Windermere's inadequate scheme of values and lack of self-knowledge rather than plead Mrs Erlynne's innate goodness;[24] it may even be his contention, as Nassaar claims (possibly too emphatically), that there are no virtuous characters in the world and that mankind shares a common evil nature through which a 'wronged' Mrs Arbuthnot may prove no better than a 'wicked' Lord Illingworth. Perhaps with fresh insight Wilde may be acquitted on the charge that he never transcended his 'stock' materials; certainly the moral complexity of his dramatic universe is only just receiving its due tribute of attention.

The ambivalence of Lord Illingworth as both hero and villain of *A Woman of No Importance* has been highlighted by Ian Gregor, one of several recent writers to explore profitably the role of the dandy, the epitome of proper aesthetic values, in Wilde's comedies. Gregor, Ganz and B.H. Fussell[25] have treated Wilde's dandies (a further embodiment of the author himself) as representing the dissentient voice of the individualist, the artist, the free thinker, in Philistine society,

and studied the problems which their successful integration into that
inimical world poses. This argument has been variously developed.
Gregor sees a conflict of rôles in all the comedies prior to *The Importance
of Being Earnest*; only in an ordered world of 'pure play' can the dandy
truly be master. Fussell shows how, by matching artificial setting to
artificial behaviour in *Earnest*, Wilde anticipates the direction taken
by the modern theatre in abandoning the social reformist comic mode
of Shaw for the farcical absurdities of Ionesco, Beckett and Pinter;
while Dennis Spininger[26] and David Parker have also illuminated the
sense of the Absurd or Nothingness in the piece. E.B. Partridge [27]
characterises Wilde's preference for the world of fantasy as simply the
expression of *sprezzatura* or graceful nonchalance, exemplifying the
aesthete's scorn for the mundane, a blow struck in defence of the life of
the free imagination.

Some of the most valuable modern work on Wilde has predictably
taken the form of a closer and more methodical analysis of both the
theatrical and linguistic means by which he achieved those effects so
often taken for granted in the past. Without lapsing into unhelpful
jargon, a number of studies have assisted us to gauge more accurately
his skill as a dramatic craftsman and a masterly composer of dialogue.
Richard Foster and Otto Reinert have explored the elements of
parody and satire respectively in *The Importance of Being Earnest;*
Harold Toliver[28] and Robert Jordan[29] have re-examined the 'trivial'
and the 'fantastic' aspects of the work, while Geoffrey Stone[30] has paid
close attention to the relationships there between language and
thought. A.E. Dyson has demonstrated how Wilde's penchant for
ironic paradox not only enables him to expose and castigate hypocrisy
and cant, but to challenge our own attitudes and habits of thought;
and L.A. Poague[31] has also developed the enquiry into this aspect.
Explorations of the analogies between Wilde's plays and Restoration
comedy by James M. Ware,[32] Parker, Shewan and others have related
his art to a recognised tradition.

If *The Importance of Being Earnest* – with its complexities of *genre*,
meaning, tone, structure and stylistic texture – has received the
lion's share of attention in recent years and thus emerges with
enhanced status, what modern investigations and discussions of all the
plays reveal most clearly is that there are still richer strata of meaning
and interest to be uncovered than former commentators ever dreamed
of. The appearance of books devoted exclusively to the plays is further
testimony to the unguessed depths these works continue to disclose.
We should not yet rest content therefore with any suggestion that
Wilde's dramatic achievement has been finally and definitively asses-
sed. When all the reservations and rejections have been voiced, his

comedies still possess sufficient merit and vitality to enable them to be enjoyed in the theatre, to stimulate debate outside it, and to survive into the foreseeable future. On 2 March 1895 *Punch*, in reviewing *The Rivals* at Cambridge, enquired rhetorically:

> Will the elaborate Wildean paradoxes have to a future generation the freshness and laughter-provoking qualities of Mrs Malaprop's derangements? I doubt it. At Cambridge the other day I saw a learned Doctor of Letters in convulsions over the Malapropian sallies. Will a Doctor of Letters towards the end of the next century be seen to smile over OSCAR's inversions?

Perhaps a Bachelor of Letters, albeit an Oxonian, may dare to reply in the affirmative.

NOTES

1. Laurence Irving, *Henry Irving: The Actor and His World* (London, 1951), p. 536.
2. A.B. Walkley, in *The Speaker* (27 Feb. 1892), pp. 257–8.
3. *Punch* (29 Apr. 1893), p. 193.
4. *The Speaker* (29 Apr. 1893), pp. 484–5.
5. Vyvyan Holland in his Explanatory Foreword to *The Original Four-Act Version of 'The Importance of Being Earnest'* (London, 1957), pp. *v–vii*. The most reliable text of 'the four-act version' is contained in Sarah Augusta Dickson's two-volume edition (New York, 1956).
6. G. Bernard Shaw, in *The Saturday Review* (12 Jan. 1895), pp. 4–5.
7. Ibid. (23 Feb. 1895), pp. 249–50.
8. William Archer, letter to Charles Archer (1 May 1895), printed in Karl Beckson (ed.), *Oscar Wilde: The Critical Heritage* (London, 1970), p. 201.
9. Edouard Roditi, *Oscar Wilde* (Norfolk, Conn., 1947).
10. James Agate, 'Wilde and the Theatre', *Masque*, 3 (1947), pp. 5–23.
11. St John Ervine, *Oscar Wilde: A Present-Time Appraisal* (London, 1951).
12. Louis Kronenberger, *The Thread of Laughter* (New York, 1952), p. 222.
13. Upton Sinclair, in *Pearson's Magazine*, XXXIX (July 1918), pp. 167–9; reprinted in Beckson, op. cit., pp. 389–93.
14. George Woodcock, *The Paradox of Oscar Wilde* (London and New York), 1949.
15. Harris Merton Lyon, in *Green Book Magazine* (Nov. 1914).
16. Geoffrey Stone, 'Serious Bunburyism: The Logic of *The Importance of Being Earnest*', *Essays in Criticism*, XXVI (1976), pp. 28–41.
17. J.W. Marriott, *Modern Drama* (London, [1934]), p. 104.
18. Alan Harris, 'Oscar Wilde as Playwright: A Centenary View', *Adelphi*, XXX (1954), pp. 212–40; quote from p. 224.
19. '. . . funniest farce . . .': J.W. Krutch, in *The Nation* (16 Oct. 1954), pp. 331–2; '. . . verbal opera . . .': W.H. Auden, in *The New Yorker* (9 Mar. 1963), pp. 155–77.
20. Arthur H. Nethercot, 'Oscar Wilde and the Devil's Advocate', *PMLA*, LIX (1944), pp. 833–50.
21. A.G. Woodward, 'Oscar Wilde', *English Studies in Africa*, II (1959), pp. 218–31.
22. E.H. Mikhail, 'Self-Revelation in *An Ideal Husband*', *Modern Drama*, XI (1968–69), pp. 180–6.

23. Richard Ellmann, 'Romantic Pantomime in Wilde', *Partisan Review*, XXX (1963), pp. 342–55.

24. See also Morse Peckham, 'What did Lady Windermere Learn?', *College English*, XVII (1956), pp. 11–14, for the suggestion that the rigidly moral Lady Windermere fails to profit from Mrs Erlynne's maternal gesture.

25. B.H. Fussell, 'The Masks of Oscar Wilde', *Sewanee Review*, LXXX (1972), pp. 124–39.

26. Dennis J. Spininger, 'Profiles and Principles: The Sense of the Absurd in *The Importance of Being Earnest*', *Papers on Language and Literature*, XII (1976), pp. 49–72.

27. E.B. Partridge, 'The Importance of Not Being Earnest', *Bucknell Review*, IX (1960–61), pp. 143–58.

28. Harold E. Toliver, 'Wilde and the Importance of "Sincere and Studied Triviality"', *Modern Drama*, 5 (1963), pp. 389–99.

29. Robert J. Jordan, 'Satire and Fantasy in Wilde's *The Importance of Being Earnest*', *Ariel:* I, 3 (1970), pp. 101–9.

30. Geoffrey Stone, op. cit. (Note 16 above).

31. L.A. Poague, '*The Importance of Being Earnest*: The Texture of Wilde's Irony', *Modern Drama*, 16 (1973), pp. 251–7.

32. James M. Ware, 'Algernon's Appetite: Oscar Wilde's Hero as Restoration Dandy', *English Literature in Transition*, XIII (1970), pp. 17–26.

PART ONE

Creation and Reception

1. *LADY WINDERMERE'S FAN* (1891–93)

WILDE TO GEORGE ALEXANDER, 2 February 1891

. . . I am not satisfied with myself or my work. I can't get a grip of the play yet: I can't get my people real. The fact is I worked at it when I was not in the mood for work, and must first forget it, and then go back quite fresh to it. I am very sorry, but artistic work can't be done unless one is in the mood; certainly my work can't. Sometimes I spend months over a thing, and don't do any good; at other times I write a thing in a fortnight. . . .

With regard to the cheque for £50 you gave me, shall I return you the money, and end the agreement, or keep it and when the play is written let you have the rights and refusal of it? That will be just as you wish. . . .

SOURCE: *Letters,* * p. 282.

GEORGE ALEXANDER TO WILDE, *c.* February 1892

. . . The end of the 2nd act is now better, but it would be better still and you could make it so if you took the trouble. I have pointed this out to you at almost every rehearsal but you only received my suggestions with contempt. . . .

I am perfectly certain, too, that for the good of the play the audience should know very early in the second act, or at any rate at the end of it, that Mrs Erlynne is the mother – this too I have impressed upon you over and over again, but you have refused even to discuss it. The interest would be increased by this knowledge and Mrs Erlynne and Lord Windermere would not be in a false position. . . .

SOURCE: quoted in A. E. W. Mason, *Sir George Alexander and the St James's Theatre* (London, 1925), pp. 36, 37–8.

* Rupert Hart-Davis (ed.), *The Letters of Oscar Wilde* (London, 1962): the abbreviation *Letters* is observed throughout Part One.

WILDE TO GEORGE ALEXANDER, mid-February 1892

. . . With regard to the speech of Mrs Erlynne at the end of Act II, you must remember that until Wednesday night Mrs Erlynne rushed off the stage leaving Lord Augustus in a state of bewilderment. Such are the stage directions in the play. When the alteration in the business was made I don't know, but I should have been informed at once. It came on me with the shock of a surprise. I don't in any degree object to it. It is a different effect, that is all. It does not alter the psychological lines of the play. . . . To reproach me on Wednesday for not having written a speech for a situation on which I was not consulted and of which I was quite unaware was, of course, a wrong thing to do. With regard to the new speech written yesterday, personally I think it adequate. I want Mrs Erlynne's whole scene with Lord Augustus to be a 'tornado' scene, and the thing to go as quickly as possible. However, I will think over the speech, and talk it over with Miss Terry[1]. Had I been informed of the change I would of course have had more time and when, through illness caused by the worry and anxiety I have gone through at the theatre, I was unable to attend the rehearsals on Monday and Tuesday, I should have been informed by letter.

With regard to your other suggestion about the disclosure of the secret of the play in the second act, had I intended to let out the secret, which is the element of suspense and curiosity, a quality so essentially dramatic, I would have written the play on entirely different lines. I would have made Mrs Erlynne a vulgar horrid woman and struck out the incident of the fan. The audience must not know till the last act that the woman Lady Windermere proposed to strike with her fan was her own mother. The note would be too harsh, too horrible. When they learn it, it is after Lady Windermere has left her husband's house to seek the protection of another man, and their interest is concentrated on Mrs Erlynne, to whom dramatically speaking belongs the last act. Also it would destroy the dramatic wonder excited by the incident of Mrs Erlynne taking the letter and opening it and sacrificing herself in the third act. If they knew Mrs Erlynne was the mother, there would be no surprise in her sacrifice – it would be expected. But in my play the sacrifice is dramatic and unexpected. The cry with which Mrs Erlynne flies into the other room on hearing Lord Augustus's voice, the wild pathetic cry of self-preservation, 'Then it is I who am lost!' would be repulsive coming from the lips of one known to be the mother by the audience. It seems natural and is very dramatic coming from one who seems to be an adventuress, and who while anxious to save Lady Windermere thinks of her own safety when a crisis comes. Also it would destroy the last act: and the chief merit of my last act is to me the fact that it does not contain, as most plays do, the explanation of what the audience knows already, but that it is the sudden explanation of what the audience desires to know, followed immediately by the revelation of a character as yet untouched by literature.

The question you touch on about the audience misinterpreting the relations of Lord Windermere and Mrs Erlynne depends entirely on the acting. In the first act Windermere must convince the audience of his absolute sincerity in what he says to his wife. The lines show this. He does not say to his wife 'there is nothing in this woman's past life that is against her;' he says openly, 'Mrs Erlynne years ago sinned. She now wants to get back. Help her to get back.' The suggestions his wife makes he doesn't treat trivially and say, 'Oh, there is nothing in it. We're merely friends, that is all.' He rejects them with horror at the suggestion.

At the ball his manner to her is cold, courteous but somewhat hard — not the manner of a lover. When they think they are alone Windermere uses no word of tenderness or love. He shows that the woman has a hold on him, but one he loathes and almost writhes under.

What is this hold? That is the play.

I have entered at great length into this matter because every suggestion you have made to me I have always carefully and intellectually considered. Otherwise it would have been sufficient to have said, what I am sure you yourself will on reflection recognise, and that is that a work of art wrought out on definite lines, and elaborated from one definite artistic standpoint, cannot be suddenly altered. It would make every line meaningless, and rob each situation of its value. An equally good play could be written in which the audience would know beforehand who Mrs Erlynne really was, but it would require completely different dialogue, and completely different situations. I have built my house on a certain foundation, and this foundation cannot be altered. I can say no more. . . .[2]

SOURCE: *Letters*, pp. 308–9.

NOTES

1. Marion Terry (1858–1930) who played Mrs Erlynne; she was the younger sister of the more celebrated Ellen Terry. [Ed.]

2. Following newspaper criticisms (see Part Two: 1 below), Wilde altered Lord Windermere's penultimate sentence in Act I to 'I dare not tell her this woman

is her own mother!'; but the wisdom of revealing Lady Windermere's parentage so early remains a matter for debate. [Ed].

HENRY JAMES TO MRS HUGH BELL, 23 February 1892

. . . Oscar's play (I was there on Saturday)[1] strikes me as a mixture that will run (I feel as if I were talking to a laundress), though infantine to my sense, both in subject and in form. As a drama it is of a candid and primitive simplicity, with a perfectly reminiscential air about it – as [of] things *qui ont traîné* [which have been met with before],* that one has always seen in plays. In short it doesn't, from that point of view, bear analysis or discussion. But there is so much drollery – that is 'cheeky' paradoxical wit of dialogue, and the pit and gallery are so pleased at finding themselves clever enough to 'catch on' to four or five of the ingenious – too ingenious – *mots* in the dozen, that it makes them feel quite 'décadent' and raffiné [able to appreciate subtlety] and they enjoy the sensation as a change from the stodgy. Moreover they think they are hearing the talk of the *grand monde* (poor old *grand monde*) and altogether feel privileged and modern. There is a perpetual attempt at *mots* and many of them *rater* [misfire]: but those that hit are very good indeed. This will make, I think, a success – possibly a really long run (I mean through the Season) for the play. There is of course absolutely no characterization and all the people talk equally strained Oscar – but there is a 'situation' (at the end of Act III) that one has seen from the cradle, and the thing is conveniently acted. The 'impudent' speech at the end was simply inevitable mechanical Oscar – I mean the usual trick of saying the unusual – complimenting himself and his play. It was what he was there for and I can't conceive the density of those who seriously reprobate it. The tone of the virtuous journals makes me despair of our stupid humanity. Everything Oscar does is a deliberate trap for the literalist, and to see the literalist walk straight up to it, look straight at it and step straight into it, makes one freshly avert a discouraged gaze from that unspeakable animal. . . .

SOURCE: Leon Edel (ed.), *Henry James: Letters, III* (Cambridge, Mass., 1980; London, 1981).

* Words within square brackets are inserted for clarification, here and elsewhere in the selection.

NOTE

1. By 1892 James had lived intermittently in England for sixteen years, and his observations on the English theatre and drama at this period are invaluable. [Ed.]

WILDE TO THE EDITOR, *ST JAMES'S GAZETTE,* 27 February 1892

Allow me to correct a statement put forward in your issue of this evening, to the effect that I have made a certain alteration in my play in consequence of the criticism of some journalists who write very recklessly and very foolishly in the papers about dramatic art. This statement is entirely untrue, and grossly ridiculous[1].

The facts are as follows. On last Saturday night, after the play was over, and the author, cigarette in hand, had delivered a delightful and immortal speech, I had the pleasure of entertaining at supper a small number of personal friends: and, as none of them was older than myself, I naturally listened to their artistic views with attention and pleasure. The opinions of the old on matters of Art are, of course, of no value whatsoever. The artistic instincts of the young are invariably fascinating; and I am bound to state that all my friends, without exception, were of opinion that the psychological interest of the second act would be greatly increased by the disclosure of the actual relationship existing between Lady Windermere and Mrs Erlynne – an opinion, I may add, that had previously been strongly held and urged by Mr Alexander. As to those of us who do not look on a play as a mere question of pantomime and clowning, psychological interest is everything, I determined consequently to make a change in the precise moment of revelation. This determination, however, was entered into long before I had the opportunity of studying the culture, courtesy, and critical faculty displayed in such papers as the *Referee, Reynolds,* and the *Sunday Sun.* . . .

SOURCE: *Letters,* pp. 312–13.

NOTE

1. *St James's Gazette* (26 Feb. 1892), p.6: 'Mr Oscar Wilde, it appears, is open to conviction. Determined, on one point at least, to be unconventional, he withheld from his audience all information regarding the relationship existing between Lady Windermere and Mrs Erlynne almost until the end of his play produced on Saturday evening at the St James's. But the critics have proved too strong for him, and the secret is now disclosed in the first act. The sacrifice has not been made in vain, for the piece

gains vastly by the alteration, however the author's views may have been disconcerted by its introduction. . .'. [Ed.]

WILDE TO AN UNIDENTIFIED CORRESPONDENT,
c. 23 February 1893

. . . The psychological idea that suggested to me the play is this. A woman who has had a child, but never known the passion of maternity (there are such women), suddenly sees the child she has abandoned falling over a precipice. There wakes in her the maternal feeling – the most terrible of all emotions – a thing that weak animals and little birds possess. She rushes to rescue, sacrifices herself, does follies – and the next day she feels 'This passion is too terrible. It wrecks my life. I don't want to know it again. It makes me suffer too much. Let me go away. I don't want to be a mother any more.' And so the fourth act is to me the psychological act, the act that is newest, most true. For which reason, I suppose, the critics say 'There is no necessity for Act IV'. But the critics are of no importance. They lack instinct. They have not the sense of Art. You have it, and I thank you again for your courteous and charming letter. . . .

SOURCE: *Letters*, pp. 331–2.

2. *A WOMAN OF NO IMPORTANCE* (1892–93)

WILDE'S REVISION OF ACT III (*c.* 1892–93)

. . . That Wilde would accept an actor's advice is proved by the omission of Illingworth's speech to his natural son Gerald Arbuthnot at the commencement of Act III. The dramatist had allowed his own feelings to run away with his character, and had made the cyncial self-possessed peer almost passionate in a diatribe on Puritanism:

My dear boy, the real enemy of modern life, of everything that makes life lovely and joyous and coloured for us, is Puritanism, and the Puritan spirit. *There* is the danger that lies ahead of the age, and most of all in England. Every now and then this England of ours finds that one of its sores shows through its rags and shrieks for the noncomformists. Caliban for nine months of the year, it is Tartuffe for the other three. Do you [not] despise a creed that starves the body, and does not feed the soul? Why, I tell you, Gerald, that the profligate, the wildest profligate who spills his life in folly, has a better, saner, finer philosophy of life than the Puritan has. He, at any rate, knows that the aim of life is the pleasure of living, and does in some way realize himself, be himself. Puritanism is the hideous survival of the self-mutilation of the savage, man in his madness making himself the victim of his monstrous sacrifice. Profligate, Gerald, you will never be; you will choose your pleasures too carefully, too exquisitely for that. But Puritanism you will always reject. It is not a creed for a gentleman. And, as a beginning, you will make it your ideal to be a dandy always.[1]

Tree did not think that a crusade against Puritanism in favour of profligacy should be launched in the middle of a scene in which the speaker is delivering wordly-wise epigrams, and Wilde cut the last part of the speech (beginning 'Why, I tell you, Gerald'), substituting for it: 'Puritanism is not a theory of life. It is an explanation of the English middle classes, that is all.' But Tree was not satisfied and wanted the rest to go. All of it went, and did not reappear in the published play. . . .

SOURCE: extract from Hesketh Pearson, *Beerbohm Tree, His Life and Laughter* (London, 1956), pp. 69–70.

NOTE

1. In fact, the draft version of *A Woman of No Importance* contains a longer version of this speech. [Ed.]

3. *AN IDEAL HUSBAND* (1894–95)

WILDE TO GEORGE ALEXANDER, (?) January 1894

. . . I shall always remember with pride and with pleasure the artistic manner in which you produced my first play, and the artistic care you showed, down to the smallest detail of production, that my work should be presented in the best manner possible, and it would be a great delight to me to have some other play of mine produced by you at your charming theatre, but I have always been anxious to have some work of mine produced by [John] Hare, whose wonderful stagecraft no one appreciates more than you do. . . .

SOURCE: *Letters*, pp. 349–50.

WILDE TO FRED TERRY, *c.* 1894

. . . Morell[1] writes to me that your charming wife[2] is a little afraid that the part of 'Lady Chiltern' in my play is not the best part – of the female characters.

Let me assure you that it is what I believe is called the part of the 'leading lady'; it is the important part, and the only sympathetic part. Indeed, the other woman [Mrs Cheveley] does not appear in the last act at all.

I am greatly pleased that I have the good fortune to have your wife in the caste – and on her much of the fortune of the play will depend.

SOURCE: undated holograph letter, in the possession of Mr Donald Sinden.

NOTES

1. H.H. Morell Mackenzie (1865–1916), formerly Tree's manager, and Waller's partner in presenting *An Ideal Husband*. [Ed.]
2. Julia Neilson (1868–1957): she had played Hester Worsley, and her husband Fred Terry (1864–1932) Gerald Arbuthnot, in *A Woman of No Importance*. [Ed.]

WILDE EDUCATING HIS CRITICS, January 1895

. . . 'The enemy has said that your plays lack action.'

'Yes; English critics always confuse the action of a play with the incidents of a melodrama. I wrote the first act of *A Woman of No Importance* in answer to the critics who said that *Lady Windermere's Fan* lacked action. In the act in question there was absolutely no action at all. It was a perfect act.'

'What do you think is the chief point the critics have missed in your new play?'

'Its entire psychology – the difference in the way in which a man loves a woman from that in which a woman loves a man, the passion that women have for making ideals (which is their weakness) and the weakness of a man who dare not show his imperfections to the thing he loves. The end of Act I, the end of Act II, and the scene in the last act, when Lord Goring points out the higher importance of a man's life over a woman's – to take three prominent instances – seem to have been quite missed by most of the critics. They failed to see their meaning; they really thought that it was a play about a bracelet. We must educate our critics – we really must educate them', said Mr Wilde, half to himself.

'The critics subordinate the psychological interest of a play to its mere technique. As soon as a dramatist invents an ingenious situation they compare him with Sardou[1]. But Sardou is an artist not because of his marvellous instinct of stage-craft, but in spite of it: in the third act of *La Tosca*, the scene of the torture, he moved us by a terrible human tragedy, not by his knowledge of stage-methods. Sardou is not understood in England because he is only known through a rather ordinary travesty of his play *Dora*, which was brought out here under the title of *Diplomacy*. I have been considerably amused by so many of the critics suggesting that the incident of the diamond bracelet in Act III of my new play was suggested by Sardou. It does not occur in any of Sardou's plays, and it was not in my play until less than ten days before production. Nobody else's work gives me any suggestion. It is only by entire isolation from everything that one can do any work. . . .

SOURCE: extract from Gilbert Burgess, 'A Talk with Mr Oscar Wilde', *The Sketch* (9 Jan. 1895), p. 495.

NOTE

1. Victorien Sardou (1831–1908) was a master of the 'well-made play'; his best-known piece *La Tosca* (1887) formed the basis for Puccini's opera, while *Diplomacy* – Clement Scott's adaptation of *Dora* – enjoyed great popularity from 1878 onwards. [Ed]

4. *THE IMPORTANCE OF BEING EARNEST* (1894–1900)

WILDE TO GEORGE ALEXANDER, (?) July 1894

. . . The real charm of the play, if it is to have a charm, must be in the dialogue. The plot is slight but, I think, adequate. . . . Well, I think an amusing thing with lots of fun and wit might be made. If you think so too, and care to have the refusal of it – do let me know – and send me £150. If when the play is finished, you think it too slight – not serious enough – of course you can have the £150 back. I want to go away and write it – and it could be ready in October, as I have nothing else to do. . . . In the meanwhile, my dear Aleck, I am so pressed for money that I don't know what to do. Of course I am extravagant – you have always been a good wise friend to me – so think what you can do.

SOURCE: extracts from letter quoted in A.E.W. Mason, *Sir George Alexander . . .*, op. cit., p.74.

ROBERT ROSS TO ADELA SCHUSTER, 23 December 1900

. . . you may think with others that his personality and conversation were far more wonderful than anything he wrote, or that his written works give only a pale reflexion of his power. Perhaps that is so, and of course it will be impossible to reproduce what [is] gone for ever; I am not alas a Boswell, as some friends have kindly suggested I should become[1]. But I only met him in 86 and only became intimate with him when he was writing *Lady Windermere,* but there were long intervals when I never saw him and he never corresponded with me regularly until after the downfall. I stayed with him [in] 87 for two months and used then to write down what he said, but to tell you a *great secret* which I ought not to do, I gave him my notes and he used a great deal of them for one of his later plays which was written in a great hurry and against time as he wanted money. This of course is *private*. . . .

SOURCE: Margaret Ross (ed.), *Robert Ross, Friend of Friends* (London, 1952), p.68.

NOTE

1. Robert Ross (1869–1918) was one of Wilde's most loyal friends; as his literary executor he succeeded in paying off all the writer's debts in eight years. [Ed.]

WILDE TO LORD ALFRED DOUGLAS, (?) August 1894

. . . My play is really funny: I am quite delighted with it. But it is not shaped yet. It lies in Sibylline leaves about the room, and Arthur [the Wildes' manservant] has twice made a chaos of it by 'tidying up'. The result, however, was rather dramatic. I am inclined to think that Chaos is a stronger evidence for an Intelligent Creator than Kosmos is: the view might be expanded. . . .

SOURCE: *Letters*, p.362.

WILDE TO C.S. MASON, August 1894

. . . I am in a very much worse state for money than I told you. But am just finishing a new play which, as it is quite nonsensical and has no serious interest, will I hope bring me in a lot of red gold. . . .

SOURCE: *Letters*, p. 364.

WILDE TO GEORGE ALEXANDER, (?) September 1894

. . . I can't make out what could have become of your letter. I thought from your silence that you thought the play too farcical in incident for a comedy theatre like your own, or that you didn't like my asking you to give me some money. I thought of telegraphing to you, but then changed my mind.

As regards the American rights: when you go to the States, it won't be to produce a farcical comedy. You will go as a romantic actor of modern and costume pieces. My play, though the dialogue is sheer comedy, and the best I have ever written, is of course in idea farcical: it could not be made part of a repertoire of serious or classical pieces, except for fun – once – . . .

I would be charmed to write a modern comedy-drama for you, and to give you rights on both sides of the disappointing Atlantic Ocean, but you, of all our young actors, should not go to America to play farcical comedy. . . . Besides, I hope to make at least £3000 in the States with this play, so what sum could I ask you for, with reference to double rights? Something that you, as a sensible manager, would not dream of paying. No : I want to come back to you. I would like to have my play done by you (I must tell you candidly that the two young men's parts are equally good), but it would be neither for your artistic reputation as a star in the States, nor for my pecuniary advantage, for you to produce it for a couple of nights in each big American town. It would be throwing the thing away. . . .

SOURCE: *Letters,* pp. 368–9.

WILDE TO GEORGE ALEXANDER, *c.* 25 October 1894

. . . I have been ill in bed for a long time, with a sort of malarial fever, and have not been able to answer your kind letter of invitation. I am quite well now, and, as you wished to see my somewhat farcical comedy, I send you the first copy of it. It is called *Lady Lancing* on the cover : but the real title is *The Importance of Being Earnest.* When you read the play, you will see the punning title's meaning. Of course, the play is not suitable to you at all : you are a romantic actor : the people it wants are actors like Wyndham[1] and Hawtrey[2]. Also, I would be sorry if you altered the definite artistic line of progress you have always followed at the St James's. But, of course, read it, and let me know what you think about it. I have very good offers from America for it. . . .

SOURCE: *Letters,* pp. 375–6.

NOTES

1. Charles Wyndham (1837–1919), light comic actor and manager of the Criterion Theatre, 1876–1919. [Ed.]

2. Charles Hawtrey (1858–1923) excelled in light comedy parts, playing Lord Goring in *An Ideal Husband*. He and Charles Brookfield (who played Phipps) helped gather evidence used against Wilde at his trials. [Ed.]

ROBERT ROSS IN DIALOGUE WITH WILDE, January 1895

'Do you think that the critics will understand your new play, which Mr George Alexander has secured?'

'I hope not.'

'I dare not ask, I suppose, if it will please the public?'

'When a play that is a work of art is produced on the stage what is being tested is not the play, but the stage; when a play that is *not* a work of art is produced on the stage what is being tested is not the play, but the public.'

'What sort of play are we to expect?'

'It is exquisitely trivial, a delicate bubble of fancy, and it has its philosophy.'

'Its philosophy!'

'That we should treat all the trivial things of life very seriously, and all the serious things of life with sincere and studied triviality.'

'You have no leanings towards realism?'

'None whatever. Realism is only a background; it cannot form an artistic motive for a play that is to be a work of art.'

'Still I have heard you congratulated on your pictures of London society.'

'If Robert Chiltern, the Ideal Husband, were a common clerk, the humanity of his tragedy would be none the less poignant. I have placed him in the higher ranks of life merely because that is the side of social life with which I am best acquainted. In a play dealing with actualities to write with ease one must write with knowledge. . . .'

SOURCE: unsigned article, 'Mr Oscar Wilde on Mr Oscar Wilde', *St James's Gazette* (18 Jan. 1895), pp. 4–5.

BERNARD SHAW AND WILDE, January 1895

. . . Our sixth meeting . . . was the one at the Café Royal[1]. On that occasion he was not too preoccupied with his danger [arising from the Queensberry trial] not to be disgusted with me because I, who had praised his first plays handsomely, had turned traitor over *The Importance of Being Earnest*. Clever as it was, it was his first really heartless play. In the others the chivalry of the eighteenth century Irishman and the romance of the disciple of Theophile Gautier[2] (Oscar was really old-fashioned in the Irish way, except as a critic of morals) not only gave a certain kindness and gallantry to the serious passages and to the handling of women, but provided that proximity of emotion without which laughter, however irresistible, is destructive and sinister. In *The Importance of Being Earnest* this had vanished; and the play, though extremely funny, was essentially hateful. I had no idea that Oscar was going to the dogs, and that this represented a real degeneracy produced by his debaucheries. I though he was still developing; and I hazarded the unhappy guess that *The Importance of Being Earnest* was in idea a young work written or projected long before under the influence of Gilbert and furbished up for Alexander as a potboiler. At the Café Royal that day I calmly asked him whether I was not right. He indignantly repudiated my guess and said loftily (the only time he ever tried on me the attitude he took to John Gray and his more abject disciples) that he was disappointed in me. I suppose I said, 'Then what on earth has happened to you?' but I recollect nothing more on that subject except that we did not quarrel over it.

SOURCE: extract from 'My Memories of Oscar Wilde', in the 1918 edition of Frank Harris's *Oscar Wilde: His Life and Confessions* (1st edition, London, 1916); reprint (New York, 1930), pp. 391–2.

NOTES

1. Frank Harris (1856–1931) gave a lunch party for Wilde and others in an attempt to persuade him to leave England before the Queensberry trial. Harris edited in turn the *Evening News*, the *Fortnightly Review* and the *Saturday Review;* his book on Wilde, first published in 1916, is lively and compassionate, though often fanciful and inaccurate. [Ed.]

2. French author (1811–72), and staunch advocate of 'Art for Art's sake'. [Ed.]

ANDRÉ GIDE AND WILDE, January 1895

. . . On one of those final evenings in Algiers[1], Wilde seemed to have made up his mind not to utter one single serious word. Eventually I grew rather irritated by the exaggerated wit of his paradoxical remarks, and I began to say, 'You have got better things to say than this nonsense; you are addressing me this evening as if I were the general public. You ought rather to speak to the public in the way that you talk to your friends. Why is it that your plays are no better? The best of what lies in you, you express in conversation; why don't you write it down?' 'Oh, come now,' he exclaimed straightaway, 'I know my plays are no good at all, and I don't think much of them. . . But if you only realised how much amusement they give people! They are nearly all the result of bets. So is *Dorian Gray* ; I wrote that in a few days because a friend of mine claimed that I could never write novels. Writing bores me so much!'

And then, suddenly leaning towards me, he said, 'Would you care to know the great drama of my life? It's that I've put my genius into my life – I have put only my talent into my works.'

SOURCE: extract from 'In Memoriam Oscar Wilde', in *Prétextes* (Paris, 1903); pp. 284–5 in the 1926 edition (extract translated by William Tydeman).

NOTE

1. Gide accidently met up with Wilde and Lord Alfred Douglas at Blidah in late January 1895.

WILDE TO FRANK HARRIS, 18 February 1899

. . . I have again written to Smithers[1], my publisher, to ask him to let me have something on account of my play, just published, which I think he can hardly refuse doing : though I do not fancy the play will have anything like the success of *The Ballad [of Reading Gaol]*.[2] It is so trivial, so irresponsible a comedy : and while the public liked to hear of my pain – curiosity and the autobiographical form being elements of interest – I am not sure that they will welcome me again in airy mood and spirit, mocking at morals, and defiance of social rules. There is, or at least in their eyes there should be, such a gap between the two Oscars. . . .

SOURCE: *Letters*, p. 780.

NOTES

1. Leonard Smithers (1861–1909) published *The Ballad of Reading Gaol* (1898), *An Ideal Husband* (1899) and *The Importance of Being Earnest* (1899).
2. Published on 13 February 1898, the poem was in a sixth printing by 21 May.

PART TWO

Contemporary Reviews

1. ON LADY WINDERMERE'S FAN (1892)

Sunday Times   (21 February 1892)

. . . *Lady Windermere's Fan* is clever and interesting enough to justify attention on its merits, and though by no means a perfect or unconventional play as far as the development of character and incident goes, it has a strong story which interests, and it is brilliantly written. Mr Wilde has the gift of writing witty and memorable dialogue, full of paradoxical surprises, and pregnant with the wisdom of the boudoir and the cynicism of the club smoking room, while under all this there frequently lurk deeper truths of a wider range. One of his characters [Lord Darlington in Act I] says, 'I think life far too important a thing ever to talk seriously about it', and this is the keynote of much of the cynicism of this play, in which the author has attempted to depict a certain phase of life, but has not taken it quite seriously. This is, perhaps, no great drawback, for as one of the characters [Darlington in his next speech] says, 'to be intelligible is to be found out', and that is a catastrophe which Mr Wilde would be scarcely likely to court. Therefore, he keeps his audience as perplexed as possible without actually mystifying them. He carefully preserves his 'secret' till the last act, and he makes at least one of his characters a psychological puzzle. . . .

Mr Wilde can be brilliantly cynical, but when he handles sentiment, he seems to lack the essential of sympathy. He can be thoroughly interesting though, and brilliant, and these are qualities which go far towards making *Lady Windermere's Fan* a success. To develop character in action is surely the highest aim of dramatic writing. And Mr Wilde attempts this, at least with the women of his play, but his developments do not always seem true. The character of Lady Windermere is decidedly perplexing, according to the logic of ordinary life – though women are often extraordinary creatures. The men are not conspicuous successes as characters, though they all talk interestingly and amusingly, except Lord Windermere. He says nothing amusing, and he is very serious. And this is the character Mr Alexander has elected to play. He has only to be earnest, and Mr Alexander's earnestness is one of his most valued artistic gifts. . . . [Unsigned review, p. 5.]

Daily Telegraph   (22 February 1892)

. . . In one important respect Mr Oscar Wilde would have done well to have closely observed the dramatic method of his gifted predecessors who have studied the stage and the principles of dramatic effect. Neither Sheridan nor Dumas nor Sardou[1] was ever to our knowledge guilty of the heresy known as the 'stage surprise'. They never fogged their audience for three acts in order to startle them with a bombshell in Act IV. But this is exactly what Mr Wilde elects to do in the teeth of precedent, and with the full knowledge that no play has ever yet interested or wholly enthralled an audience unless the author at once gets that assembly into his confidence and allows it to act as the conscience of the drama. A play with three acts of mist and mystery and one of enlightenment is that most unpardonable of dramatic errors. The truth of this has once more been proved, though proof was wholly unnecessary.

For two-thirds of the evening people were asking one another, Who is she? What is he? Why does she do this? How does he come to do that? Is this adventuress a mistress, or can she be a mother? when by the addition of a couple of lines in the opening scene, the whole gratuitous difficulty would have melted into thin air. Not a moment should be lost in writing in these important lines if future audiences are not to be irritated, as was the complimentary company of Saturday. Further obstinacy in such a matter would be suicidal.[2] . . .

The play is a bad one, but it will succeed. No faults of construction, no failure in interest, no feebleness in character drawing, no staleness in motive, will weigh in the scale against the insolence of its caricature. Society loves best those who chaff it most, and society will rush to see Lady Windermere, and will cringe to be tickled by her fan. It is the way of the world. When they are sitting in the theatre they will laugh because their enemies are being ridiculed, and when they come home they will ridicule the author. And that is exactly what pleases him most. His appearance addressing society with a deferential tone and a lighted cigarette in his hand was a triumph of a career of humorous audacity!   [Unsigned review, p.3.]

NOTES

1. Alexandre Dumas *fils* (1824–95), natural son of Alexandre Dumas, the great French novelist, was a prolific dramatist. His best-known play, *La Dame aux Camélias*, was staged in 1852. For Sardou, see Note at end of Section 3, Part One, above. [Ed.]

2. See Note 2 to Wilde's letter to Alexander, mid-February 1892 – section 1, Part One, above. [Ed.]

WILLIAM ARCHER   *World*   (24 February 1892)

. . . I [am not] going to quarrel with Mr Wilde for writing drawing-room romance, or to waste time in enumerating all the plays which this play would resemble if it were not entirely different. Personally, I like drawing-rooms – on the stage – and am grateful to Mr Wilde for reporting to me the manners and customs of their denizens. Even if he embellishes a little and tells a few traveller's tales, there is no great harm done. . . . Accepting the environment, then, what shall we say of the romance? Well, in itself it is no great matter. It abounds in external improbabilities and psychological inconsistencies. No man in his senses would act as Lord Windermere does in inviting Mrs Erlynne to the ball. He does not even tell his wife explicitly: 'There *is* a mystery which, for your own sake, I can't explain to you; I appeal to your faith and generosity, and beg you to do this thing without understanding its reasons.' Of course he in effect makes some such appeal, but he entirely discounts it by professing to be surprised and injured because his wife's attitude renders it necessary. (Similarly, Mrs Erlynne, in the third act, appears no less astonished than shocked at the bare idea that Lady Windermere should have placed what she must know to be the one obvious and common-sense interpretation on her relations with Lord Windermere.) And, having succeeded in infuriating instead of winning over her ladyship, how can Lord Windermere dream of suffering Mrs Erlynne to come to the ball in the face of his wife's threat? There is every likelihood that she will carry it out – how can he stake everything on the off-chance that she may change her mind? He has all to lose, and we do not see that he or anyone has so very much to gain. If his sole object is to get the adventuress married to Lord Augustus Lorton (a delightfully cynical 'happy ending' by the way), he is simply burning his house to heat his shaving-water – or rather Mrs Erlynne's curling-tongs. He says himself, when Mrs Erlynne appears, 'You ought not to have come'; why, then did he send her the invitation? This is the chief of what I have called the external improbabilities; the psychological inconsistencies, if less glaring, are of more real moment. I do not reckon among them the odd mixture of cynicism and sentiment in Mrs Erlynne's character. It is a little bewildering, and we have, strictly speaking, a right to demand that even under the conditions of the stage, the artist should in some way resolve such a discord; but the apparent contradiction is evidently intentional, and after the all-of-a-piece heroines and villainesses of commonplace drama, a character in two pieces in a welcome change, even if they do not seem quite to dovetail. The fatal inconsistency is in the

character of Lady Windermere. In the first act, at five p.m., she is a
woman carved in alabaster, from whom, in her own conceit, all possible soilure seems infinitely remote. . . . She is a happy wife and
mother, without even the dimmest suspicion of her husband's faith;
not, like Dumas's Francillon[1], a woman who has speculated on the
theory of conjugal infidelity, and made up her mind what to do should
the case present itself. Yet this very woman, seven hours later, is prepared to abandon her child without a thought (does Mr Wilde wish us
to believe that she actually forgets its existence?) and then to throw
herself into the arms of a man for whom she feels nothing but a very
unimpassioned friendship? When Lord Darlington began to make
love to Lady Windermere in the ball-room, I wondered at what
seemed to me his tactless and self-defeating precipitancy; when Lady
Windermere for a moment listened to him, I could not believe my
ears; when she went off to join him, I pinched myself to make sure that
I was not dreaming. Even in the maddest access of jealousy a woman
could not thus, all of a sudden, fly in the face of her every habit of
thought and action. If Lady Windermere had set to work to swear like
a trooper and smash the furniture, her conduct would have been just
as rational, and no whit more improbable. 'Rational!' Mr Wilde may
say; 'do you expect a woman under these circumstances to follow the
dictates of pure reason?' Certainly not; but everything that is
unreasonable is not, therefore, probable. For another woman, of course,
Lady Windermere's course would be possible enough. That is precisely my point: that the Lady Windermere of the second and third
acts is a totally different woman from the Lady Windermere of the
first act, who is evidently the Lady Windermere of Mr Wilde's fundamental conception. He ought either to have modified that conception
to suit the situation in the third act, or, better, to have totally altered
the situation to suit the character. Best of all to have got on without
any situation, in the sense of a trick tableau, but that is a counsel of
perfection on which I do not insist. Even Mr Wilde, with all his contempt for the commonplace, prefers humdrum success to illustrious
failure. I do not blame him, and still less, I fancy, does Mr Alexander. . . .   [Signed review, pp. 20–1.]

NOTE

1. Dumas *fils*'s *Francillon* was his last play, staged in 1887.

2. ON *A WOMAN OF NO IMPORTANCE* (1893)

Daily News   (20 April 1893)

If *Lady Windermere's Fan* deserved the complaints that were made of the paucity of action as compared with the quantity of words, what shall be said of *A Woman of No Importance*, brought out last night at the Haymarket Theatre? In this play in four acts, occupying in the representation about three hours and a quarter, Mr Oscar Wilde has introduced really only one dramatic situation, and that is nothing more than one of the most familiar commonplaces of the French stage. A gay, unscrupulous nobleman, Lord Illingworth, has dared to insult a pretty American girl of Puritanical tendencies by forcibly kissing her in a garden, and for this act he is instantly called to account by his youthful secretary Gerald Arbuthnot, who is on the point of laying violent hands upon the middle-aged Lothario when the exclamation, 'Hold Gerald! he is your father!' stays his uplifted arm. The voice which thus arrests Gerald's stern purpose is, we need hardly say, that of his own mother, the secret which she has hitherto guarded from her son being thus for the first time revealed to him. Beyond this scene, which brings to a close the third act, Mr Wilde's play may be described as mainly a collection of epigrams, some of which it must be admitted are amusing, while others are decidedly lacking in the most conspicuous attribute of 'the quality of Mercy'. The proposition that the Peerage is 'decidedly the best thing in fiction that the English have done', may as a cynical witticism fairly pass; but when the heartless and frivolous little world sit bandying hour by hour such observations . . . it must be confessed that the patience of an indulgent first-night audience is put to a rather severe test. Mr Wilde's theme, so far as his play has a serious purpose, is one of obvious dramatic capabilities. It is that of the hollowness of the conventional morality which treats the profligate seducer with infinitely more indulgence than the victim of his arts. . . .   [Unsigned review, p.3.].

Sunday Times   (23 April 1893)

A Woman of No Importance, the new four-act play which won the vocifer-ous applause of an exceptionally brilliant audience at the Haymarket on Wednesday night, can scarcely, with justice, be said to advance Mr Oscar Wilde's position as a dramatist. From the point of view of dramatic interest it is, perhaps, of less account even than *Lady Windermere's Fan*; but, for all that, it is a very entertaining piece of work, redolent from first to last of its clever author. Its primary quality is showiness; its cynicism and its emotion are both excessively showy, and Mr Wilde obviously intended that they should be so. If we are to accept Mr Beerbohm Tree's dictum that *A Woman of No Importance* is a work of art, we must do so with the reservation that Mr Wilde has been at no pains to conceal his art. By deliberately setting himself to write avowedly cynical talk, to use up any serviceable witty and sur-prising paradoxes he has himself uttered and remembered from time to time, to startle, to tickle, to amuse his audience, regardless of relevancy to the dramatic development of his story, he departs from the customary methods of the dramatic artist, but the means he employs are too apparent to make this seem to us a better artistic way. The very essence of a play is its drama, though, perhaps, this truism, not being paradoxical, will scarcely find favour with Mr Wilde. Hence in his new play it is the epigram and the paradoxes that we remember with interest rather than the relation of one character to another, with the incidents that arise therefrom. . . . If Mr Wilde would only keep his passion for paradox, persiflage, and proverbial perversity within the legitimate limits of his dramatic theme, what a good play he might write. . . .   [Unsigned review, p.6.]

Observer (23 April 1893)

. . . If *A Woman of No Importance*, with its inconsistent characterisation and its inconclusive motives, with its inverted conundrums doing duty for epigrams and strung together on a thin thread of perfunctory plot, with its choice of a painfully hackneyed theme and its abortive straining after originality of treatment – if this be indeed a satisfactory work of dramatic art, then must we revise the standards by which we have been wont to test such achievements. That there is much daring cleverness in Mr Wilde's writing here, just as there was in his *Dorian Grey* [*sic*][1] and in his *Lady Windermere's Fan*, would be denied by no one with an ear for sharp sayings and an eye for quick turns of thought. But, if we may adopt one of Mr Wilde's pet paradoxes, we make bold to assert that nothing on the stage can be quite so stupid as cleverness: and, unfortunately, *A Woman of No Importance* is too clever by half. Its literary form has no doubt a style as well as a finish sufficiently rare to secure them an appreciative welcome at the hands of all playgoers of culture and taste. But its author's employment of his resources is so lacking in discrimination that he not only wastes them, but actually uses them to his own disadvantage. What can be more fatal to the individuality of *dramatis personae* than to make them all talk exactly alike? What more irritating than the perpetual waiting for the paradoxical answer to the ingenious riddle about life, or society, or woman, or love? In *Lady Windermere's Fan*, Mr Wilde kept in some sort of check his tendency towards repeating himself in his creations, whose smart sayings were for the most part characteristic of the speakers as well as of the playwright. In *A Woman of No Importance* the quip and crank of the commonplace book are showered out upon the dialogue as from a pepper-pot, so that every dish in the banquet has precisely the same flavour. So much for the talk; of the action of the piece there is less to be said, for there is much less of it, and what there is has no claim to novelty. . . .   [Unsigned review, p.6.]

NOTE

1. *The Picture of Dorian Gray* first appeared in June 1890. [Ed.]

WILLIAM ARCHER   *World*   (26 April 1893)

. . . the one essential fact about Mr Oscar Wilde's dramatic work is that it must be taken on the very highest plane of modern English drama, and furthermore, that it stands alone on that plane. In intellectual calibre, artistic competence − ay, and in dramatic instinct to boot − Mr Wilde has no rival among his fellow-workers for the stage. He is a thinker and a writer; they are more or less able, thoughtful, original playwrights. This statement may seem needlessly emphatic, and even offensive; but it is necessary that it should be made if we are to preserve any sense of proportion in criticism. I am far from exalting either *Lady Windermere's Fan* or *A Woman of No Importance* to the rank of a masterpiece; but while we carp at this point and cavil at that, it behoves us to remember and to avow that we are dealing with works of an altogether higher order than others which we may very likely have praised with much less reserve.

Pray do not suppose that I am merely dazzled by Mr Wilde's pyro-technic wit. That is one of the defects of his qualities, and a defect, I am sure, that he will one day conquer, when he begins to take himself seri-ously as a dramatic artist. At present, he approaches his calling as cynically as Mr George R. Sims[1]; only it is for the higher intellects, and not the lower, among the play-going public, that Mr Wilde shows his polite contempt. He regards prose drama (so he has somewhere stated) as the lowest of the arts; and acting on this principle – the falsity of which he will discover as soon as a truly inspiring subject occurs to him – he amuses himself by lying on his back and blowing soap-bubbles for half an evening, and then pretending, during the other half, to interest himself in some story of the simple affections such as audiences, he knows, regard as dramatic. Most of the soap bubbles are exceedingly pretty, and he throws them off with astonishing ease and rapidity –

> One *mot* doth tread upon another's heels,
> So fast they follow[2]

but it becomes fatiguing, in the long run, to have the whole air a-shim-mer, as it were, with iridescent films. Mr Wilde will one day be more sparing in the quantity and more fastidious as to the quality of his wit, and will cease to act up to Lord Illingworth's motto that 'nothing suc-ceeds like excess'. It is not his wit, then, and still less his knack of paradox-twisting, that makes me claim for him a place apart among living English dramatists. It is the keenness of his intellect, the indi-viduality of his point of view, the excellence of his verbal style, and, above all, the genuinely dramatic quality of his inspirations. I do not hesitate to call the scene between Lord Illingworth and Mrs Arbuthnot at the end of the second act of this play the most virile and intelligent – yes, I mean it, intelligent – piece of English dramatic writing of our day. It is the work of a man who knows life, and knows how to transfer it to the stage. There is no situation-hunting, no post-uring. The interest of the scene arises from emotion based upon thought, thought thrilled with emotion. There is nothing conven-tional in it, nothing insincere. In a word, it is a piece of adult art. True, it is by far the best scene in the play, the only one in which Mr Wilde does perfect justice to his talent. But there are many details of similar, though perhaps not equal, value scattered throughout. How fine and simple in its invention, for instance, is the scene in which the mother tells her son the story of Lord Illingworth's treachery, only to hear him defend the libertine on the ground that no 'nice girl' would have let herself be entrapped! This exquisite touch of ironic pathos is worth half a hundred 'thrilling tableaux' like that which follows almost immediately upon it.

For it is not to be denied that in his effort to be human – I would say 'to be popular', did I not fear some subtle and terrible vengeance on the part of the outraged author – Mr Wilde has become more than a little conventional. How different is the 'He is your father!' tableau at the end of Act III from the strong and simple conclusion of Act II – how different, and how inferior! It would be a just retribution if Mr Wilde were presently to be confronted with this tableau in all the horrors of chromolithography [colour printing], on every hoarding in London, with the legend, 'Stay, Gerald! He is your father!' in crinkly letters in the corner. Then, indeed, would expatriation – or worse – be the only resource of his conscience-stricken soul.[3] His choice would lie between Paris and prussic acid. The conventional element seems to me to come in with the character of Mrs Arbuthnot. Why does Mr Wilde make her such a terribly emphatic personage? Do ladies in her (certainly undesirable) position brood so incessantly upon their misfortune? I have no positive evidence to go upon, but I see no reason why Mrs Arbuthnot should not take a more common-sense view of the situation. That she should resent Lord Illingworth's conduct I quite understand, and I applaud the natural and dignified revenge she takes in declining to marry him. But why all this agony? Why all this hatred? Why can 'no anodyne give her sleep, no poppies forgetfulness'? With all respect for Mrs Arbuthnot, this is mere empty phrase-making. I am sure she has slept very well, say, six nights out of the seven, during these twenty years; or, if not, she has suffered from a stubborn determination to be unhappy, for which Lord Illingworth can scarcely be blamed. After all, what material has she out of which to spin twenty years of unceasing misery? She is – somehow or other – in easy circumstances; she has a model son to satisfy both her affections and her vanity; it does not even appear that she is subjected to any social slights or annoyances. A good many women have led fairly contented lives under far more trying conditions. Perhaps Mr Wilde would have us believe that she suffers from mild religious mania – that it is the gnawing thought of her unpardonable 'sin' that nor poppy nor mandragora can soothe. But she herself admits that she does not repent the 'sin' that has given her a son to love. Well then, what is all this melodrama about? Does not Mrs Arbuthnot sacrifice our interest, if not our sympathy, by her determination 'in obstinate condolement to persever'[4]? May we not pardonably weary a little (to adapt Lord Illingworth's saying) of 'the Unreasonable eternally lamenting the Unalterable'? Mrs Arbuthnot is simply a woman who has been through a very painful experience, who has suffered a crushing disappointment in the revelation of the unworthiness of the man she loved, but for whom life, after all, has turned out not so very intolerably. That is the rational view of her situation; and she herself might quite well take that view without the sacrifice of one scene or speech of any real value. The masterly scene at the end of the second act would remain practically intact, and so would the scene between mother and son in the third act; for the complacent cruelty of Gerald's commentary on her story could not but cause a bitter pang to any mother. It is only in the fourth act that any really important alteration would be necessary, and there it could only be for the better. The young man's crude sense of the need for some immediate and heroic action is admirably conceived, and entirely right; but how much better, how much truer, how much newer, would the scene be if the mother met his Quixotism with sad, half-smiling dignity and wisdom, instead of with passionate outcries of unreasoning horror! There is a total lack of irony, or, in other words, of commonsense, in this portion of the play. Heroics respond to heroics, until we feel inclined to beg both mother and son (and daughter-in-law, too, for that matter) to come down from their stilts and look at things a little rationally. Even Mr Wilde's writing suffers. We are treated to such noble phrases as 'I am not worthy [either] of her or of you', and it would surprise no one if Master Gerald were to drop into blank verse in a friendly way. How much more telling, too, would the scene between Mrs Arbuthnot and Lord Illingworth become if she took the situation more ironically and less tragically, if she answered the man of the world in the tone of a woman of the world! How much more complete, for one thing, would be his humiliation! As it is, the vehemence of her hatred can only minister to his vanity. From the point of view of vanity, to be hated for twenty years is just as good as to be loved. It is indifference that stings. It was all very well, in the second act, for Mrs Arbuthnot not to be vehement in her protest against the father's annexation of the son; in the fourth act, when that danger is past, a tone of calm superiority would be ten times as effective. In short, the play would have been a much more accomplished work of art if the character of Mrs Arbuthnot had been pitched in another key. . . .   [Signed review, pp. 26–7.]

NOTES

1. George R. Sims, (1847–1922); popular dramatist and versifier. [Ed.]

2. Cf. *Hamlet*, IV vii 164–5. [Ed.]

3. Wilde had threatened to emigrate to France after the banning of *Salome* in 1892. [Ed.]

4. Cf. *Hamlet*, I   ii   92–3. [Ed.]

W. MOY THOMAS   *Graphic*   (29 April 1893)

To say that the most stirring situation in Mr Oscar Wilde's new play
at the Haymarket is one of the most familiar commonplaces of the
French stage is only to say that the author of *A Woman of No Importance*
adheres to the opinion that he is understood to entertain on the subject of dramatic invention. 'Let me see', said a spectator in the stalls to
his neighbour, on the first night, 'in what French melodrama is it that
we have a mother who stays the uplifted arm of her illegitimate son by
exclaiming – 'Hold, Henri, he is your father"?' The answer was
'Ask, rather, in what French melodrama is it not?' The sarcasm, however, would be lost on Mr Wilde, who, so far from fearing the charge of
poverty of invention, will go out of his way to show his contempt for
ingenuity of design by dipping for his materials in the very oldest 'bag of
tricks' of the hack playwright. As the great cook is not he who can
delight with choice viands, but rather the genius of the kitchen who
knows how to make a ragout of shoe-leather which shall be appetising
and nutritious, it may be allowed that there is some truth in
Mr Wilde's alleged theories. It is certain that many a play has afforded
pleasure in spite of an intrigue that is destitute of novelty or even of
plausibility. Clever characterisation, brilliant dialogue, shrewd
satire, human relations that throw a sudden light on the problems of life
and the philosophy of society, may, it is clear, go very far to console us
for a threadbare theme. . . . But, unfortunately, Mr Wilde has done
little more than suggest a noble theme and garnish it with cynical
epigrams which, regarded as mere exercises of wit and sprightly
fancy, are not always – I may even say, not often – worthy of praise.

So far as there is a serious purpose in Mr Wilde's play, it appears to
be that of rebuking the rich and idle class of society for its love of pleasure, its cynicism, its mean profligacy, its contempt of principle, its
hatred of enthusiasm, its profound disbelief in the existence of anything better than itself. The protagonist of this Schopenhauerian[1]
world is Lord Illingworth, the middle-aged *roué* who speaks of the girl
whom he has cheated and betrayed some twenty years earlier as 'a
woman of no importance'; the chorus is the New England maiden,
played by Miss Neilson, with her Puritanical ideas of honesty and
honour, which she takes frequent opportunity of communicating to
her aristocratic hostess and friends, even venturing on one occasion
upon a vehement tirade in which she contrasts American virtue with
English vice in a way that must have put a rather severe strain upon
the obligations of hospitality. But the working out of the story brings
with it few of the moral lessons which lurk in most presentments of

human life wherein the conflict of passions and of interests is followed
to its natural issues. In the end, the machinery of the dramatist seems
to have been set in motion merely to provide Mrs Arbuthnot with the
triumph of rejecting Lord Illingworth's tardy offer of 'reparation',
together with the vulgar gratification of smacking his face for being
insolent, and of dismissing him with the retort that *he* is a 'person of no
importance' . . .   [Signed review, p.475]

NOTE

1. Arthur Schopenhauer (1786-1860), the pessimistic German philosopher, who
viewed the universe as being governed by Will. [Ed.]

3. ON *AN IDEAL HUSBAND* (1895)

Morning Advertiser   (4 January 1895)

Anyone happening to look in at the Haymarket Theatre on the fall of the curtain last night would have come to the conclusion that Mr Oscar Wilde had written a brilliant play, and no doubt many of those who cheered so lustily were quite of that opinion. But viewed dispassionately, *An Ideal Husband* was a thing of shreds and patches, a stringing together of a number of inconsequent incidents whose only dramatic value was that they have been in use for years past, and are therefore to be borne with as we bear with the ancient jokes of an elderly, highly respectable and, above all, wealthy member of one's family. There is nothing in it which gives Mr Wilde the right to class himself as a playwright either of promise or experience. He does not dispute the conventions of the stage after the manner of the Norwegian school,[1] for his memory, which serves him so well in other things, stands faithfully by him when in need of theatrical tricks, and there is enough stale business in his latest achievement to make up a tolerably decent one act in a Surrey melodrama.[2] But, worst of all, his paradoxes fall tamely on the ear, and now the author of *The Green Carnation*[3] has shown us how easily those smart sayings may be twisted and coined, we seem to see the hand of the mechanic in every distorted sentence. In Mr Wilde's maiden efforts they attracted and amused by reason of their novelty, but now when we are told that London society is composed of 'beautiful idiots and brilliant lunatics' we know the writer has got his phrase-book upside down, and is reproducing them by means of the convenient typewriter. Now and then Mr Wilde gets home a good shot, but his dialogue, compared to that of either Mr Pinero, Mr Jones, or Mr Grundy,[4] is the veriest French paste. . . . [Unsigned review, p.5.]

NOTES

1. Ibsen and his followers. [Ed.]

2. The Surrey Theatre in Lambeth was one of the traditional homes of sensational melodramas in the nineteenth century. [Ed.]

3. A satire on Wilde and his friends, written by Robert Smythe Hitchens, which appeared in September 1894. [Ed.]

4. Arthur Wing Pinero, Henry Arthur Jones and Sydney Grundy were leading playwrights of the period. [Ed.]

Morning Post   (4 January 1895)

When, in response to the overwhelming enthusiasm of the house, Mr Oscar Wilde came last night a second time before the curtain, he thanked the audience and the actors, and added that he 'had enjoyed the evening immensely'. In so saying he gave expression to the general feeling. Not only had Mr Wilde enjoyed the performance – the public had enjoyed it also. The minority, doubtless, had not been wholly satisfied. There had been an *amari aliquid* [something bitter] in their cup. *An Ideal Husband*, as a dramatic work, is as inferior to *A Woman of No Importance* as *A Woman of No Importance* was inferior to *Lady Windermere's Fan*. Mr Wilde is not progressing in the dramatist's art. There is more mere 'story' in *An Ideal Husband* than there was in its two predecessors, but that story is not so well worked out. The plot of *Lady Windermere's Fan* was a *pasticcio* [muddled concoction], but it was unfolded with some tact. Even *A Woman of No Importance* had, in the latter half of it, some dramatic moments. But though in *An Ideal Husband* the story begins earlier than is usual with Mr Wilde, it also ends earlier, the play concluding virtually just before the curtain falls upon the third of the four acts. At the close of the third act Mr Wilde starts a new complication, but in the fourth he quickly lets it drop, and the remainder of the work is a series of disjointed and ineffective incidents. The strength of *An Ideal Husband* is certainly not in the narrative it lays before us. . . . *An Ideal Husband* was not a first-night success by reason of the absorbing interest of its story or the masterly fashion in which that story was handled. It was a success in spite of its framework. It was a success, perhaps, in the first place, because evidently the audience was sympathetically disposed towards both Mr Wilde and the new sub-lessees of the theatre, Mr Waller and Mr Morell; and in the second place, because much of the characterisation and a good deal of the dialogue is admirable either in its truth to life or in its literary cleverness. Mr Wilde knows the fashionable world, and supplies of it a graphic and effective picture. . . .   [Unsigned review, p.3]

Sketch   (9 January 1895)

One curious fact must strike anyone who compares Mr Oscar Wilde's new work with *A Woman of No Importance* or *Lady Windermere's Fan*. Everyone expected, and correctly, that the jokes in the latest piece would show a falling-off in quality, would seem a mere after-crop; but, on the other hand, it was imagined that *An Ideal Husband* would exhibit a decided advantage so far as the actual drama is concerned, and this proved to be by no means the case. Indeed, one cannot discover any aspect of the piece in which it does not display great inferiority to the earlier works. It certainly is surprising that in so young a dramatist one should find a decided falling-off.

However, it may be remarked that perhaps the relative inferiority of *An Ideal Husband* is due, to some extent, to change of method. *Lady Windermere's Fan* and *A Woman of No Importance* were ingenious plays of character – perhaps not human, but Wilde character – with stagey scenes rather cleverly handled to give movement to them. *An Ideal Husband* is a mere play of intrigue. One could believe easily that it was written by a disciple of Mr Wilde, who had been studying, insufficiently, the school of Scribe[1], as well as the joke-manufacturing process of the famous pseudo-epigrammatist. It may seem strange that Mr Wilde's play should be old-fashioned, since the author is supposed to be ultra-modern; yet no one could well deny that the sense of weariness it sometimes causes is due partly to the fact that it is antiquated in method, and that the method is not well handled.

There is hardly a character in the piece in whom one detects any signs of life. Ere now the author has shown a curious gift for presenting characters not founded on observation or exactly truthful, but effective and interesting. I should be very sorry, for instance, not to have had the pleasure of becoming acquainted with Mrs Erlynne. In *An Ideal Husband*, unfortunately, there is no Mrs Erlynne. Of the four characters of importance, not one is interesting. . . .   [Unsigned review, p.496.]

NOTE

1. Eugène Scribe (1791–1861), inventor of the *'pièce bien faite'* and prolific playwright and librettist. [Ed.]

4. ON *THE IMPORTANCE OF BEING EARNEST* (1895)

The Times   (15 February 1895)

From serious comedy or frivolous drama Mr Oscar Wilde has passed to farce, a piece of this description being produced in his name last night at the St James's Theatre, under the title of *The Importance of Being Earnest*. Perhaps it may be alleged that as M. Jourdain spoke prose,[1] so Mr Oscar Wilde has hitherto been writing farce, unawares; but in truth *The Importance of Being Earnest* is somewhat more extravagant than the other pieces which have so far proceeded from his pen. A strange effect is thereby produced. It may only be the result of custom, but Mr Oscar Wilde's peculiar view of epigram does not accord too well with flippant action. Its proper setting is among serious people, in the drawing-room after dinner, or so at least we have been taught to think. In a farce it gives one the sensation of drinking wine out of the wrong sort of glass; it conveys to the palate a new sensation which in the end, however, is discovered to be not unpleasing. The public took very kindly last night to this further instalment of Mr Oscar Wilde's humour, and there is now little prospect of its true nature being discovered, until some one attempts to translate it into French. Whether in farce or drama, plot continues to be Mr Oscar Wilde's most vulnerable point. The story of this latest production is, indeed, almost too preposterous to go without music. Yet it sets a keynote of extravagance, which, being taken up by the actors, is speedily communicated to the house, and the result is an harmonious whole which is not unlikely to entertain the public of St James's for many months to come. . . . [Unsigned review, p.5].

NOTE

1. See Act II of Molière's *Le Bourgeois Gentilhomme* (1670). [Ed.].

Daily Telegraph   (15 February 1895)

In the days to come, when the dramatic historian of the future sits down to give his account of our theatrical era, he will note 1895 as the year in which Mr Oscar Wilde produced his first farce; and further, if he be a faithful chronicler, he will add that a brilliant audience welcomed the work to the footlights at the St James's Theatre on the evening of St Valentine's Day with not a little cordiality. In truth, there need be no hesitating over the manner in which we are to class the new piece.

Mr Oscar Wilde, in his usual perverse way, insists upon styling his play, 'a trivial comedy for serious people'; but, as a matter of fact, the 'serious people' might have been left out of the question. *The Importance of Being Earnest* is 'trivial comedy' if you will; for ourselves we prefer to term it extravagant farce. With all his leaning towards paradoxical dialogue, and the flippant inversion of commonplace phrase, Mr Wilde has in his previous essays written for the stage devoted a certain portion of his theme to serious incident, and worked – faultily it may be, but with some approach to sincerity – in the direction of a definite dramatic end. But in the play that Mr George Alexander offered his patrons last evening there is no trace of solemn theatrical intention. The dramatist has given himself a holiday, as it were, and rested content with putting forth, with all his characteristic volubility, a story whose extravagance is fairly matched by the tone of the dialogue which serves to tell it. . . .

Certainly, the quality of his work in the present case is, in many respects, brilliant. There is laughter in abundance in the three acts of *The Importance of Being Earnest;* and if we begin to feel as the end approaches, that the pace is too hot to last, and that these scintillating flashes of wit cannot be kept up any longer, such feeling is quickly dissipated by some brisk scene that comes to wipe out of the memory an interlude of comparative tameness. . . .   [Unsigned review, p.3.].

Daily Graphic   (15 February 1895)

The empire of Mr Gilbert over Topseyturveydom is at last successfully challenged, and Mr Wilde may claim to reign

Beyond dispute
O'er all the realms of nonsense absolute.[1].

His three-act novelty at the St James's Theatre, announced as 'a trivial comedy for serious people', is a veritable specimen of what, in a more propitious season, might be called midsummer madness. It has not a relish of reason or sparkle of sanity; it is absurd, preposterous, extravagant, idiotic, saucy, brilliantly clever, and unedifyingly diverting. The idea on which Voltaire constructed his *Ingénu*, that of an innocent and guileless savage speaking the truth in all presences and under all conditions – a notion subsequently elaborated upon by Mr Gilbert in the *Palace of Truth* – is once more employed.[2] This time, however, everybody speaks truth through no magical influence of place, but through a hardened belief that what they think, do, and say is the same as is thought, done and said by the rest of the world. . . .

What really constitutes the attraction is less the scenes of *équivoque* [misunderstanding], though these abound, than the absolutely delicious things which people say to each other. A scene in the second act, in which the two heroines meet for the first time, embrace and on a sudden thought swear eternal friendship, then, finding that they are both betrothed, as they think, to the same man, the imaginary Ernest, proceed to exercise on each other the coldest civility, or the most cutting irony, is one of the drollest things ever witnessed on the stage. A little too much repetition of motive in the second act is, indeed, all in the way of approximation to dulness with which the play can be charged. Each successive scene elicited roars and hoots of approval, and the audience grew absolutely impatient to hear each succeeding witticism or impertinence the author had in store. Mr Wilde has the power to make even his *fadeurs* [pointless jokes] diverting. There is not a line without a laugh, and joke, epigram and parody jostle each other unendingly. Mr Wilde seems, indeed, to have introduced the piece in part as an Apologia, and makes one of his characters say, when taxed with talking nonsense: 'It is much better and rarer to talk nonsense than to listen to it'. It is, however, a mistake that everybody, down to the servants, talks in the same vein of *persiflage*. A similar kind of indictment has, however, been brought against Sheridan. . . .

[Unsigned review, p.7.]

NOTES

1. cf. Dryden, *Mac Flecknoe* (1682), lines 5–6.

2. Voltaire's *Ingénu* first appeared in 1767; Gilbert's *The Palace of Truth* had its *première* in 1870. [Ed.]

Observer   (17 February 1895)

The Importance of Being Earnest, which is the awkward name of the new play by Mr Oscar Wilde, just produced with so much success by Mr George Alexander, is a title wherein lies concealed one of its author's characteristic jokes. Of course, Mr Wilde does not really mean that it is important to be earnest; he would be much more likely to urge the importance of being frivolous. He employs the adjective 'earnest' by way of a pun upon the Christian name 'Ernest', whereby a couple of eccentric, if attractive, girls are anxious to call their future husbands. It does not strike us as a particularly good joke, or one altogether worthy of the bright piece of nonsense to which it belongs. But at any rate it suggests clearly enough that in his latest work Mr Oscar Wilde has deliberately abandoned what he believes to be the methods of genuine comedy for those of avowed farce. He has provided a fresh and, to our way of thinking, a far more appropriate medium for the humour typified in the quasi-epigrams which he places in the mouths of all his *dramatis personae*, old men and maidens, lords and ladies, masters and servants indiscriminately. He has devised extravagant motives and extravagant proceedings to match their extravagant style of conversation and views of life. He has in fact accepted the situation, and since the public has shown itself most appreciative of his efforts as a drawing-room jester he has determined to jest without any laborious pretence of being serious. The plot on which Mr Wilde here hangs his airy witticisms and his favourite contradictions of accepted axioms is as slight as the web which may serve as setting for drops of dew. His epigrammatic heroes in the irreproachable frock-coats of contemporary civilisation are creations as fanciful as any clown who ever donned the motley. His lady-like heroines, with the diaries in which they take down their lovers' proposals from dictation, are as frankly creatures of burlesque as though they wore the garb of fairy queens and spoke in couplets of limping rhyme. The only two persons in the play who bear any relationship to comedy as distinguished from Gilbertian extravagance are the cynical dowager Lady Bracknell and the cynical man-servant Lane. . . , and even with these it is noticeable that their respective utterances of cynicism are in precisely the same key. But if the characters of Mr Wilde's 'trivial comedy for serious people' all talk exactly alike it must be admitted that their talk is extremely entertaining, until through the monotony of its strain it becomes just a trifle wearisome. . . .   [Unsigned review, p.6.]

WILLIAM ARCHER   *World*   (20 February 1895)

. . . It is delightful to see, it sends wave after wave of laughter curling and foaming round the theatre; but as a text for criticism it is barren and delusive. It is like a mirage-oasis in the desert, grateful and comforting to the weary eye — but when you come close up to it, behold! it is intangible, it eludes your grasp. What can a poor critic do with a play which raises no principle, whether of art or morals, creates its own canons and conventions, and is nothing but an absolutely wilful expression of an irrepressibly witty personality? Mr Pater, I think (or is it some one else?), has an essay on the tendency of all art to verge towards, and merge in, the absolute art — music. He might have found an example in *The Importance of Being Earnest*, which imitates nothing, represents nothing, means nothing, is nothing, except a sort of *rondo capriccioso*, in which the artist's fingers run with crisp irresponsibility up and down the keyboard of life. Why attempt to analyse and class such a play? Its theme, in other hands, would have made a capital farce; but 'farce' is too gross and commonplace a word to apply to such an iridescent filament of fantasy. Incidents of the same nature as Algy Moncrieffe's[1] 'Bunburying' and John Worthing's invention and subsequent suppression of his scapegrace brother Ernest have done duty in many a French vaudeville and English adaptation; but Mr Wilde's humour transmutes them into something entirely new and individual. Amid so much that is negative, however, criticism may find one positive remark to make. Behind all Mr Wilde's whim and even perversity, there lurks a very genuine science, or perhaps I should say instinct, of the theatre. In all his plays, and certainly not least in this one, the story is excellently told and illustrated with abundance of scenic detail. Monsieur Sarcey[2] himself (if Mr Wilde will forgive my saying so) would 'chortle in his joy' over John Worthing's entrance in deep mourning (even down to his cane) to announce the death of his brother Ernest, when we know that Ernest in the flesh — a false but undeniable Ernest — is at that moment in the house making love to Cicely. The audience does not instantly awaken to the meaning of his inky suit, but even as he marches solemnly down the stage, and before a word is spoken, you can feel the idea kindling from row to row, until a 'sudden glory' of laughter fills the theatre. It is only the born playwright who can imagine and work up to such an effect. . . .   [Signed review, p-p. 24–5.]

NOTES

1. Algy's surname was spelt thus in the programme for the first night. [Ed.]
2. Francisque Sarcey (1827–99) was a highly exacting French dramatic critic. [Ed.]

PART THREE

Critical Comment, 1900–1967

Max Beerbohm   (1900; 1904; 1909)

1900

. . . his death, is, in a lesser degree, than his downfall, a great loss to the drama of our day. His work was distinct from that of most other playwrights in that he was a man who had achieved success outside the theatre. He was not a mere maker of plays. Taking up dramaturgy when he was no longer a young man, taking it up as a kind of after-thought, he brought to it a knowledge of the world which the life-long playwright seldom possesses. But this was only one point in his ad-vantage. He came as a thinker, a weaver of ideas, and as a wit, and as the master of a literary style. It was, I think, in respect of literary style that his plays were most remarkable. In his books this style was perhaps rather too facile, too rhetorical in its grace. Walter Pater, in one of his few book-reviews,[1] said that in Mr Wilde's work there was always 'the quality of the good talker'. This seems to me a very acute criticism. Mr Wilde's writing suffered by too close a likeness to the flow of speech. But it was this very likeness that gave him in dramatic dialogue as great an advantage over more careful and finer literary stylists as he had over ordinary playwrights with no pretence to style. The dialogue in his plays struck the right mean between literary style and ordinary talk. It was at once beautiful and natural, as dialogue should always be. With this and other advantages, he brought to dramaturgy as keen a sense for the theatre as was possessed by any of his rivals, except Mr Pinero. Theatrical construction, sense of theatri-cal effects, were his by instinct. I notice that one of the newspapers says that his plays were 'devoid of consideration as drama,' and suggests that he had little or no talent for construction.[2] Such criticism as this merely shows that what Ben Jonson called 'the dull ass's hoof,'[3] must have its backward fling. In point of fact, Mr Wilde's instinct for construction was so strong as to be a disadvantage. The very ease of his manipulation tempted him to trickiness, tempted him to accept current conventions which, if he had had to puzzle things out labori-ously and haltingly, he would surely have discarded, finding for him-self a simpler and more honest technique. His three serious comedies were marred by staginess. In *An Ideal Husband* the staginess was most apparent, least so in *A Woman of No Importance*. In the latter play, Mr Wilde allowed the psychological idea to work itself out almost unmolested, and the play was, in my opinion, by far the most truly dramatic of his plays. It was along these lines that we, in the early 'nineties, hoped Mr Wilde would ultimately work. But, even if he had confined his genius to the glorification of conventional drama, we should have had much reason to be grateful to him. His conventional comedies were as superior to the conventional comedies of other men as was *The Importance of Being Earnest* to the everyday farces whose scheme was so frankly accepted in it. At the moment of Mr Wilde's downfall, it was natural that the public sentiment should be one of repulsion. But later, when he was released from prison, they remembered that he had at least suffered the full penalty. And now that he is dead, they will realise also, fully, what was for them involved in his downfall, how lamentable the loss to dramatic literature.

SOURCE: extract from article in *Saturday Review* (8 Dec. 1900), p. 720.

NOTES

1. *Bookman* (Nov. 1891), I, pp. 59–60. [Ed.]
2. *Pall Mall Gazette* (1 Dec. 1900), p.2. [Ed.]
3. Jonson's 'An Ode: To himselfe', line 36. [Ed.]

1904

. . . He did not, at first, take the theatre seriously. He was content to express himself through the handiest current form of play. And that form happened to be Sardouesque comedy. It is inevitable, therefore, that *Lady Windermere's Fan* should seem to us, now that we see it again at the St James's Theatre,[1] after the lapse of twelve years, old-fashioned in scheme. But it is old-fashioned only in the sense in which a classic is old-fashioned. Partly by reason of the skill with which the scheme is treated – that perfect technique which comes to other men through innumerable experiments, but came all unearned to Oscar Wilde – and much more by reason of the dialogue itself, which is incomparable in the musical elegance and swiftness of its wit, *Lady Windermere's Fan* is a classic assuredly. As time goes on, those artificialities of incident and characterisation (irritating to us now, because we are in point of time so near to this play that we cannot discount them) will have ceased to matter. Our posterity will merely admire the deftness of the construction. And no lapse of time will dim the lustre of that wit which won for the play so much enthusiasm last Saturday. One may note, by the way, that the critics have doffed the glory with which, twelve years ago, they covered themselves by declaring that the author's wit was not genuine wit, but merely a mechanical trick which anyone could master. Perhaps they have been experimenting in the interval. . . .

SOURCE: extract from article in *Saturday Review* (26 Nov. 1904), p. 665.

NOTE

1. The play was revived on 19 November 1904.

1909

The Importance of Being Earnest has been revived by Mr Alexander at the St James's Theatre, and is as fresh and as irresistible as ever. It is vain to speculate what kind of work Oscar Wilde would have done had the impulse for play-writing survived in him. It is certain that a man of such variegated genius, and a man so inquisitive of art-forms, would not, as some critics seem to think he would, have continued to turn out plays in the manner of *The Importance of Being Earnest*. This, his last play, is not the goal at which he would have rested. But, of the plays that he wrote specifically for production in London theatres, it is the finest, the most inalienably his own. In *Lady Windermere's Fan* and *A Woman of No Importance* and *An Ideal Husband*, you are aware of the mechanism – aware of Sardou. In all of them there is, of course, plenty of humanity, and of intellectual force, as well as of wit and humour; and these qualities are the more apparent for the very reason that they are never fused with the dramatic scheme, which was a thing alien and ready-made. The Sardou manner is out-of-date; and so those three plays do, in a degree, date. It is certain that Oscar Wilde would later have found for serious comedy a form of his own, and would have written serious comedies as perdurable as his one great farce.

In *The Importance of Being Earnest* there is a perfect fusion of manner and form. It would be truer to say that the form is swallowed up in the manner. For you must note that not even in this play had Oscar Wilde invented a form of his own. On the contrary, the bare scenario is of the tritest fashion in the farce-writing of the period. Jack pretends to his niece, as an excuse for going to London, that he has a wicked brother whom he has to look after. Algernon, as an excuse for seeing the niece, impersonates the wicked brother. Jack, as he is going to marry and has no further need of a brother, arrives with the news of the brother's death; and so forth. Just this sort of thing had served as the staple for innumerable farces in the 'sixties and 'seventies and 'eighties – and would still be serving so if farce had not now been practically snuffed out by musical comedy. This very ordinary clod the magician picked up, turning it over in his hands – and presto! a dazzling prism for us.

How was the trick done? It is the tedious duty of the critic to ask such questions, and to mar what has been mere delight by trying to answer them. Part of the play's fun, doubtless, is in the unerring sense of beauty that informs the actual writing of it. The absurdity of the situation is made doubly absurd by the contrasted grace and dignity of everyone's utterance. The play abounds, too, in perfectly chiselled apothegms – witticisms unrelated to action or character, but so good in themselves as to have the quality of dramatic surprise. There are perhaps, in the course of the play, a dozen of those merely verbal inversions which Oscar Wilde invented, and which in his day the critics solemnly believed – or at any rate solemnly declared – to be his only claim to the title of wit. And of these inversions perhaps half-a-dozen have not much point. But, for the rest, the wit is of the finest order. . . . But, of course, what keeps the play so amazingly fresh is not the inlaid wit, but the humour, the ever-fanciful and inventive humour, irradiating every scene. Out of a really funny situation Oscar Wilde would get dramatically the last drop of fun, and then would get as much fun again out of the correlative notions aroused in him by that situation. When he had to deal with a situation which, dealt with by any ordinary dramatist, would be merely diagrammatic, with no real fun at all in it, always his extraneous humour and power of fantastic improvisation came triumphantly to the rescue. Imagine the final scenes of this play treated by an ordinary dramatist! How tedious, what a signal for our departure from the theatre, would be the clearing-up of the mystery of Jack Worthing's parentage, of the baby in the handbag, the manuscript in the perambulator! But the humour of the writing saves the situation, makes it glorious. Lady Bracknell's recital of the facts to the trembling Miss Prism – 'Through the elaborate investigations of the Metropolitan police, the perambulator was discovered at midnight, standing by itself in a remote corner of Bayswater. It contained the manuscript of a three-volume novel of more than usually revolting sentimentality' – and Miss Prism's subsequent recognition of the handbag by 'the injury it received through the upsetting of a Gower Street omnibus in younger and happier days' and by 'the strain on the lining caused by the explosion of a temperance beverage, an incident that occurred at Leamington' – these and a score of other extraneous touches keep us laughing whole-heartedly until the actual fall of the curtain.

Or again, imagine an ordinary dramatist's treatment of the great scene in the second act — the scene when Jack Worthing, attired in deepest mourning, comes to announce the death of the imaginary brother who is at this moment being impersonated on the premises by Algernon. I call this a 'great' scene, for, though it is (as I have hinted) essentially stale, it is so contrived as to be quite fresh. It is, indeed, and will always be cited as, a masterpiece of dramatic technique. If the audience knew at the beginning of the act that Jack was presently to arrive in deep mourning, the fun would be well enough. On the other hand, if, when he arrived, it had to be explained to them why he was in deep mourning, and what was his mission, there would be no fun at all. But the audience is in neither of these states. In the first act, Jack has casually mentioned, once or twice, that he means to 'kill off' his imaginary brother. But he doesn't say when or how he is going to do it. As the second act opens and proceeds, the audience has forgotten all about his intention. They are preoccupied by Algernon. And so, when the sable figure of Jack at length appears, they are for a moment bewildered, and then they vaguely remember, and there is a ripple of laughter, and this ripple swells gradually to a storm of laughter, as the audience gradually realises the situation in its full richness. None but a man with innate instinct for the theatre could have contrived this effect. But the point is that only Oscar Wilde, having contrived the effect, could have made the subsequent scene a worthy pendant to it. Miss Prism's comment on hearing that the cause of the brother's death was a chill, 'As a man sows, so shall he reap'; Dr Chasuble's offer to conduct the funeral service, and Jack's hasty explanation that his brother seems 'to have expressed a desire to be buried in Paris', and Dr Chasuble's 'I fear that hardly points to any very serious state of mind at the last' — these are of the things that have kept the play young, and have won for it, in dramatic literature, a place apart.

Source: extracts from article in *Saturday Review* (11 Dec. 1909), pp. 725–6.

J.T. Grein   (1901)

In 1895, when *The Importance of Being Earnest* saw the light at the St James's Theatre, it was voted a perfect farce, and, but for the catastrophe it would have been played for centuries of evenings. I recall this not merely as a chronological fact but more particularly in order to emphasise the exceeding cleverness of the play, since the duality of its fibre escaped most of the critics, and certainly the majority of the public. The practised eye discovered at once that the first and second acts and the third act were not of the same mould. They made the impression of wines of different vintages served in the same glasses. Those two acts – perfect, not only as farce, but as comedy, too, for they reflect the manners of the period, and are richly underlaid with humorous current.– were written in days when the poet basked in the hot sun of popularity, when his every saying darted like an arrow through the land, when the whole of the English speaking world echoed sallies which, though they were not always Oscar Wilde's, were as *ben trovato* [happily conceived] as if they had been his. The third act was – I know it authoritatively – composed under stress of circumstances, when the web was tightening round the man, and menaces of exposure must have rendered his gaiety forced, like that of a being condemned to the stocks. Under pressure a lofty mind often does excellent work, and it is undeniable that in the third act of *The Importance of Being Earnest* there is more cleverness than in one round dozen English comedies *en bloc*. There are epigrams in it for the paternity of which some people would give a few years of their lives, and as a solution to a tangle well-nigh inextricable it is by no means unhappy. Yet it is not of the same quality as those other two acts, in which the real, the probable, and the impossible form a *ménage à trois* of rare felicity. And as we listen to the play, what strikes us most of all is not so much the utterances of a mind which could not fail to be brilliant, but the prospect that this comedy – for I prefer to call it a comedy – will enjoy a kind of perennial youth somewhat akin to Congreve's work or that of Sheridan. It is a bold thing to say, I know, but if there is exaggeration, let it pass, for the sake of the argument that when the artist's working powers were shut off he had not yet thoroughly felt his feet, but was only just beginning to plough his furrow in a new field. *The Importance of Being Earnest* ranks high, not only on account of its gaiety – a gaiety which in many produces the smile of intimate understanding, and in the less *blasé* guffaws straight from a happy mood – but because it satirises vividly, pointedly, yet not unkindly, the mannerisms and foibles of a society which is constantly before the public eye. I need not dive into details, for the plot is, or ought to be, known to every lover of the Theatre. And I do not quote epigrams, for it is but a poor glory to feather one's own cap with another man's cleverness. Anon, when the play is revived at the St James's Theatre,[1] when the book of an author whose name one need no longer express with bated breath, is sold by the thousand, there will be ample opportunity to refresh one's memory, and spend a joyful hour with *The Importance of Being Earnest*. . . .

SOURCE: article in *Sunday Special* (8 Dec. 1901), p.6.

NOTE

1. Wilde's comedy was first revived at the Coronet Theatre on 2 December 1901, then transferred to its original home, the St James's, on 7 January 1902. [Ed.]

'Leonard Cresswell Ingleby' (1907)

When Mr George Alexander produced *Lady Windermere's Fan* at the St James's Theatre, in the spring of 1892, it created an unprecedented furore among all ranks of the playgoing public, and placed the author at once upon a pedestal in the Valhalla of the Drama; not on account of the plot, which was frankly somewhat *vieux jeu*, nor yet upon any striking originality in the types of the personages who were to unravel it, but upon the sparkle of the dialogue, the brilliancy of the epigrams, a condition of things to which the English stage had hitherto been entirely unaccustomed. The author was acclaimed as a playwright who had at last succeeded in clothing stagecraft with the vesture of literature, and with happy phrase and nimble paradox delighted the minds of his audience. What promise of a long succession of social comedies, illuminated by the intimate knowledge of his subject that he so entirely possessed, was held out to us! Here was a man who treated society as it really exists; who was himself living in it; portraying its folk as he knew them, with their virtues and vices coming to them as naturally as the facile flow of their conversation; conversation interlarded with no stilted sentences, no well- (or ill-) rounded periods, but such as that which falls without conscious effort from the lips of people who, in whatever surroundings they may be placed, are, before all things, and at all times, thoroughly at their ease. It may be objected that people in real life, even in the higher life of the Upper Ten, do not habitually scatter sprightly pleasantries abroad as they sit around the five-o'clock tea-table. That Oscar Wilde made every personage he depicted talk as he himself was wont to talk. *Passe encore.* [Well and good.] The real fact remains that he *knew* the social atmosphere he represented, had breathed it, and was familiar with all its traditions and mannerisms. He gave us the *tone* of Society as it had never before been given. He was at home in it. He could exhibit a ball upon the stage where real ladies and gentlemen assembled together, quite distinct from the ancient 'Adelphi guests',[1] who had hitherto done yeoman's service in every form of entertainment imagined by the dramatist. The company who came to his great parties were at least *vraisemblables*, beings who conducted themselves as if they really might have been there. And so it was in every scene, in every situation. His types are drawn with the pen of knowledge, dipped in the ink of experience. That was his secret, the keynote of his success. And with what power he used it the world is now fully aware. It is not too much to say that Oscar Wilde revolutionised dramatic art. Henceforth it began to be understood that the playwright who would obtain the merit of a certain plausibility must endeavour to infuse something of the breath of life into his creations, and make them act and talk in a manner that was at least possible.

It has been a popular *pose* among certain superior persons, equally devoid of humour themselves as of the power of appreciating it in others, that Oscar Wilde sacrificed dramatic action to dialogue; that his plays were lacking in human interest, his plots of the very poorest; a fact that was skilfully concealed by the sallies of smart sayings and witty repartee, which carried the hearers away during the representation, so that in the charm of the style they forgot the absence of the substance. But such is by no means the case. The author recognised, with his fine artistic *flair*, that mere talk, however admirable, will not carry a play to a successful issue without a strong underlying stratum of histrionic interest to support it. There are situations in his comedies as powerful in their handling as could be desired by the most devout stickler for dramatic intention. There are scenes in which the humorist lays aside his motley, and becomes the moralist, unsparing in his methods to enforce, *à l'outrance* [to the utmost], the significance of his text. In each of his plays there are moments in which the action is followed by the spectator with absorbed attention; incidents of emotional value treated in no half-hearted fashion. Such are the hall mark of the true dramatist who can touch, with the unerring instinct of the poet, the finest feelings, the deepest sympathies of his audience, and which place Oscar Wilde by the side of Victorien Sardou. As has been

well written by one of our most impartial critics: 'No other among our
playwrights equals this distinguished Frenchman, either in imagination or in poignancy of style.'

Again, it has been contended, with a sneer, that the turning out of
witty speeches is but a trick, easy of imitation by any theatrical scribe
who sets himself to the task. But how many of Wilde's imitators –
and there have been not a few – have accomplished such command
of language, such literary charm, such 'fineness' of wit? Who among
them all has ever managed to hold an audience spellbound in the
same way? How many have succeeded in drawing from a miscellan-
eous crowd of spectators such spontaneous expressions of delighted
approval as 'How brilliant! How true!' first muttered by each under
the breath to himself, and then tossed loudly from one to the other in
pure enjoyment, as the solid truth, underlying the varnish of the
paradox, was borne home to them? Surely, not one can be indicated.
Nor is the reason far to seek. For in all Oscar Wilde's seemingly
irresponsible witticisms it is not only the device of the inverted epigram that is made a characteristic feature of the dialogue; there is
real human nature behind the artificialities, there is poetry beneath
the prose, the grip of the master's hand in seemingly toying with truth.
And it is the possession of these innate qualities that differentiates
the inventor from his imitators, and leaves them hopelessly behind in
the race for dramatic distinction.

To invent anything is difficult, and in proportion to its merits
praiseworthy. To cavil at that which has been devised, to point with
the finger of scorn at its imperfections, to 'run it down', is only too easy
a pastime. Oscar Wilde was before all an inventor. Whatever he
touched he endowed with the gracious gift of style that bore the stamp
of his own individual genius. He originated a new treatment for
ancient themes. For there is no such thing as an absolutely new 'plot'.
Every play that has been written is founded on doings, dealings, incidents that have happened over and over again. Love, licit or illicit, the
mainspring of all drama, is the same to-day as it was yesterday, and
will be for ever and ever in this world. One man and one woman, or
one woman and two men, or again, as a pleasant variant, two women
and one man. Such are the eternal puppets that play the game of Love
upon the Stage of Life; the unconscious victims of the sentiment which
sometimes makes for tragedy. They are always with us, placed in the
same situations, and extricating themselves (or otherwise) in the same
old way. So that when a new playwright is condemned by the critics as
a furbisher-up of well-known *clichés* he is hardly treated. He cannot
help himself. He must tread the familiar paths, *faute de mieux*. And the
public, with its big human heart and unquestioning traditions, knows

this, and is satisfied therewith. Nothing really pleases people so much as to tell them something they already know. What an accomplished dramatist can do is to rehabilitate his characters by the power of his own personality, and by felicitous treatment invest his action with fresh interest. And this is what Oscar Wilde effected in stagecraft. He vitalised it. . . .

(Signed review. The 'Ingleby' pen-name was one of those used by C. Ranger Gull: see Notes on Contributors below. – Ed.)

SOURCE: extract from *Oscar Wilde* (London [1907]), pp.95–100.

NOTE

1. The 'extras' in the predominantly melodramatic productions at the Adelphi Theatre were a frequent target for satire. [Ed.]

Archibald Henderson   (1907)

. . . there is no term which so perfectly expresses the tone of Wilde's comedies as nonchalance. The astounding thing is, that in his sincere effort to amuse the public, he best succeeded with that public by holding it up to scorn and ridicule with the lightest satire. One of the most self-revelative of his paradoxes is the opinion that life is far too serious ever to be discussed seriously. 'If we are to deliver a philosophy', says Mr Chesterton, in speaking of contemporary life, 'it must be in the manner of the late Mr Whistler[1] and the *ridentem dicere verum*.[2] If our heart is to be aimed at, it must be with the rapier of Stevenson, which runs through without either pain or puncture.' If our brain is to be aroused, he might have added, it must be with the scintillating paradox and enlivening epigram of Oscar Wilde. Horace Walpole once said that the world is a comedy for the man of thought, a tragedy for the man of feeling. He forgot to say that it is a farce for the man of wit. It was Wilde's creed that ironic imitation of the contrasts, absurdities and inconsistencies of life, its fads and fancies, its quips and cranks, its follies and foibles, give far more pleasure and amusement than faithful portraiture of the dignity of life, its seriousness and profundity, its tragedy, pity and terror. His comedies are marked, not by consistency in the characters, continuity of purpose, or unity of action, but only by persistence of the satiric vein and prevalence of the comic mood. Like Flaubert, Wilde gloried in demoralizing the public,

and he denied with every breath Sidney Lanier's[3] dictum that art has
no enemy so unrelenting as cleverness. His whole literary career was
one long, defiant challenge to Zola's pronunciamento: *'L'homme de
génie n'a jamais d'esprit'* [the man of genius never possesses wit].

While the dialogue of Wilde's comedies, as the brilliant Viennese
critic, Hermann Bahr, has said, contains more verve and *esprit* than all
the French, German and Italian comedies put together, nevertheless
our taste is outraged because Wilde makes no effort to paint character
and employs a conventional and time-worn technique. Wilde's figures are lacking in vitality and humanity; it is impossible to believe
in their existence.

They are mere mouthpieces for the diverting ratiocinations of their
author, often appearing less as personalities than as personified customs, embodied prejudices and conventions of English life. By means
of these pallid figures, Wilde has at least admirably succeeded in
interpreting certain sides of the English national character. The form of
his comedies approximates to that of the best French farces, but his
humor sounds a genuine British note. There is no escaping the impression, however, that his characters are automatons and puppets –
masks which barely suffice to conceal the lineaments of Wilde. Here
we see the *raisonneur* [disputant] as we find him in Dumas *fils*, or in
Sudermann[4]. It is in this way that Wilde identifies his characters, not
with their prototypes in actual life, but with himself.

Jean Joseph Renaud and Henri de Regnier have paid eloquent tri-
butes to Wilde as a master of the *causerie* [chat]. A great lady once said
of him: 'When he is speaking, I see round his head a luminous
aureole.' The mere exaggeration of the phrase is testimony to Wilde's
maestria [mastery] in utterance of golden words. He was a slave to the
Scheherazade of his fancy, and was unsparingly lavish in the largess of
his wit. He realized that he was a past-master in the gentle art of making conversation, and he nonchalantly ignored Goethe's precept:
'Bilde, Künstler, rede nicht!' [Create art, you artists, don't discuss it].
The result is, that he does not construct, but only sets off a mime. His
art is the expression of his enjoyment of verbal pyrotechnics. To use
Baudelaire's phrase, he wrote comedies *pour étonner les sots*, and the
height of his pleasure was *épater les bourgeois* [to surprise the fools. . .to
amaze the conventional]. The result in his comedies, while vastly
diverting, is deplorable from the standpoint of dramatic art. For the
conversations are disjointed, and, in the dramatic sense, incoherent,
in that they live only for the moment, and not at all for the sake of
elucidation and propulsion of the dramatic process. The comparison
with Shaw in this particular immediately suggests itself, but the fundamental distinction consists in the fact that whereas in Shaw's

comedies the conversation, witty and epigrammatic to a degree is strictly germane to the action, with Wilde the conversation, with all its sparkling brilliancy, is in fact subsidiary and beside the mark. As Hagemann has justly said, in Wilde's comedies the accent and stress are thrown wholly upon the epigrammatic content of the dialogue.

What, after all, is the secret of Wilde's success? What is the quintessence of his art as a dramatist? For, say what one will, Wilde's comedies were – and are – immensely successful; and his plays, whether comedy or tragedy, are art even if they are not always drama. Hermann Bahr refused to consider Wilde as frivolous, maintaining that his paradoxes rest upon a profound insight into humanity. 'Wilde says serious and often sad things that convulse us with merriment, not because he is not "deep", but precisely because he is deeper than seriousness and sadness, and has recognized their nullity.'

. . . Wilde called one of his plays *The Importance of Being Earnest*. In his inverted way, he aimed at teaching the world the importance of being frivolous. Only from this standpoint is it possible to appreciate, in any real sense, Wilde the comic dramatist. . . .

SOURCE: extracts from 'The Theatre of Oscar Wilde', *Overland Monthly*, L (1907), pp. 9–18.

NOTES

1. James McNeill Whistler (1834–1903), the American artist and wit. He and Wilde frequently accused the other of cribbing his ideas and witticisms. [Ed.]

2. Cf. Horace, *Satires* I 1 24: 'speaking the truth in a jesting manner'. [Ed.]

3. American poet and critic (1842–81). [Ed.]

4. For Dumas *fils*, see Note 1, Section 1, Part Two above; Hermann Sudermann was a German novelist and playwright (1857–1928), author of *Die Ehre* (1890). [Ed.]

C.E. Montague   (1908)

Lady Windermere's Fan was Wilde's first success with a world which it half mocked and half flattered. Its plot was propelled by theatrical commonplaces. The incident of the fan had just been used by Mr Haddon Chambers in *The Idler*.[1] Lady Windermere's doctrine of tit-for-tat in conjugal infidelity had been expounded in full by at least one heroine of the younger Dumas. The reappearance of a divorced wife to rescue a daughter, who does not know her, from risk of a similar fate, had been used in the *Révoltée* of Lemaître,[2] if not elsewhere. Wilde in this play gave the public a great deal of what it was already known to like; but also he made it like − at least made it accept − one thing which was not such sure merchandise − the coherent treatment of Mrs Erlynne's character to the end. The dialogue was sometimes forced and tedious. In the third act the play's action made an almost dead halt to accommodate a string of highly worked-up witticisms, machine-made, second-rate, crude, and unprepared in the manner of their introduction. But much of the play was amusing. Surprisingly like many plays of no moment, adapted from middling French writers by middling English ones, it was still always better than these wherever it did differ from them; and at the end of the first act the dialogue was salt and rapid, the real dialogue of comedy.

Then came *A Woman of No Importance*, and for a long time after the rise of the curtain one wondered, Would there be a play at all? There was talking, not drama. On the terrace of a country house persons were shown launching at each other illustrated reminiscences of Wilde's *Intentions*, a critical volume in which the best ways to flout and puzzle the Philistine mind are fully explained. From their clothes and the qualities of their voices one gathered that there were a few broad differences between the persons on the terrace. Some were men, some women, one an Archdeacon, one an American. But, except for these shallow, if broad, distinctions of sex, country and business, they were nearly all identical in character for a good while. They did not build themselves individualities in their talk; they only took turns to talk in the same way. They passed the whole act in the composition of couplets of speeches; first a question, then its answer − first couplet; then a quite disconnected second question, drawing its answer − second couplet. 'What is a bad man?' asked some character − you soon forgot which. 'The sort of man who admires innocence', answered another, quite pat. Then the audience gaped; here and there a spectator felt that he saw it, and he raised an isolated laugh, a little late. Then the game began again. Was it not the frivolity of the wife, somebody asked, that most often spoilt marriages? Somebody else took three steps across the carpet and, planting himself in the midst of the party said with solemnity: 'More marriages are ruined nowadays by the common sense of the husband than by anything else.' A slight sound from the auditorium would follow this sally, not exactly applause or mirth, but what is suggested by the parenthetic phrase in police reports, 'sensation in court'. On the stage, meanwhile, they went at it again, always in the form of a disjointed catechism, burlesquing the catch phrases of conventional morals or of mechanical friendliness.

It was mostly clever, not always new – how often had we heard, even then, that 'good Americans, when they die, go to Paris'? – and generally the effect of labour had not been smoothed out or tidied away. Most of the questions and answers might, without loss of aptness, have been taken from their appointed utterers, shaken up in a bag and distributed anew. As 'criticism of life' they would then have been only equally futile; as means of explaining character or forwarding the play's action they were insignificant anyhow. After more than one act of this stationary, ingenious, and obscure entertainment, Wilde began a play with a telling final scene, and, when that scene came, he wrote it capitally, kept his audience intent, and achieved in his heroine a strain of noble disdain finer than anything he had yet done in dramatic emotion. But this change to real drama caused a dreadful mortality among the undramatic figures of the first act. As the play went on, all but three of its characters disappeared. As soon as dramatic business was meant there was clearly no place for them; they had to pack up their epigrams and go.

In *An Ideal Husband*, Wilde's next play to be acted, his comic genius was not to reach its full height, but at least it was to prove how indolently a man of comic genius may write a comedy and yet not fail. Its plot, its incidents, the main lines of its characters are half invented, half cribbed, as lazily or hurriedly as anything in Shakespeare or Molière, those arch-cribbers. As a mainspring for plays the blackmailing lady who keeps whole catacombs of dark pasts, steals jewels freely, and is received at embassies, may indeed be junior to the everlasting hills – it depends on the age of the hills – but the world of stormed barns and penny gaffs has no older inhabitant. Then the tangle of the plot is not really disentangled at all; it is merely exorcised; miracles happen whenever Wilde cannot undo one of his knots. For example: A has to know, in order to make things get on, that B is hiding in the next room, so B kicks down a chair, noisily. C, for the same good end, has to force upon D the physical possession of a brooch; so the brooch becomes convertible, against the nature of brooches, into a bracelet, and the bracelet has a secret spring, and C knows the spring and D does not, and thus, by heaping improbability upon improbability, the literal fetter that is needed for the lady's arm is called out of the vasty deep. Or consider the idleness of the thinking; compare the cutting of the ethical knot here, when the wife and husband are relieved, not from his past act of profitable baseness, but from the mere fear of its detection, with the facing of the same difficulty by Ibsen in *A Doll's House*.

On this heap of stale loans Wilde sheds wit and mischief till the old stuff gleams and twinkles with comic lights direct and refracted, a dancing lustre unlike any other, and somewhat exotic. For people quite English do not talk like these people of Wilde's. Of course the paradoxical line is followed in England, as elsewhere, often enough. Paradox is inevitable in social groups where saltness of speech is a point of honour and where wit is not universal; for paradox is usually the announcement of a sense of the necessity of brilliancy, with or without the power to achieve it. But the play of mind in Wilde's Londoners of quality is usually that of English men and women whom a quick-witted Frenchman or Irishman is coaching, prompting, briefing, and at the same time watching, delicately mocking. Behind the immediate gaiety and irony of their talk you feel a reserve of irony not given to them for their use, but used against them, playing upon them, and playing, through them, on the audience, too: it comes out in the more obvious epigrams, thrown down like little bombs, as if in a derisive offer to match with their shouted emphasis some understood dullness and literalness in the hearer's mind; and again it comes out in the reticent gravity with which Chiltern, the accepted public man, the phrasing dullard, is presented, as if Wilde half thought that the public might take him seriously, and, for mischief's sake, would not give them the hint not to do so. The play is so drenched in comedy that it cannot but keep an audience laughing; but with the laughter there seems to go some perplexity; one fancies, an uneasy sense of something alien to the spectator's blood, and of a blurring of the confines of lawful fun and levity.

In his last acted comedy, *The Importance of Being Earnest*, Wilde's art does not quite shed its faults, but he gains the upper hand of them as he did nowhere else. He still turns out some machine-made or Gilbertian humours of simple inversion; he still fusses now and then about keeping up his name for paradox; he still gives his people some things to say that are not expressive of just those people, merely because they have come into his head and he cannot deny himself their use or will not wait to find something apter; and some of the characters – the parson, the governess, the she-dragon from Debrett – are old stage dummies. But Wilde's other comedies were made of such failings; they are mere specks on the excellence of this one; here the detachable witticisms, the little candles and gilt balls and calico blossoms tied on, as it were, to a Christmas tree, are relatively few, and the real flowers, the jests and telling things that grow out of the stem of the play, and express and expand it, are relatively many. In the French slang of the theatre, the *mots d'esprit* have become *mots de situation*, also, and, to some extent, *mots de caractère*, too; the verbal good things, besides their first glitter, take value from where they are placed in the play, and often give value by making someone's mood or character divertingly apparent.

All of this comedy is instantly amusing; you laugh, or at least your mental interior beams, at almost every speech. Mr Shaw says it wastes your time because it does not touch you as well as amuse. But one may hold that laughter, like bread, is a thing that has worth in itself so far as it goes; the bread may also sustain a gallant garrison, or the laughter may also conduce to Christian charity and brotherhood; but, even without these higher offices, bread and laughter are good. And this play is no mere rib-tickler, like some string of puns. All the early talk of Jack and Algernon is quite veracious social portraiture. Among a portion of the comfortable English unemployed, some years ago, there was current just that vein of chaff, a special blend of the knowing and the infantine, a kind of cynic simplicism. Perhaps it is extinct. If so, here is your document. Wilde catches the mental (not vocal) drawl, the pose of an adult egoism aping childlike naïveté in appetite, as cleverly as Swift, in his *Polite Conversations*,[3] seems to have hit off the frank parade of imbecility and grossness common in some modish people of his time. Again, it has been said that there is too much of mere stock farcical mechanics in the play – the symmetrical lying and counter-lying, the sham mourning, the dual christening, the fight for the muffins, and so on. But it is rather hard to say exactly when fun is mechanical and when it is not. You might call Trinculo's fun with the bottle mechanical, and Sganarelle's fun with the same beloved object, and much of the Bob Acres fun at the duel, and Tony Lumpkins's fun at the inn. It all depends on the account to which you turn your mechanism, and Wilde's use of his in this play is the work of a comic genius – Worthing's entry, for instance, in deep mourning for the brother whom he had only pretended to have, and whom he now pretends to have lost, to the house in which his friend is at the moment personating that fictitious brother. That entry is an example of true theatrical invention. To an audience, knowing what it knows, the mere first sight of those black clothes is convulsingly funny; it is a visible stroke of humour, a witticism not heard but seen, and it is precisely a richness in this gift of scenic or spectacular imagination that most distinguishes dramatists from other imaginative writers.

SOURCE: article in *Manchester Guardian* (13 Apr. 1908), p.9; reprinted in *Dramatic Values* (London, 1911), pp. 175–89.

NOTES

1. *The Idler*, a four-act melodrama by Charles Haddon Chambers (1860–1921), was staged at the St James's Theatre by George Alexander on 26 February 1891.

2. Jules Lemaître (1853–1914), French critic and playwright, published his *Revoltée* in 1889.

3. Swift's *A Complete Collection of Genteel and Ingenious Conversations* appeared in 1738.

St John Hankin (1908)

. . . The difficulty about Wilde as a playwright was that he never quite got through the imitative phase. *The Importance of Being Earnest* is the nearest approach to absolute originality that he attained. In that play, for the first time, he seemed to be tearing himself away from tradition and to be evolving a dramatic form of his own. Unhappily it was the last play he was to write, and so the promise in it was never fulfilled. Had his career not been cut short at this moment, it is possible that this might have proved the starting-point of a whole series of 'Trivial Comedies for Serious People', and that thenceforward Wilde would have definitely discarded the machine-made construction of the Scribe-Sardou theatre which had held him too long and begun to use the drama as an artist should, for the expression of his own personality, not the manufacture of clever *pastiches*. It would then have become possible to take him seriously as a dramatist. For, paradoxical as it may sound in the case of so merry and light-hearted a play, *The Importance of Being Earnest* is artistically the most serious work that Wilde produced for the theatre. Not only is it by far the most brilliant of his plays considered as literature. It is also the most sincere. With all its absurdity, its psychology is truer, its criticism of life subtler and more profound, than that of the other plays. And even in its technique it shows, in certain details, a breaking away from the conventional well-made play of the 'seventies and 'eighties in favour of the looser construction and more naturalistic methods of the newer school.

Consider its 'curtains' for a moment and compare them with those of the conventional farce or comedy of their day or of Wilde's other plays. In the other plays Wilde clung tenaciously to the old-fashioned 'strong' curtain, and I am bound to say he used it with great cleverness, though the cleverness seems to me deplorably wasted. The curtain of the third act of *Lady Windermere's Fan*, when Mrs Erlynne suddenly emerges from Lord Darlington's inner room, and Lady

Windermere, taking advantage of the confusion, glides from her hiding-place in the window and makes her escape unseen, is theatrically extremely effective. So is that of the third act of *An Ideal Husband,* when Mrs Cheveley triumphantly carries off Lady Chiltern's letter under the very eyes of Lord Goring, who cannot forcibly stop her because his servant enters at that moment in answer to her ring. It is a purely theatrical device only worthy of a popular melodrama. But it produces the requisite thrill in the theatre. On the analogy of these plays one would expect to find in *The Importance of Being Earnest* the traditional 'curtains' of well-made farce, each act ending in what used to be called a 'tableau' of comic bewilderment or terror or indignation. Instead of this we have really no 'curtains' at all. Acts I and II end in the casual, go-as-you-please fashion of the ultra-naturalistic school. They might be the work of Mr Granville Barker. Of course, there is nothing really go-as-you-please about them save in form. They are as carefully thought out, as ingenious in the best sense, as the strong 'curtain' could possibly be. But this will not appear to the superficial observer, who will probably believe that these acts 'end anyhow'. Here is the end of Act I:

ALGERNON Oh, I'm a little anxious about poor Bunbury, that is all.
JACK If you don't take care, your friend Bunbury will get you into a serious scrape some day.
ALGERNON I love scrapes. They are the only things that are never serious.
JACK Oh, that's nonsense, Algy. You never talk anything but nonsense.
ALGERNON Nobody ever does.

(Curtain)

This may seem an easy, slap-dash method of ending an act, and one which anybody can accomplish, but it is very far from being so easy as it looks. To make it effective in the theatre – and in *The Importance of Being Earnest* it is enormously effective – requires at least as much art as the more elaborate devices of the earlier comedies. Only in this case it is the art which conceals art which is required, not the art which obtrudes it.

In *The Importance of Being Earnest,* in fact, Wilde really invented a new type of play, and that type was the only quite original thing he contributed to the English stage. In form it is farce, but in spirit and in treatment it is comedy. Yet it is not farcical comedy. Farcical comedy is a perfectly well recognised class of drama and a fundamentally different one. There are only two other plays which I can think of which belong to the same type – *Arms and the Man* and

The Philanderer. Arms and the Man, like *The Importance of Being Earnest,* is psychological farce, the farce of ideas. In it Mr Shaw, like Wilde, has taken the traditional farcical form – the last of both plays are quite on traditional lines in their mechanism – and breathed into it a new spirit. Similarly, *The Philanderer* is psychological farce, though here there is less farce and more psychology. . . .

The same imitative quality which prevents one from taking *The Duchess of Padua* seriously as a work of art mars the comedies also. As far as plot and construction are concerned they are frankly modelled on the 'well-made play' of their period. Indeed, they were already old-fashioned in technique when they were written. The long soliloquy which opens the third act of *Lady Windermere's Fan* with such appalling staginess, and sends a cold shiver down one's back at each successive revival, was almost equally out of date on the first night. Ibsen had already sent that kind of thing to the right-about for all persons who aspired to serious consideration as dramatists. Luckily the fame of Wilde's comedies does not rest on his plots or his construction. It rests on his gifts of characterisation and of brilliant and effective dialogue. Both these gifts he possessed in a pre-eminent degree, but in both of them one has to recognise grave limitations. His minor characters are generally first-rate, but he never quite succeeded with his full-length figures. He is like an artist who can produce marvellously life-like studies or sketches, but fails when he attempts to elaborate a portrait. Windermere and Lady Windermere, Sir Robert and Lady Chiltern, none of them is really human, none of them quite alive. As for the principal people in *A Woman of No Importance,* Lord Illingworth himself, Mrs Arbuthnot and her son, Hester Worsley, they are all dolls. The sawdust leaks out of them at every pore. That is the central weakness of the play, that and its preposterous plot. But when you turn to the minor characters, to Lady Hunstanton and Lady Caroline Pontefract and Sir John and the Archdeacon, how admirably they are drawn! Did anybody ever draw foolish or pompous or domineering old ladies better than Wilde? Think of Lady Hunstanton's deliciously idiotic reply to poor Miss Worsley when that American young lady, with impassioned fervour, has just been proclaiming to the assembled company the domestic virtues of her countrymen who are 'trying to build up something that will last longer than brick or stone'. 'What is that, dear?' asks Lady Hunstanton with perfect simplicity. 'Ah yes, an Iron Exhibition, is it not, at that place which has the curious name?' How it sets before us in a flash the whole character of the speaker, her gentleness, her stupidity, her admirable good breeding as contrasted with Miss Worsley's crude provincialism! Or again, think of that other reply of hers when Mrs Allonby tells her that in the Hunstanton

conservatories there is an orchid that is 'as beautiful as the Seven
Deadly Sins'. 'My dear, I hope there is nothing of the kind. I will certainly speak to the gardener.'

Lady Caroline is equally well drawn, with her sharp tongue and
her shrewd masculine common sense. She also has a brief encounter
with Miss Worsley, in which the latter is again put to rout, but by
quite different means. Lady Hunstanton conquered by sheer gentle
futility. Lady Caroline administers a deliberate snub, all the more
crushing because it is given with a deadly semblance of unconscious-
ness. Here is the scene:—

HESTER Lord Henry Weston! I remember him, Lady Hunstanton. A man with a
hideous smile and a hideous past. He is asked everywhere. No dinner-party is complete
without him. What of those whose ruin is due to him? They are outcasts. They are
nameless. If you met them in the street you would turn your head away. I don't complain of their punishment. Let all women who have sinned be punished.

LADY HUNSTANTON My dear young lady!

HESTER It is right that they should be punished, but don't let them be the only ones
to suffer. If a man and a woman have sinned, let them both go forth into the desert to
love or loathe each other there. Let them both be branded. Set a mark, if you wish, on
each, but don't punish the one and let the other go free. Don't have one law for men and
another for women. You are unjust to women in England. And till you count what is a
shame in a woman to be an infamy in a man, you will always be unjust, and Right, that
pillar of fire, and Wrong, that pillar of cloud, will be made dim to your eyes, or be not
seen at all, or if seen, not regarded.

LADY CAROLINE *Might I, dear Miss Worsley, as you are standing up, ask you for my cotton
that is just behind you? Thank you.*

It must be admitted that in order to get his effect, Wilde has exaggerated the rhetoric of Miss Worsley's speech to an unfair degree,
thereby 'loading the dice' against her in the encounter. But the effect
is so admirable in the theatre that one forgives the means.

When I say that it was only in his 'minor characters' that Wilde
was completely successful, I do not mean unimportant characters, or
characters who only make brief appearances in his plays, such as the
walking ladies and gentlemen in his evening parties, or the impassive
men-servants who wait upon Lord Goring and Mr Algernon Mon-
crieff. I include under the description all the people who are not
emotionally of prime importance to the plot. Lady Bracknell and the
Duchess of Berwick are very important parts in the plays in which
they appear, and Wilde obviously took an immense amount of trouble
with them, but they are not emotionally important as Lady Windermere is or Mrs Erlynne. In that sense they are minor characters. It is
in the drawing of such characters that Wilde is seen absolutely at his
best. Who can ever forget Lady Bracknell's superb scene with Mr
Worthing in *The Importance of Being Earnest,* when she puts that gentle-

man through a series of questions as he is 'not on her list of eligible bachelors, though she has the same list as the dear Duchess of Bolton'? Who can forget the inimitable speech in which she sums up the sorrows of the modern landowner?—

What between the duties expected of one during one's lifetime, and the duties exacted from one after one's death, land has ceased to be either a profit or a pleasure. It gives one position, and prevents one from keeping it up. That is all that can be said about land.

Yes, Lady Bracknell is an immortal creation. She is in some ways the greatest achievement of the Wilde theatre, the fine flower of his genius. It is impossible to read any of her scenes – indeed, it is impossible to read almost any scene whatever in *The Importance of Being Earnest* – without recognising that for brilliancy of wit this play may fairly be ranked with the very greatest of English comedies. But though Lady Bracknell is wonderfully drawn, she is not profoundly drawn. As a character in so very light a comedy, there is, of course, no reason why she should be. I merely mention the fact lest she should be claimed as an exception to the statement that Wilde's more elaborate portraits are all failures. Lady Bracknell is brilliantly done, but she is a brilliant surface only. She has no depth and no subtlety. Wilde has seen her with absolute clearness, but he has seen her, as it were, in two dimensions only, not in the round. That is the weak point of all Wilde's character drawing. It lacks solidity. No one can hit off people's external manifestations, their whims and mannerisms, their social insincerities, more vividly or more agreeably than he. But he never shows you their souls. And when it is necessary that he should do so, if you are really to understand and to sympathise with them, as it is in the case of Mrs Arbuthnot, for example, or Lady Chiltern, he fails.

Why he failed I do not know. Possibly it was from mere indolence, because he was not sufficiently interested. Possibly he could not have succeeded if he tried. To analyse character to the depths requires imaginative sympathy of a very special kind, and I am not sure whether Wilde possessed this, or at least possessed it in the requisite degree of intensity. He had a quick eye for the foibles of mankind and a rough working hypothesis as to their passions and weaknesses. Beyond that he does not seem to me to have gone, and I doubt it ever occurred to him to examine the springs of action of even his most important characters with any thoroughness. So long as what they did and the reasons assigned for their doing it would pass muster in the average English theatre with the average English audience, he was content.

That is not the spirit in which the great characters of dramatic literature have been conceived. . . .

SOURCE: extract from *Fortnightly Review* (1 May 1908), pp. 791–
802.

P.P. Howe   (1911)

When Wilde wrote about the Decay of Lying[1] he wrote of course to
deplore the desuetude into which an art had fallen. Wilde admired the
art – indeed, he practised it. What is *Lady Windermere's Fan* but one
elaborate, self-conscious lie, based throughout on the doctrines of his
'new aesthetics'? Art must never express anything but itself, said
Wilde; all bad art came from returning to Life and Nature, and elevating them into ideals; it was desirable rather that Life should imitate
Art than the contrary. Those were the doctrines, roughly; and, since
Wilde was not your mere paradox-monger, he proceeded to base his
plays upon them. When the remark has been made – as Wilde made
it – that it is very much easier to be bold and enterprising as a critic
than as an artist, these will be found to be the doctrines on which *Lady
Windermere's Fan* is based. Everyone in the play talks the purest Wilde.
Certainly it is not in the least true to life. As for Life imitating *Lady
Windermere's Fan* – well, probably in certain of its walks there was
some such tendency in 1892, but we have fortunately outlived all that.
No, one's inclination on visiting the St James's Theatre nineteen
years later is to make use of Wilde's phrase a little differently, and to
see in the revival the Decay of Lying exemplified. For the play has not
been able to stand the test of time. There is food for thought in this
reflection that, however golden the lie, it must come to dust. One finds
oneself emerging from the theatre with a mumbled tag upon one's
lips about the greatness of Truth and the certainty that it shall
prevail. . . .
     . . . If *Lady Windermere's Fan* were a new play, put on last week for
the first time, I think criticism could only have one thing to say, that it
was a very bad play. Only criticism would have to add with its next
breath that it was very well written. I do not mean well constructed;
the badness of its construction is such, even if the play were given as
Wilde wrote it [i.e. without the revelation of Mrs Erlynne's identity at

the end of Act I – Ed.], as to lead one to the belief that Wilde never bothered sufficiently to become in any strict sense of the word a dramatist at all. And yet if no single figure stood against one but that of Ernest entering at the wicket-gate in mourning for the brother who was not his brother and who was not dead, it would be impossible to deny Wilde a sense of the theatre. *The Importance of Being Earnest* is good to read, but it is better to see and to listen to in the theatre; and the same, if on account of its dialogue alone, must be said of *Lady Winder- mere's Fan*. How much better if Wilde did lazily kick at the work involved in mastering the theatre, had he written nothing for it save fantastic comedy, in which he might have uttered a mint of golden lies and never been found out! But his 'good woman' who goes back to her half-world after ensuring that her unconscious daughter shall not idly throw away the enjoyment of her whole one – pooh, he never mas- tered stagecraft enough even to make her stand firmly on her feet! You may count nine large soliloquies at the St James's Theatre any even- ing; indeed the characters explain themselves to us, when explanation is imperative, by no other means. Yet a good 'producer' may do much with such a play, so well worth reviving, so certain of a place in the repertory of a National Theatre. . . .

SOURCE: extracts from article in *Outlook* (21 Oct. 1911), p. 536.

NOTE

1. First published in *Nineteenth Century* (Jan 1889), and revised for *Intentions* (1891). [Ed.]

Arthur Ransome (1912)

. . . There was a continuity in Wilde's interest in the theatre wholly lacking in his passing fancies for narrative or essay-writing. This, with the fact that his plays brought him his first financial success, has made it usual to consider him as a dramatist whose recreations are rep- resented by his books. Even Mr Symons, in his article on Wilde as 'An Artist in Attitudes', finds that his plays, 'the wittiest that have been seen upon the modern stage,' expressed, 'as it happened by acci- dent, precisely what he himself was best able to express.'[1] I cannot help feeling that this is a little unjust to him. His most perfectly successful works, those which most exactly accomplish what they attempt, without sacrificing any part of themselves, are, perhaps, *The Import-ance of Being Earnest* and *Salome*. Both these are plays. But neither of them seems to me so characteristic, so inclusive of Wilde as *Intentions, De Profundis, The Portrait of Mr W. H.,* or even *The Picture of Dorian Gray*. His plays are wilfully limited, subordinated to an aim outside them-selves, and, except in the two I have just mentioned, these limitations are not such as to justify themselves by giving freedom to the artist. Some limitations set an artist free for an achievement otherwise impossible. But the limitations of which I complain only made Wilde a little contemptuous of his work. They did not save his talent from preoccupations, but compelled it to a labour in whose success alone he could take an interest.

It is impossible not to feel that Wilde was impatient of the methods and the meanings of his first three successful plays, like a juggler, con-scious of being able to toss up six balls, who is admired for tossing three. These good women, these unselfish, pseudonymous mothers, these men of wit and fashion discomfited to make a British holiday; their temptations, their sacrifices, their defeats, are not taken from any drama played in Wilde's own mind. He saw them and their adventures quite impersonally; and no good art is impersonal. Salome kissing the pale lips of Iokanaan may once have moved him when he saw her behind the ghostly footlights of that secret theatre in which each man is his own dramatist, his own stage-manager, and his own audience. But Lady Windermere did not return to her husband for Wilde's sake, and he did not feel that Sir Robert Chiltern's future mat-tered either way. He cared only that an audience he despised should be relieved at her return, and that to them the career of a politician should seem to be important. Not until the production of *The Impor-tance of Being Earnest* did he share the pleasure of the pit. I know a travelling showman who makes 'enjoy' an active verb, and speaks of 'enjoying the poor folk' when, for coppers, he lets them ride on merry-go-rounds, and agitate themselves in swing-boats, which offer him no manner of amusement. In just this way Wilde 'enjoyed' the London audiences with his early plays. He did not enjoy them himself.

Hazlitt said of Congreve that 'the workmanship overlays the materials; in Wycherley the casting of the parts and the fable are alone sufficient to ensure success'. Wilde may not have read Hazlitt on *The English Comic Writers*, but his earlier plays suggest a determination to 'ensure success' after the manner of Wycherley, and to overlay the bare material necessary for that purpose with wit's fine workmanship after the manner of Congreve. The fables, the characters, the settings, were chosen on account of their experience; all were veterans with reputa-tions untarnished by any failure in popularity. Some were taken from the English stage, some from the French; all served as the machinery to keep an audience interested and carry Wilde's voice across the foot-lights. In the theatre, as in storytelling, he was not unready to work to *bouts-rimés* [prescribed patterns].

I say, to carry Wilde's voice across the footlights: that is exactly what his plays do. Those neat, polished sentences, snapping like snuff-boxes, are often taken from the books that hold what he chose to preserve of his conversation. An aphorism that has served the author of *The Soul of Man* and shone for a moment in *Dorian Gray* is given a new vitality by Lord Illingworth, and what is good enough for Lady Narborough is a little better in the mouth of Dumby. Wilde was never without the power, shared by all amateurs of genius, of using up the odds and ends from one pastime to fill out the detail of another. Doing things, like Merimée,[2] for wagers with himself, he would make plays that should be powerful in their effect on other people, but he would reserve the right to show, even while making them, that he could do something else. He learnt from Musset,[3] and believed, with For-tunio, that 'a pun is a consolation for many ills, and a play upon words as good a way as another of playing with thoughts, actions, and people.' He consoled himself for his plots by taking extraordinary liberties with them, and amused himself with quips, bons-mots, epi-grams and repartee that had really nothing to do with the business in hand. Most of his witty sayings would bear transplanting from one play to another, and it is necessary to consult the book if we would remember in whose mouth they were placed. This is a very different thing from the dialogue of Congreve on the one hand or of J. M. Synge on the other. The whole arrangement in conversation, as he might appropriately have called either *Lady Windermere's Fan, An Ideal Husband,* or *A Woman of No Importance,* was very much lighter than the story that served as its excuse and sometimes rudely interrupted it. It was so sparkling, good-humoured and novel that even the audience for whom he had constructed the story forgave him for putting a brake upon its speed with this quite separate verbal entertainment.

I suppose that this forgiveness encouraged him to believe that the situations and emotional appeals he borrowed from melodrama were not necessary to his success. In *The Importance of Being Earnest* he threw them bravely overboard, and wrote a play whose very foundation was a pun. Nothing could be a better proof of the inessential nature of those tricks with which he had been making sure of his audience than the immense superiority of this play to the others. Free from the neces-sity of living up to any drama more serious than its conversation, it preserves a unity of feeling and of tone that sets it upon a higher level. Wit is a little heartless, a little jarring, when flashed over a crisis of conscience, even when we know that the agitated politician is only a figure cut from an illustrated paper and mounted on cardboard. And passion, whether of repentance or of indignation, is a little *outré* in a picture-gallery where Lord Illingworth has said that a well-tied tie is the first serious step in life. In those first three plays, even when Wilde makes a serious effort to get dramatic value out of, for example, Lord Illingworth's wordly wisdom, he is quite unable to disguise the fact that it is an effort and serious. Those plays are interesting, amusing, clever, what you will, but their contradictions have cost them beauty. It is not in the least surprising that *The Importance of Being Earnest*, the most trivial of the social plays, should be the only one of them that gives that peculiar exhilaration of spirit by which we recognise the beautiful. It is precisely because it is consistently trivial that it is not ugly. If only once it marred its triviality with a bruise of passion, its beauty would vanish with the blow. But it never contradicts itself, and it is worth noticing that its unity, its dovetailing of dialogue and plot, so that the one helps the other, is not achieved at the expense of the conversation, but at that of the mechanical contrivances for filling a theatre that Wilde had not at first felt sure of being able to do without. The dialogue has not been weighted to trudge with the plot; the plot has been lightened till it can fly with the wings of the dialogue. The two are become one, and the lambent laughter of this comedy is due to the radio-activity of the thing itself, and not to glow-worms incongruously stuck over its surface.

It is not easy to define the quality of that laughter. It is not uproarious enough to provide the sore throat of farce. It is not thoughtful enough to pass Meredith's test of comedy.[4] It is not due to a sense of superior intellect, like much of Mr Shaw's. It is the laughter of complicity. We do not laugh at but with the persons of the play. We would, if we could, abet the duplicity of Mr Worthing, and be accessories after the fact to the Bunburying of Algernon. We would even encourage Lady Bracknell's determined statement, for we are in the secret, and we know—

> She only does it to amuse,
> Because she knows it pleases.[5]

The simultaneous speech of Cecily and Gwendolen is no insult to our intelligence, nor do we boggle for a moment over the delightful impossibility of Lane. We are caught from the beginning by a spirit of delicate fun. We busy ourselves in the intrigues, and would on no account draw back. *The Importance of Being Earnest* is to solid comedy what filigree is to a silver bowl. We are relieved of our corporeal envelopes, and share with Wilde the pleasure of sporting in the fourth dimension.

SOURCE: from *Oscar Wilde: A Critical Study* (London, 1912), pp. 133–40.

NOTES

1. Arthur Symons, *Studies in Prose and Verse* (London, 1904), pp. 124–8. [Ed.]
2. Prosper Mérimée (1803–70), French novelist and essayist. [Ed.]
3. Alfred de Musset (1810–57), French author of plays, poems and novels. [Ed.]
4. See George Meredith, *On the Idea of Comedy* (1877). [Ed.]
5. Cf. Lewis Carroll, *Alice's Adventures in Wonderland*, ch. VI. [Ed.]

A.B. Walkley   (1923)

'In matters of grave importance', says a young lady in the blithest and most brilliant of Oscar Wilde's comedies, 'style, not sincerity, is the vital thing'. She must have been thinking of her author's plays. Superficially, these are all style and no sincerity. But we must distinguish. Without sincerity there can be no style: only flatulence, stereotypes, empty verbiage, what in Paris they call *le poncif*. Without, that is to say, the artist's sincerity of presentation, the true expression of his intuitions. You cannot have perfect form without genuine feeling. Wilde was a dramatic artist who had a keen feeling on the dramatic virtues of insincerity – the sudden surprise of its paradoxes, its inverted commonplaces, its pouring of old wine into old bottles – and he sincerely presented it in a delightful style, terse, tense, witty, urbane. And so, when all his personages are insincere, as all are in *The Importance of Being Earnest,* he is most sincere, his style is at his best, and the result is a comedy worthy of the same shelf as *Marriage à la Mode* or *The Way of the World*. Nor am I 'dragging in' Dryden and Congreve. For not only in the happy, easy elegance of his form is Wilde in the direct line of these masters of style; he is of their lineage, too, in his triumphantly sincere expression of insincerity.

Conversely, there is such a thing as the insincere presentation of sincerity. Wilde, it is clear enough, was much under the influence of two great Frenchmen, Augier[1] and the younger Dumas, whose authority in the theatre, though on the wane, was even then scarcely to be ignored. From Augier he took his 'natural' sons who unwittingly raise an arm against their father, and his 'adventuresses' vainly attempting to force the portals of 'society'; from Dumas *fils* he took what no English dramatist can afford even to touch, the *tirade*. Both these men were serious at heart, where Wilde never was; both did sincerely present sincerity, which Wilde never could. Both, in short, were romantic, with the perfervid emotionalism of the romantic tradition; and it was with an eye on its tendency to degenerate into the mere simulation of emotion that Sainte-Beuve said, *l'écueil particulier du genre romantique, c'est le faux*.[2] You will find *le faux* in Wilde so soon as you turn to any of his presentations of the sincere. The husband and wife in *Lady Windermere's Fan* are mere mechanical dolls, who are none the more human for behaving like lunatics. The mother and son and the Puritan maiden in *A Woman of No Importance* discredit virtue and seriousness by their hopeless inferiority in interest to the vicious and frivolous of the company. The Puritan maiden delivers a Dumasian tirade against English society, with variations by Wilde ('It lives like a leper in purple. It sits like a dead thing smeared with gold') which is not only rhetoric, but 'twopence coloured' rhetoric. For mark the peculiar penalty of insincerity: it not merely makes a nonentity of the author's personage, but ruins his style!

Take those two other insincere presentations of sincerity, Sir Robert and Lady Chiltern in *An Ideal Husband*. Wilde was never tired of railing at the newspapers. By a kind of Nemesis, his own Sir Robert always talks the most pompous journalism. Thirty years ago, at any rate, this was not the lingo of an English cabinet minister. As for Lady Chiltern, she is not, at a domestic crisis, above borrowing the favourite literary *cliché* of the kitchen. 'Don't touch me!' Such were the misadventures of Wilde's fine culture, and fastidious taste, when sincerity failed him!

Style *with* sincerity, then 'is the vital thing', and, when all is said, Wilde had enough of it to keep his work alive. His conversations of the frivolous are inimitable. They out-Chamfort Chamfort.[3] Many of his epigrams have become legendary. 'The Book of Life begins with a man and a woman in a garden; it ends with Revelations.' Women are 'Sphinxes without secrets.' 'I can resist everything, except temptation.' 'To be intelligible is to be found out.' 'The English country gentleman galloping after a fox – the unspeakable in full pursuit of the uneatable.' These are sheer wit. But others are wisdom, too. As: 'In this world there are only two tragedies. One is not getting what one wants, and the other is getting it.' And: 'All thought is immoral. Its very essence is destruction. Nothing survives being thought of.'

Evidently the author of *obiter dicta* such as these could do something more than manufacture epigrams by the mechanical process of turning commonplaces upside down or inside out. But he was sometimes reduced to that extremity, because, at all costs, epigrams he must have. He believed, you see, like a true artist, in unity of tone; but unity of tone, when artificially prolonged, is called monotony.

His plots are as artificial as his weaker epigrams; almost as artificial, indeed, as the plots of Congreve. His stage situations are striking rather than inevitable, or even plausible. There is no real reason for Lord Windermere's persistence in bringing Mrs Erlynne into his wife's drawing-room. Arbuthnot's desire to inflict the death-penalty, on the spot, on Lord Illingworth is somewhat excessive – and is really created by the author's sore need for a situation wherein the relationship of the two men shall be strikingly divulged. The story of *An Ideal Husband* is a mere list of articles of stolen property – letters, Cabinet secrets, bracelets, more letters. In plot, as in characterisation, when Wilde tried to be serious he succeeded only in being artificial. . . .

SOURCE: extract from Introduction to vol. VII of *The Complete Works of Oscar Wilde* (New York, 1923), pp. *ix–xiv*.

NOTES

1. Emile Augier (1820–89), French playwright whose works include *Les Effrontés* (1861). [Ed.]

2. Trans. : 'The particular danger of the romantic style is falsity.' [Ed.]

3. Sebastién Chamfort (1740–94), famous French conversationalist and wit, who also wrote poetry. [Ed.]

John Drinkwater   (1923)

. . . Once . . . Wilde's own nature, with all its limitations, worked clearly in delight of itself, and achieved what is in its own province a perfect work of art. *The Importance of Being Earnest* is not really a comedy of manners in the sense of being primarily a criticism of the follies into which a society is betrayed by its conventions, and a tearing off of the masks. Nor is it primarily a comedy of wit, sure and sustained as the wit is. Attempts have been made to derive the play in some measure from the Restoration masters, but without much conviction, and while the manner employed by Wilde has clearly influenced some later writers notably St John Hankin, *The Importance of Being Earnest* really forms a class in English drama by itself. It is in mere simplicity that one says that it seems to be the only one of Wilde's works that really has its roots in passion. Every device of gaiety and even seeming nonsense is employed to keep the passion far back out of sight, and, if it were otherwise, the play would not be the masterpiece it is. But the passion is there. That is to say that the play is directly an expression of that part of Wilde's own experience which was least uncontaminated and in which he could take most delight. And this meant that all his great gifts as a craftsmen were for once employed in work where, with insincerity almost as the theme, there was more sincerity than in anything else he did. Plays like *Salome* and *The Florentine Tragedy* are at best little more than virtuosity, while *The Woman of No Importance, Lady Windermere's Fan* and *The Ideal Husband,* although they may have many of the qualities that mark Wilde's one great achievement, are on the whole frank surrenders to a fashion of the theatre which Wilde had too good a brain not to despise. But in *The Importance of Being Earnest* there is neither virtuosity nor concession. It is a superb and original piece of construction, with several moments of stage mastery which can hardly be excelled in comedy, and packed throughout with a perfect understanding of dramatic speech. One has only to recall any scene in the play and place it beside almost any of the successful comedies that one sees in the ordinary run of theatre production, to see how definitely apart that greatness is set which comes of having not three words in seven dramatically right but seven in seven. But when art comes to this excellence of form it can only mean excellence of life at the springs, and flowing through *The Importance of Being Earnest* is the surest and clearest part of Wilde's life. There was much, perhaps everything, in the more profoundly moving story of man that Wilde saw always imperfectly or not at all. But he did see, with a subtlety that can hardly be matched in our dramatic literature, that the common intrigues of daily life are not really the moralist's province at all, but interesting only for the sheer amusement that can be got out of them. Shakespeare gave to the English stage a comedy as full of poetic passion as great tragic art, Ben Jonson the comedy of humours, and Congreve and his fellows the true comedy of manners, but Wilde in his one masterpiece brought into the same company of excellence the comedy of pure fun.

SOURCE: extract from Introduction to vol. VIII of *The Complete Works of Oscar Wilde* (New York, 1923), pp. *ix–xiv.*

Ashley Dukes   (1923)

. . . Wilde's plays, with the exception of *The Importance of Being Earnest*, show lamentable signs of wear. They have many virtues that our stage can ill afford to lose. They please the ear always, the mind very often. They help to maintain a standard of dramatic writing. The emptiest of their epigrams are not altogether worthless, because they reflect a world where all is artificial. Like dandies and well-dressed women, they gratify a sense of fitness. Glancing at them, we feel with Dulaure's marchioness:[1] 'Depend upon it, sir, God thinks twice before damning a man of that quality.' Time, we must hope, will think twice before forgetting Lord Goring and others of Wilde's gallery. But such figures apart, how can *An Ideal Husband* escape oblivion? Or *Lady Windermere's Fan*? Or *A Woman of No Importance*? Wilde chose to write august and wooden melodramas spangled with wit and comedy; and he did so, not because he was wholly insincere, but because there was a strain of the second-rate in his talent. He offended just where he claimed never to offend – in lack of discrimination, in artistic taste. The final paradox of his career is that we forgive him his seriousness for the sake of his triviality. We forget Salome and remember Bunbury. . . .

SOURCE: extract from *The Youngest Drama: Studies of Fifty Dramatists* (London, 1923), pp. 55–6.

NOTE

1. Jacques-Antoine Dulaure (1755–1835), French politician and historian.

Vincent O'Sullivan   (1936)

. . . I believe he thought his plays the most important things he had done. The plays, with the exception of *The Importance of Being Earnest* and *Salome,* derive very definitely from a French school long out of fashion, represented by Scribe, Augier, George Sand, the second Dumas and Sardou. The substance is melodramatic. What saves them, what makes them viable, what casts a glamour over them, is the style and the wit which, say what they will, was Wilde's very own, not only different from what any of his contemporaries produced, but different from what any one at any time in the history of literature has produced. In his peculiar form of wit, Wilde had imitators, but no predecessors.

Sometimes Whistler's wit is compared to Wilde's. It was quite something else. Whistler was malignant. Whistler's wit was like the prongs of a rake which, dragged across the subject of it, left a poisonous wound, as it was meant to do. Wilde's is full of tolerance and good-humour and high spirits, as the man was himself. It is not meant to be a stab, but a cocktail.

With that, and his sense of dramatic situation, and a shallow, not altogether original, but very clear and consistent philosophy, easily grasped, his plays make a good show, and it is not surprising that they are now played in various languages, while those of Dumas, which have dramatic situation and wit, and also a preaching philosophy, but no tolerance and good-humour, are not played out of France, and not much in it, and those of Scribe, which have only dramatic situation, are not played anywhere. As with the two others, as with Pinero who belongs to the same school, Wilde's dramatic situations may be called artificial. In life, we say, things don't happen so neatly as that. Still, the moment we touch the theatre we touch convention. In all plays is the element of make-believe: that is what the spectators are there for. A plain photographic and stenographic report of life would be unbearable on the stage. And life does really offer dramatic situations – too many of them. Even Tchekov, the master of writing in minors, who does his best to be drab, has to fall back on the revolver shot.

The best stage-play writers at present do no more attempt to get rid of the dramatic situation than did Sardou or Wilde. What they try for is to go round it and to treat it quietly. In the hands of a very modern French or German dramatist, 'Mrs Arbuthnot' would not hit her ex-lover across the face with a glove. But she would show that she had it in her to do it, or something equivalent more cerebrally cruel. Which is closer to life it were hard to decide. Perhaps both. But, as was said, it is not the business of the drama to deal with life as it is lived. Do that and you bore your public; and a play that does not please a large public does not exist as a play. On the stage the incessant calamity of the times can only be shown in samples more abrupt, more immediate, than reality.

In a theatre Wilde's plays are found interesting by those who are there not for an evening's instruction, or an evening's shock, or an evening's patriotism, or for anything else than an evening's entertainment. I read some of them again not long ago and found, rather to my surprise, that they were pleasant to read. Once the theatricalism is accepted, the nimble intelligence, the surprising wit, the general good form, carry the acts happily along. And in his plays, at any rate, it cannot be said of Wilde, *sufflaminandus erat* [he was apt to be impeded]. For a man so enveloped in words, who wrote so easily, who had such huge battalions of phrases at command, he shows a noteworthy restraint. He wanders far less away from the business in hand than any of the Russians except Gogol; less than Strindberg too, or Bernard Shaw. This is due to the fact that when he sat down to write, his intention was simply to make a play, and not to preach, or to enforce a doctrine, or to explode against social wrongs, or to right wrongs in the wrong way. I once read that *A Woman of No Importance* was a powerful accusation of the treatment meted out to the unmarried mother; but that surely is to lean too heavily on a dramatic situation which had the run of the streets long before Wilde's time.

In reality Wilde has only a small number of ideas in his plays and they are very simple. He disliked hypocrisy in social intercourse, he glorified individualism, he denied the moral right of the community to sacrifice the life of any member of it. These ideas he hardly ever expressed directly like Dumas *fils* and Augier. He was either more afraid of his audiences, or he had not the same confidence in their patience if they were preached at. When the American girl in *A Woman of No Importance* gives what seems to be a sincere deliverance of what Wilde really thought, he cuts short the tirade with a joke, and, seeming to mock his own sincerity, he nullifies the effect of it. He resigned himself to be the amuser from fear of being the bore. In this he was wrong; he wronged himself, and he deprived his plays of a permanent element. For just at that time the drama of ideas was coming into vogue in England, and Wilde lost the chance of being a pioneer. He left it to Bernard Shaw, and to Archer with his translations from Ibsen. He was satisfied with scattering not so much ideas as notions of ideas amid the witty and amusing dialogue, and they appear in fragments, in the course of a reply, not causing the least delay in the exposure of the anecdote, not detaching attention from the plot. Besides, the characters as conceived are not vehicles for ideas, not even in the play where he allows himself to think. . . .

SOURCE: extract from *Aspects of Wilde* (London, 1936), pp. 13–18.

Eric Bentley   (1946)

The Importance of Being Earnest (1895) is a variant, not of domestic drama like *Candida* or of melodrama like *Brassbound*, but of farce, a genre which, being the antithesis of serious, is not easily put to serious uses. In fact nothing is easier than to handle this play without noticing what it contains. It is so consistently farcical in tone, characterisation and plot that very few care to root out any more serious content. The general conclusion has been that Wilde merely decorates a silly play with a flippant wit. Like Shaw he is dismissed as 'not really a dramatist at all'. Unlike Shaw he does not have any such dramatic structure to offer in refutation of his critics as underlies a *Major Barbara* or a *Candida*. We cannot turn to him for the dialectical steel frame of a Molière or a Shaw. Yet we shall only display our own insensitivity if we dismiss him.

Insensitivity to slight and delicate things is insensitivity *tout court*. That is what Wilde meant when he declared that the man who despises superficiality is himself superficial. His best play is connected with this idea. As its title confesses, it is about *earnestness,* that is, Victorian solemnity, that kind of false seriousness which means priggishness, hypocrisy and lack of irony. Wilde proclaims that earnestness is less praiseworthy than the ironic attitude to life which is regarded as superficial. His own art, and the comic spirit which Congreve embodied and which Meredith had described, were thereby vindicated. Wilde calls *The Importance of Being Earnest* 'a trivial comedy for serious people', meaning, in the first place, a comedy which will be thought negligible by the earnest and, in the second, a *comedy of surface* for connoisseurs. The latter will perceive that Wilde is as much of a moralist as Bernard Shaw but that, instead of presenting the problems of modern society directly, he flits around them, teasing them, declining to grapple with them. His wit is no searchlight into the darkness of modern life. It is a flickering, a coruscation, intermittently revealing the upper class of England in a harsh bizarre light. This upper class could feel about Shaw that at least he took them seriously, no one more so. But the outrageous Oscar (whom they took care to get rid of as they had got rid of Byron) refused to see the importance of being earnest.

One does not find Wilde's satire embedded in plot and character as in traditional high comedy. It is a running accompaniment to the play and this fact, far from indicating immaturity, is the making of a new sort of comedy. The plot is one of those Gilbertian absurdities of lost infants and recovered brothers which can only be thought of to be laughed at. Yet the dialogue which sustains the plot, or is sustained by it, is an unbroken stream of comment on all the themes of life which the plot is so far from broaching. Perhaps *comment* is too flat and downright a conception. Wildean 'comment' is a pseudo-irresponsible jabbing at all the great problems, and we would be justified in removing the prefix 'pseudo' if the Wildean satire, for all its naughtiness, had not a cumulative effect and a paradoxical one. Flippancies repeated, developed, and, so to say, elaborated almost into a system amount to something in the end – and thereby cease to be flippant. What begins as a prank ends as a criticism of life. What begins as intellectual high-kicking ends as intellectual sharp-shooting.

The margins of an annotated copy of *The Importance* would show such headings as: death; money and marriage; the nature of style; ideology and economics; beauty and truth; the psychology of philanthropy; the decline of aristocracy; nineteenth-century morals; the class system. The possibility of such notations in itself means little. But if we bear in mind that Wilde is skimming steadily over mere topics all through *The Importance*, we can usefully turn to a particular page to see precisely how this works. To choose the opening page is not to load the dice in a dramatist's favor, since that page is usually either heavy-going exposition or mere patter which allows the audience to get seated. . . .

[Bentley quotes the first seventeen speeches of the play – Ed.]

This passage is enough to show the way in which Wilde attaches a serious and satirical allusion to every remark. The butler's 'I didn't think it polite to listen, sir' is a prelude to the jokes against class society which run through the play. Algernon's first little speech touches on the foolish opposition of life and sentiment, science and art. Talk of science and life leads by Wildean transition back to the action and the cucumber sandwiches. Champagne takes the action to speculation on servants and masters, and thence to marriage and morals. A little dialectical climax is reached with the answer to the question: 'Is marriage so demoralising as that?' when Lane coolly replies: 'I believe it *is* a very pleasant state, sir', and adds, by way of an explanation no less disconcerting by Victorian standards, 'I have had very little experience of it myself up to the present. I have only been married once.' Which is followed by the explanation of the explanation: 'That was in consequence of a misunderstanding . . .'. It cannot be said that marriage in this passage receives the 'staggering blows' which the ardent reformer is wont to administer. But does it not receive poisoned pin pricks that are just as effective? Are not the inversions and double inversions of standards managed with dexterous delicacy? 'No, sir. It is not a very interesting subject.' A delicious turn in the argument! And then the little moralistic summing-up of Algernon's: 'Lane's views

on marriage seem somewhat lax. Really, if the lower orders don't set
us a good example . . .' And so it ripples on.

We are accustomed to plays in which a serious plot and theme are
enlivened – 'dramatised,' as we say – by comic incident and
witticism. Such plays are at best sweetened pills. 'Entertainment
value' is added as an afterthought, reminding one of the man who,
having watched for weeks the construction of a modern Gothic building, cried one day: 'Oh, look, they're putting the architecture on now!'
Oscar Wilde's procedure is the opposite of all this. He has no serious
plot, no credible characters. His witticisms are, not comic, but serious
relief. They are in ironic counterpoint with the absurdities of the
action. This counterpoint is Wilde's method. It is what gives him his
peculiar voice and his peculiar triumph. It is what makes him hard to
catch: the fish's tail flicks, flashes and disappears. Perhaps *The Importance*
should be defined as 'almost a satire'. As the conversations in *Alice in
Wonderland* hover on the frontier of sense without ever quite crossing it,
so the dialogue in *The Importance* is forever on the frontier of satire,
forever on the point of breaking into bitter criticism. It never breaks.
The ridiculous action constantly steps in to prevent the break. That is
its function. Before the enemy can denounce Wilde, the agile outburst
is over and we are back among the cucumber sandwiches.

The counterpoint or irony of Wilde's play expresses itself theatrically in the contrast between the elegance and *savoir-faire* of the actors
and the absurdity of what they actually do. This contrast too can be
dismissed as mere Oscarism and frivolity. Actually it is integral to an
uncommonly rich play. The contrast between smooth, assured
appearances and inner emptiness is, moreover, nothing more nor less
than a fact of sociology and history. Wilde knew his England. He
knew her so well that he could scarcely be surprised when she laughed
off his truisms as paradoxes and fastened a humorless and baleful eye
on all his flights of fancy. Wilde had his own solution to the problem
stated by Meredith, the problem of finding a vantage point for satire
in an unaristocratic age. It was the solution of Bohemianism. For
Wilde the Bohemian attitude was far from being a philosophy in
itself – a point which most of his friends and enemies, beginning at
the Wilde trial, seem to have missed. Bohemianism was for Wilde a
mask. To wear masks was Wilde's personal adjustment to modern
life, as it was Nietzsche's. Hence we are right in talking of his pose as
we are right in talking of Nietzsche's vanity. The mistake is in believing
that these men deceived themselves. If we patronise them the joke is
on us. If Wilde seems shallow when we want depth, if he seems a liar
when we want truth, we should recall his words: 'A Truth in Art is that

whose contradictory is also true. The Truths of metaphysics are the Truths of masks.' These words lead us to Pirandello.

SOURCE: from *The Playwright as Thinker* (New York, 1946), pp. 172–7.

A.E. Dyson   (1965)

. . . His most characteristic habit is one of paradox. 'Work is the curse of the drinking classes', he writes, and naturally we are delighted; but why? Partly, no doubt, because the mere intention to shock by way of reversing a respectable cliché always is amusing, not only to adolescents to whom it comes fairly naturally as a form of humour, but to the incurable iconoclast biding his time inside most of us. But the intention of shocking is only part of the story. The real joke is that the cliché Wilde reverses is itself hopelessly and perniciously stupid, so that there is irony at the expense of those who are actually shocked, as well as good-humoured laughter for those who are not. Do we really believe that drink is the curse of the working classes? Of course not. Do we say that we believe it? If we do, we deserve any fate a satirist might devise. Wilde's wit performs, therefore, the traditional task of irony, sorting its audience into sheep and goats by challenging to a response which is human and real instead of being conventional and dead. Though his pose is to shock for its own sake, the pose, in this instance, is his technique. Mistaking pose for real intention is precisely the trap Wilde sets for his readers, and the *raison d'être* of his irony.

If we examine more closely the clichés Wilde turns inside out, we shall see that almost always he has behind him either genuine insight . . . or genuine humanity (as in his great essay, *The Soul of Man Under Socialism*), or genuine detestation of cant and humbug (as in his Comedies, and much of the recorded conversation). What looks like, and is intended to look like, a prolonged flirtation with cynicism is in fact a running battle against obtuseness, hypocrisy and cant. What seems at first sight an affront to responsibility is on second sight a jest at the expense of the pseudo-responsible. Stupidity and insincerity are confronted with formulae decked out to look more deplorable than themselves, yet actually pointing back towards minimal respect for good sense and good nature which they violate.

A few quotations from Wilde's greatest, and most characteristic success, might bear out this claim. *The Importance of Being Earnest* is undoubtedly one of the funniest plays in the language. In appearance it is immensely cynical, yet the audiences who laugh are not, by and large, a crowd of cynics. The force of the wit can best be translated into questions addressed to ourselves. Are we the sort of person who parrots 'money doesn't matter', or accounts it for righteousness to those who do? 'I do not approve of mercenary marriages', says Lady Bracknell. 'When I married Lord Bracknell I had no fortune of any kind. But I never dreamed of allowing that to stand in my way.' Do we delight in telling people their faults for their own good? 'On an occasion of this kind', says Gwendolen, 'it becomes more than a moral duty to speak one's mind. It becomes a pleasure.' Do we say (not in the 1960s admittedly), that the Upper Classes should set an example? 'If the lower classes don't set us a good example', retorts Algernon, 'What on earth is the use of them?' Do we dismiss groups we cannot be admitted to as worthless? 'Never speak disrespectfully of Society, Algernon', warns Lady Bracknell, 'only people who can't get into it do that.'

Wit of this order sets a delicate problem for the critic. It no more lends itself to analysis than champagne does. Attack is bound to seem heavy-handed, sober praise rather beside the point. But risking this, as one must: what *is* going on in passages like these? On the surface, there is aristocratic flippancy in the face of virtue, and flippancy, what is worse, reverberant with class-conscious overtones. If we did not know Wilde to be a socialist and a man of humane instinct, we might think he really meant it. Yet look again, and where is the cynicism? Any of Wilde's epigrams could be transmuted into serious insights, and transplanted into the most moral of dramas or novels. Once more, the substitution of cynicism for responsibility is only apparent; the real challenge is from honesty to pretence, from generosity to meanness. No doubt some of us do disapprove of mercenary marriages, despise the fleshpots, deflate our friends disinterestedly, look for a lead to our Betters. But for each of the genuinely virtuous (and is virtue quite the right word?) there must be dozens who make use of the formulae. These, as at all times, are Wilde's real target, for it is hypocrisy he hates, and the cruelty bred of hypocrisy, never true disinterestedness or warmth of heart. His humour, though sparkling, is merciless to the moral poseur, whether Insider or Outsider, fool or knave. And why, indeed, should it not be? To attack cant with flippancy is surely less vicious than to disguise selfishness with cant; and recognising the selfishness in humanity may be no bad preliminary to recognising the unselfishness that can co-exist with it as well. Wilde's cynicism, in any event, is born of a light-hearted generosity of spirit that can be better trusted than solemn professions, and certainly than the morality of the people he deflated. The unusualness of the irony is that his norms are to be found neither in what he says, nor in the reversal of what he says, but in the confrontation of moral humbug parading as righteousness with moral good-heartedness parading as flippancy. His tone is so gay that conventional moralists could neither see, nor afford to see, what was really happening. As we know, they had a fine revenge on him in the end; and their verdict, whether we like it or not, has influenced and obscured our view of his art, as well as of himself, ever since.

Wilde made no claim to being a saint, and the claim is unlikely to be made for him now. But a remark which Lady Windermere mistakenly makes about Lord Darlington really is true, I would say, of Wilde himself: 'Believe me, you are better than most other men, and I sometimes think you pretend to be worse.' . . .

SOURCE: from *The Crazy Fabric: Essays in Irony* (London, 1965), pp. 145–7.

John Russell Taylor　　　(1967)

. . . His success in the theatre was won entirely with plays which mirrored the ordinary theatrical tastes of his day. . . .

Not only are these, apparently, ordinary society dramas, but they are society dramas of a decidedly old-fashioned kind, littered with asides and soliloquies. What then saves them, for Shaw and for us? Primarily, I think, their entire shamelessness. Wilde does not give the impression, even for a moment, that he takes all this nonsense seriously. The plots are creaking old contrivances, and far from trying to disguise the fact he glories in it. They are strong enough to hold up a glittering display of epigrams, delivered for the most part by characters – the Duchess of Berwick, Lady Hunstanton, even Lord Goring – who are irrelevant to most of the main action except as a sort of mocking chorus, and that is all that the plot is there for. Wilde's element of barefaced charlatanism appealed to Shaw: at least if he appeared to be upholding conventional morality, he was doing it with so little conviction, and with tongue so evidently in cheek, that no one could take it seriously, and therefore no one could take it amiss.

The message of Wilde's drama became even plainer in *The Importance of Being Earnest*, where at last even the slightest pretence of seriousness is dropped and joy reigns unconfined in a farcical farrago about two suitors, two girls under the erroneous impression they are engaged to a man called Ernest, a gorgon-like mother-in-law to be, an absent-minded nurse and a complicated history of a baby inadvertently left in a handbag at Victoria Station left-luggage office, the Brighton line. Of course, by the same token this might be the most serious of all Wilde's plays, but that is another matter. The point is that here all the machinery of the well-made play finds a triumphantly and unarguably proper use. The convention is paramount: nobody really talks or acts like this, or certainly not for more than a few moments at a time, but, to paraphrase Turner's remark to a lady who objected that she never saw sunsets as he painted them, don't we all wish they did? . . .

SOURCE: extracts from *The Rise and Fall of the Well-Made Play* (London 1967), pp. 89–90.

PART FOUR

Modern Studies

Ian Gregor   Comedy and Oscar Wilde (1966)

Repeated revivals of *The Importance of Being Earnest* suggest that it has generally been found a very amusing and a very satisfying play. Accounts of why it is very amusing and very satisfying are harder to come by. In fact, the play seems to be singularly unilluminated by criticism, a curious state of affairs for a work which has frequently been praised in terms which indicate that it is among the best English dramatic comedies.

In trying to understand the kind of success represented by *The Importance of Being Earnest*, two things become clear. The first is that the play has a very precise place in Wilde's development as a dramatist, and that consequently any description of it involves taking into account the nature of his earlier plays; the second, that such a critical description of Wilde's dramatic progress casts a rather unexpected light on some fairly widely held assumptions about the proper relation of the play world to the moral world, form to content, the author to his creation. For Wilde's development as a dramatist is intimately connected with his ability to translate into fully dramatic terms the importance of not being earnest; and the earlier plays contained a lesson which, when fully absorbed by him, led to his most satisfying play.

I

It is possible to regard Wilde's four principal plays as a series of attempts to resolve a particular clash between manners and morals, between style and content, between the author and his characters. The problem which faced him, as a dramatist, was a very specific one – that of finding a world fit for the dandy to live in; fit, in the sense that such a world would help to make clear the meaning of the dandy. Considered in general terms, the role of the dandy is defined largely by his alienation from the social world in which he lives. He is the visible emblem of non-attachment. His best audience is himself; his favourite view, that presented him by his mirror. Like the tramp, who was to succeed him in the mythology of a later drama, the dandy is a displaced person, but, unlike the tramp's, this displacement is voluntary, indeed it is ostentatiously sought. It is not in a pair of worn-out boots, but in a buttonhole, that the dandy proclaims himself.

For the dramatist the accommodation of such a figure presents special problems. In so far as his role is mythic and not individualised he requires for his embodiment a special form of play. Drama usually involves its characters in ethical judgements; the dandy elaborately

abjures them. Drama is an exploration of character in action; the
dandy is self-consciously static, and the art he requires of the
dramatist is precisely that which sees the mind's construction in the
face. The dramatic role of the dandy would seem to lead into a world
where, of necessity, everything was amoral, inconsequential and superficial. Was it possible to create such a figure and such a world, and
yet produce a play which itself would be none of these things? This,
basically, was Wilde's problem. He solved it only once with complete
success, in his last play, *The Importance of Being Earnest*. In the varying
achievement of the three plays which preceded it, however, we can see
what were the conditions for such a 'solution', and this enables us to
understand more clearly the nature of Wilde's single dramatic masterpiece.

Lady Windermere's Fan (1892), Wilde's first play, illustrates very
clearly the difficulties that beset a dramatist whose aesthetic ideology
includes a belief that manners take precedence over morals and style
over content. In this play there are two characters, Lord Darlington
and Mrs Erlynne, who have important sympathies with the dandy
view of life. The play, in common with *A Woman of No Importance* and
An Ideal Husband, has as a central theme the hazards of precipitate and
inflexible moral judgement − in this case a wife judging, or misjudg-
ing, the nature of her husband's liaison with another woman − and
the way in which that judgement has to be modified. And it is in this
modification that the dandy has his special role to play. The critical
problem in all the plays arises from the nature of the wisdom the
dandy dispenses and the relationship of this wisdom to the dilemmas
which constitute the plot of the play.

Lady Windermere's Fan opens with the direct confrontation of the
dandy and the moralist, Lord Darlington and Lady Windermere:

> LORD DARLINGTON I think life too complex a thing to be settled by these hard and
> fast rules.
> LADY WINDERMERE If we had 'these hard and fast rules', we should find life much
> more simple.

This is sufficiently indicative of the kind of opposition involved. But of
course it is not his attitudes that distinguish the dandy, it is the way in
which those attitudes are validated by his mode of expression.

> LORD DARLINGTON It's a curious thing, Duchess, about the game of marriage − a
> game, by the way, that is going out of fashion − the wives hold all the honours, and
> invariably lose the odd trick.
> DUCHESS OF BERWICK The odd trick? Is that the husband, Lord Darlington?
> LORD DARLINGTON It would be rather a good name for the modern husband.

DUCHESS OF BERWICK Dear Lord Darlington, how thoroughly depraved you are!
LADY WINDERMERE Lord Darlington is trivial.
LORD DARLINGTON Ah, don't say that, Lady Windermere.
LADY WINDERMERE Why do you *talk* so trivially about life, then?
LORD DARLINGTON Because I think that life is far too important a thing ever to talk seriously about it.

Here we have the usual mutual criticism of dandy and moralist with its accompanying paradoxes about things serious and trivial but the important thing to note is that Darlington's flippant tone authenticates the seriousness of his remarks. He is doing two 'serious' things here – one directed at the Duchess of Berwick and the other at Lady Windermere. The first is simple satire, aimed at the social set. Adopting a tone of raffish insouciance – 'the game', 'the odd trick', 'the modern husband' – Darlington parodies current 'advanced' views about marriage, views which the Duchess *really* thinks and acts on. Indulgently, she can assume indignation with the coy: 'Dear Lord Darlington, how thoroughly depraved you are!' It is a remark which justifies Darlington's satire without disturbing the blithe tone in which it is expressed. But Darlington is also speaking to Lady Windermere, and he intends these remarks as a warning. 'The game', 'the modern husband' now have a specific reference – to Windermere himself and his relations with Mrs Erlynne. Darlington, of course, is serious about this, because he is in love with Lady Windermere. But the dandy has his social sense of what is fitting. Public politeness is an outward sign of inward grace; his language, no less than his buttonhole, must be a testimony.

In this exchange Wilde is able to exhibit perfectly the seriousness of the dandy. But it is a precarious poise; the exigencies of the plot are to drive Darlington into an explicit declaration of love, and immediately he forfeits his right to the paradoxical language of the dandy. The fatal place for the dandy's heart to be is on his sleeve. It is interesting to notice that as Darlington fades in the role of the dandy, Wilde tries to keep this element present in the play through one of his friends, Cecil Graham. But, because Graham is nothing more than a choric voice, his wit remains unassimilated into the action of the play, and so remains a collection of cynical *obiter dicta,* some Wildean epigrams in search of a character. The transformation of Darlington and the coarsening of the dandy in Graham is caught in this exchange:

LORD DARLINGTON This woman has purity and innocence. She has everything we men have lost.
CECIL GRAHAM My dear fellow, what on earth should we men do going about with purity and innocence? A carefully thought-out buttonhole is much more effective.

If Lady Windermere disturbs Wilde's presentation of Darlington in his role of dandy, she also exercises a distorting effect on his presentation of Mrs Erlynne. Admittedly the demands of plot are strong here: Mrs Erlynne has to be seen as supposed temptress of Windermere, and devoted mother to her unsuspecting daughter. But there is no reason why this should affect her credibility, and it is not on the level of her dramatic role that she seems to make contrary demands on the audience. Rather, it is because Wilde presents her alternately as both 'inside' and 'outside' the action of the play – a protagonist in a moral plot turning, at times, into a Wildean commentator. Her role in the plot makes us react critically to sentiments which we are meant to approve – approve not because they are Mrs Erlynne's but because they are Wilde's. This crisscross role is sometimes exemplified within a single speech; here, for example, she is speaking to Windermere and leading into a blackmailing request:

> . . . You have a delightful opportunity now of paying me a compliment, Windermere. But you are not very clever at paying compliments. I am afraid Margaret doesn't encourage you in that excellent habit. It's a great mistake on her part. When men give up saying what is charming, they give up thinking what is charming. But seriously, what do you say to £2000? £2500, I think. In modern life margin is everything.

The attitude here to compliments, the notion of 'saying' controlling 'thinking', has the full Wildean approval, but juxtaposed to the blackmailing threat it merely becomes cynical. And the same applies to the final phrase, 'In modern life margin is everything', which has the authentic dandyesque ring, but which, in this context, comes over as ruthlessly casual. It is involvement in plot that affects, in varying degree, the dandyish roles allocated initially to Lord Darlington and fitfully to Mrs Erlynne. For involvement in plot means involvement in a world of judgements, a world of character.

This discussion of *Lady Windermere's Fan*, concentrating on the particular problem of accommodating the dandy to the moral world, is necessarily a partial one, and a fuller account would have to indicate that the play is *une pièce bien faite* and has an evenness about it which is lacking in *A Woman of No Importance* and *An Ideal Husband*. More important for our present purpose, however, is that in the closing episode at least Wilde succeeds in obtaining just the right tone for dramatically harmonising the parts of the dandy and the moralist. A climax in the plot is reached towards the end of the last act. Will Mrs Erlynne explain her behaviour by telling Lady Windermere the truth – that she is her mother? Will she tell Lord Windermere that his wife was thinking of leaving him? In fact she does neither. The joint happiness of the Windermeres is secured by a discreet omission in the one case and a false explanation in the other. Lady Windermere is deeply grateful, and Lord Windermere modifies his condemnation, 'She is better than one thought her'; and the play ends with them giving their respective estimates of Mrs Erlynne to her future husband:

> LORD WINDERMERE Well, you are certainly marrying a very clever woman!
> LADY WINDERMERE (*taking her husband's hand*) Ah, you're marrying a very good woman!

Wilde directs his irony perfectly. Lady Windermere is now very happy, when her honour is threatened, to see goodness in a well-intentioned lie; her 'hard and fast rules' have been quietly waved aside. Beyond this gently satiric touch, however, the lines have a greater interest, in that they establish with delicate sureness the relationship of the dandy with the orthodox moral judges. The assessments of Mrs Erlynne by the Windermeres are both wide of the mark. For the husband she is simply a good strategist; for his wife she is virtuous. She is in fact, up to a point, both. But the important fact is that her strategy is bound up with self-sacrifice in a way that Windermere does not recognise, while her virtue is quite other than Lady Windermere imagines it to be. Her behaviour in fact cannot be described exclusively in terms of either artifice or ethics. Her future husband too is satisfied that she has 'explained every demmed thing'; but she has really done nothing of the sort. Rather she has built out of her conduct a beautiful, false image of herself, which will give pleasure to Lady Windermere and sustain the couple's happiness. Her behaviour is seen as a praiseworthy and effective embodiment of the dandy's aspiration to turn his own life into a work of art, and recalls the Wildean dictum that 'lying, the telling of beautiful, untrue things, is the proper aim of Art'. But in the play as a whole this 'proper aim' is only fitfully achieved, and behind the successful conclusion lie unresolved moral and aesthetic tensions.

If the dandy as lover causes difficulty in *Lady Windermere's Fan*, the dandy as villain in *A Woman of No Importance* (1893) causes considerably more. It would seem that Wilde had not yet grasped the fatal significance of making his dandy into a character, equipped, in however simple a way, with complexity of motive and a capacity for involvement in emotional affairs. By nature a bystander, the dandy is forced in these first two plays to become a participant, and confusion results. In Darlington's case he was at least cast favourably in both roles; in Illingworth's, it seems, we have to admire him in one and dislike him in the other.

'The world says that Lord Illingworth is very, very wicked,' remarks Lady Stutfield. And Illingworth rejoins: 'But what world says that, Lady Stutfield? It must be the next world. This world and I are on excellent terms.' Unfortunately for Wilde's play it is neither Lady Stutfield nor the next world that judges Illingworth to be wicked, but Mrs Arbuthnot, the central character and, from one point of view, the heroine of the play. Wooed by Illingworth in the past, she was promised marriage and then deserted and left to bring up her child without any support. She now finds herself again in Illingworth's social circle, and her son has just been offered the prospect of a successful career as his private secretary. Indifferent to the situation of the mother, patronising to her son, flirtatious towards the girl with whom the boy is in love – the moral case against Illingworth is a strong one, and Lady Stutfield's remark, for all its archness, points to a reality. But if Illingworth is the villain of the piece, he is also, for long stretches, its hero. His intelligence, vitality and wit make the rest of the characters seem anaemic. If he can show up the triviality and malice of the social set which surrounds him, he is equally capable of making us sense the rigidity and self-satisfaction behind Hester's puritan values and Mrs Arbuthnot's religiose grief. And yet this superiority of attitude seems to exist quite apart from the moral situation in which he finds himself. This has nothing to do with complexity of character – it is not that kind of play; it arises from an ambiguity in his conception. If we look at Illingworth more carefully we shall see that this 'superiority' does not belong to him *in propria persona*; it is the author temporarily speaking through him. When it comes to advancing the plot, however, Wilde has as it were to desert Illingworth and think of him in the wicked role in which he has cast him. The more Illingworth moves into the plot, the less Wilde cares about what he says; so that his final lines, as he leaves Mrs Arbuthnot, have all the clichés of phrase and attitude of the stock-in-trade villain:

. . . Quarter to two! Must be strolling back to Hunstanton. Don't suppose I shall see you there again. I'm sorry, I am, really. It's been an amusing experience to have met amongst people of one's own rank, and treated quite seriously too, one's mistress and one's –

It seems quite fitting that Illingworth's stagey words should be brought to an end by a melodramatic gesture – and Mrs Arbuthnot duly 'snatches up glove and strikes Lord Illingworth across the face with it'. This routine melodramatic finale suggests how little Wilde's attention is really engaged with the moral questions which his plot genuinely seems to raise. Justice has to be done to Mrs Arbuthnot, but it is enough for Wilde if it is seen to be done. The centre of his interest remains in the dandy and in trying to realise the significance of the dandy in an appropriate action. In *Lady Windermere's Fan* he had become a sympathetic lover and had been rendered null; in *A Woman of No Importance* he has been a faithless lover and is degraded into a melodramatic villain.

Involvement of one kind or another was the root defect of these plays, and in writing his third play, *An Ideal Husband* (1895), Wilde seems to have taken special care to keep his dandy free from commitment. If Lord Goring is to be in love it will be with a minor figure of the play, and his 'love' will simply be there to testify to his status as hero. His connection with the central figures of the play will not be a profoundly emotional one, and will not involve him with a woman, faithfully or otherwise. And so we find Wilde giving Goring a friendship with Sir Robert Chiltern and hoping that the dandy, limited to the more fitting role of guide and philosopher, will at last find insurance against loss of wit.

Connected with Wilde's clearer insight into the dramatic requirements of the dandy was his decision to make the central plot of *An Ideal Husband* much wider, much more public in concern, than that of the earlier plays. Here, for the first and only time, a man's profession is central to the play. If Lady Chiltern demands an ideal husband this is intimately connected with the requirement that he must be an ideal politician. Corruption in the one sphere is, for her, corruption in the other.

This, then, is the world that faces the dandy; and now Wilde introduces him to us:

Enter Lord Goring. Thirty-four, but always says he is younger. A well-bred, expressionless face. He is clever, but would not like to be thought so. A flawless dandy, he would be annoyed if he were considered romantic. He plays with life, and is on perfectly good terms with the world. He is fond of being misunderstood. It gives him a post of vantage.

It is from this post of vantage that he sees an eminent politician being blackmailed, because of a past misdeed, into supporting a political scheme which he considers fraudulent; he sees his vain attempts to keep this from his wife, and her reactions when she learns the truth. At critical moments he is appealed to for help, and through his successful intervention the plot is happily resolved.

For the first time Wilde gives us a satisfactory portrait of the dandy. Unlike Darlington's and Illingworth's it is not a portrait confused by the plot. In Goring we feel that Wilde can use his own voice and remain confident that the character is appropriate to the play. But it is an appropriateness that has a significant limitation. This is a play of political intrigue, of action; and such intrigue, such action, are alien to the dandy. It is interesting to note how Wilde overcomes the difficulties which ensue. Goring has two decisive actions in the play. The first, his thwarting of Mrs Cheveley's plans of blackmail, is made possible by his finding a bracelet which she has lost and which he knows to have been stolen. The blackmailer become blackmailed. It is a significantly arbitrary device, too casually introduced by Wilde. Goring is lucky enough to be in a position to expose Mrs Cheveley. But it is good fortune which has nothing to do with his specific role as 'the first well-dressed philosopher in the history of thought'. Goring's second crucial action is to persuade Lady Chiltern to allow her husband to remain in public life and accept the seat in the cabinet which has just been offered him. And this takes the form of a set speech, in Wilde's characteristic anti-puritanical manner, prefaced by a stage-direction to the effect that Goring here shows 'the philosopher that underlies the dandy'. The action is not really resolved in dramatic terms; it is arrested, and dialectic is allowed to demolish the plot. But as Goring is inseparable from Wilde, this dialectic simply belongs to the author, and clearly it must end in victory. Goring resolves the problems in the play, certainly, but this is because Wilde has endowed him with an effortless superiority over everyone else. In Goring, then, Wilde has found an appropriate dramatic voice for himself, but he has not found a world where that voice can have a really appropriate dramatic effect.

However lightly it may be sketched in, the world of *An Ideal Husband* is a world where ambition and disgrace, love and suspicion, are possible. It is, uniquely in Wilde, a world of work. From his post of vantage the dandy may observe keenly and comment shrewdly, but he can never affect this world except through the arbitrary good fortune which the author has conferred on him. On his own, Goring is Wilde's most successful dandy; in the Chiltern-Cheveley world he is a wraith, lucky enough to be his author's Scarlet Pimpernel. His father's constant rebuke that he is wasting his time is not so easily dismissed as Wilde would like us to think.

It seems reasonable to think that, in creating a dandy satisfactorily, even though in isolation, Wilde was beginning to realise precisely the dramatic action he required. There are significant stage-directions in the third act. The first refers to a completely minor character, Goring's butler:

The distinction of Phipps is his impassivity. He has been termed by enthusiasts the Ideal Butler. The Sphinx is not so incommunicable. He is a mask with a manner. Of his intellectual or emotional life, history knows nothing. He represents the dominance of form.

The second refers to Goring:

One sees that he stands in immediate relation to modern life, makes it indeed, and so masters it. [my emphasis]

In these two directions we find, indicated abstractly, the solution to the problem that has dogged Wilde's progress as a dramatist. Repeatedly the dandy has been broken on the wheel of the every-day world, sometimes too involved a figure, sometimes incapable of being involved enough. And now Wilde begins to see that, if the dandy is to master the world, it can be only a world of his own making. Only in a *world* of dandies will his voice and actions become harmonious: a world where the categories of serious and frivolous will no longer apply, where every character can speak like the author and the author like every character, where everything that can be seen is harmonious and there is nothing that cannot be seen. The dandy can exist fully only in a world of idyll, of pure play. And at last, in *The Importance of Being Earnest* (1895), he finds himself in such a world.

II

The prevalence of cant is a constant target for Wilde, and a topic which receives significant mention in three of his four plays is the varying attitudes taken up by — and towards — men and women in matters of sexual morality. It is there in Hester's upholstered rhetoric in *A Woman of No Importance:*

. . . If a man and woman have sinned, let them both go forth into the desert to love or loathe each other there. Let them both be branded. Set a mark, if you wish, on each, but don't punish the one and let the other go free. Don't have one law for men and another for women.

More coolly, it is there in Lord Darlington's exchange with Lady Windermere:

LORD DARLINGTON ... do you think seriously that women who have committed what the world calls a fault should never be forgiven?
LADY WINDERMERE I think they should never be forgiven.
LORD DARLINGTON And men? Do you think that there should be the same laws for men as there are for women?

LADY WINDERMERE Certainly!
LORD DARLINGTON I think life too complex a thing to be settled by these hard and
fast rules.

And then we find it again towards the end of *The Importance of Being Earnest:*

JACK Unmarried! I do not deny that is a serious blow. But after all, who has the right to cast a stone against one who has suffered? Cannot repentance wipe out an act of folly? Why should there be one law for men, and another for women? Mother, I forgive you.

The most cursory reading, of course, reveals that, however similar these passages may be, the last one is markedly different in tone from the other two. And it is this difference in tone which constitutes the essential difference between *Earnest* and the plays which preceded it. It is a tone which emerges as a result of sentiments from widely different contexts being fused together into a single statement. Beginning with mock-understatement − 'I do not deny that is a serious blow' − it moves on through biblical reference to the clichés of romantic melodrama. The effect of this on the audience is to maintain a complete moral disengagement. But though Wilde's tone cuts out any ethical response to the sentiment, it makes completely real a character and a world where the sentiment seems quite appropriate. In other words, if we are kept deliberately disengaged from ever thinking of Jack's world as our own, we are kept no less deliberately engaged, by seeing the reality of Jack's world for *him*.

In the earlier plays, as we have seen, the reality of the dandy's world crumbled at the point where he became involved in the dramatic action. Now, in *Earnest*, at the height of the dramatic action, Jack's world is still perfectly viable. This testifies to Wilde's complete success in finding, in this play, the appropriate context for the dandy, and it is a characteristic touch of bravura that the testimony consists in making sustained play with the very situation which had earlier taken such toll of the dandy. We are now in a position to describe directly how Wilde has succeeded in finding a world fit for dandies to live in.

Everything starts from language. The characteristic language of the dandy is the paradox, and the essence of paradox is contradiction. This draws attention to two things − the attitude or sentiment which the paradox is concerned to reverse, and the language itself in which the reversal is done. We should say of paradox that it is a form of expression which is at once critical and self-delighting. And the same definition would apply very well to *Earnest* as a whole. Wilde is able to achieve this extension and uniformity because in this play the language of the dandy is a language appropriate to everyone. In the earlier plays, where the dandy was a figure involved with others who were not dandies, his idiom belonged to him in a very personal way: we were driven to reflect on *his* criticism, *his* self-delight. But when all the characters can speak with the author's voice they are completely insulated against each other; the criticism is then cut free to apply to a world beyond the characters, to the world of the audience. And in their turn the audience cannot think of any of the characters critically, because the delighting, and self-delighting, form of paradox creates a comic response which encloses these characters in a protective shell. Something of the way this works can be seen from the opening lines of the play; Algernon, who has been playing the piano in the next room, comes in and addresses his servant:

> ALGERNON Did you hear what I was playing, Lane?
> LANE I didn't think it polite to listen, sir.

This reveals, with splendid economy, the nature of the relationships between the characters in this play. The dandy, characteristically playing the piano and delighting in his own art, asks his servant for approval. Lane's reply is interesting. Taken in isolation it is the archetypal expression of deference from servant to master. Taken in this particular context it is of course the reverse: Lane is exercising his liberty to refuse to say what Algy expects from a servant on such an occasion. But when we take the question and answer *together*, we think neither of Algy's request nor of Lane's skilfully evasive reply, and what this may imply about them as people; we think simply of the perfect way in which they encounter each other. In other words we think of expression, of form, of the manner in which Wilde reveals the perfect servant as one who is the equal of his master.

If, at the end of the play, we are left thinking more of the dramatist than of his creation, if this were so, the play would hardly have succeeded: but rather because of the precise rhetorical means through which Wilde has obtained and controlled our attention. The use of striking linguistic display, such as paradox, instantly draws attention to the author as manipulator; it is a reminder that words are man-made things. In realistic drama the author works in the opposite way: everything is done to give the impression that the characters are autonomous; the writer puts his skill into re-creating exact speech rhythms, idiosyncratic turns of phrase. The same is true in the realm of plot. The realistic dramatist will try to follow out as faithfully as possible the subtle configurations of daily life; Wilde finds his ideal plot in farce, because he sees art as exaggeration, and 'selection, which is the very spirit of art, in nothing more than an intensified mode of over-emphasis'. Nothing is more over-emphatic than farce, permitting as it does the maximum of coincidence and unlikelihood. Paradox in language, farce in plot – these are Wilde's chief resources in directing our response away from the characters and towards the play. Because for him it is in the play as such, embodying an imaginative world of perfect harmony, that life, 'so terribly deficient in form', is given a meaning. Before exploring this, it is worth looking more exactly at the elements of farce and character in *Earnest*.

One of the ways in which Wilde defines his conception of plot and character is by making the characters themselves take on the role of plot-makers. They will shape their lives with the same complete confidence as they shape their phrases. So we find Act I opening with Jack playing the part of Ernest and coming up to town to woo Gwendolen, and closing with Algernon playing the part of Ernest and going down to the country to woo Cecily. In the second act Algernon appears as Ernest and Jack as Ernest's bereaved brother. The girls dramatise their lives in their diaries and plan to marry not the right man, but the right name – Ernest. Eventually the mythical plot takes over and is shown to be 'truer' than the real plot – Jack is, in fact, Ernest. Plot-makers of this sort can never be taken by surprise, they feel too sure of themselves for that. And consequently, at the times when things appear to be going wrong – Lady Bracknell's refusal to let Gwendolen marry Jack, Algernon's appearance as Ernest at the moment when Jack is mourning his death, the girls' discovery that 'Ernest' is a fiction – no one is abashed; there is just a momentary pause and new resources of plot are immediately called upon. Shaw found the play 'inhuman' and of course, in a sense, he was right: Wilde's whole art is calculated to prevent his characters' becoming people. If they did, they could no longer say perfectly all they have to say, they could no longer act as the masters of fortune, they could no longer co-operate with the author in validating the truth of his world, a truth founded not in reality but in imaginative cohesiveness, a truth sensed in shape.

Whenever the plot seems to be moving towards reality we see language taking it over and designing it into fantasy. There is, for example, the love-scene in Act I, which culminates like this:

GWENDOLEN . . . We live, as I hope you know, Mr Worthing, in an age of ideals. The fact is constantly mentioned in the more expensive monthly magazines, and has reached the provincial pulpits, I am told; and my ideal has always been to love someone of the name of Ernest. There is something in that name that inspires absolute confidence. The moment Algernon first mentioned to me that he had a friend called Ernest, I knew I was destined to love you.

JACK You really love me, Gwendolen?
GWENDOLEN Passionately!
JACK Darling! You don't know how happy you've made me.
GWENDOLEN My own Ernest!

It is a splendid climax, perfectly appropriate for the 'love-scene', and at the same time perfectly undercutting its reality. When Jack goes on to hint that his name might not be Ernest, Gwendolen dismisses the suggestion briskly as having 'very little reference at all to the actual facts of life, as we know them' – another ironical gloss on the question of reality.

Lady Bracknell is interesting in that we do feel, here, that we have in a quiet ordinary sense of the word a 'character'. But she too builds up her whole mode of speech out of bemusing herself with her own voice. If she exists at all, it is in an echo-chamber. She is so used to speaking in tones of imperious command that these persist regardless of what she is talking about:

Well, I must say, Algernon, that I think it is high time that Mr Bunbury made up his mind whether he was going to live or to die. This shilly-shallying with the question is absurd. Nor do I in any way approve . . . I consider . . . I am always telling . . . etc., etc.

It is not only her own tone that hypnotises her, it is often a phrase itself: 'But German sounds a thoroughly respectable language, and, indeed, I believe, is so.' The first rather curious statement gets a splendid endorsement from the would-be pedantic accuracy of the second.

A good example of 'serious' situation, tone, and individual phrase combining together in this process of de-realisation occurs when Jack arrives dressed in his mourning clothes:

CHASUBLE Dear Mr Worthing, I trust this garb of woe does not betoken some terrible calamity?
JACK My brother.
MISS PRISM More shameful debts and extravagance?
CHASUBLE Still leading his life of pleasure?
JACK (*shaking his head*) Dead!
CHASUBLE Your brother Ernest dead?
JACK Quite dead.
MISS PRISM What a lesson for him! I trust he will profit by it.

It is a rich exchange. Chasuble, reacting automatically to black, goes into his trade language – 'garb of woe', 'betoken', 'terrible calamity'. One routine response fades and is immediately replaced by another, 'Still leading his life of pleasure?' – which is an odd hypothesis as to why Jack should be in mourning. It is after 'pleasure' that Jack drops his monosyllable, 'dead'. Chasuble, still in the same mechanically solicitous tone, repeats, 'Your brother Ernest dead?' Jack then returns his splendidly superfluous '*quite* dead'. Interspersed with these exchanges are those of Miss Prism, who is as eccentrically unresponsive to the situation as Chasuble is eccentrically responsive. The effect of this triple play – Jack solemnly in mourning for a fiction, the other two quite incapable of making an appropriate response to the announcement – is to make form everything and content nothing. The interesting point that emerges from looking at this passage is that here Wilde is exercising his linguistic control for a purpose very different from the one revealed in the Jack-Gwendolen passage which we looked at earlier. There, the rhetorical situation kept feeling at bay, it was impossible to think of the scene as either passionate or heartless; now the rhetoric keeps farce at bay. The fact that Ernest is a fictitious character, and that Jack is solemnly arrayed in mourning for him, certainly goes far towards creating a *merely* farcical situation; but Wilde's scrupulous attention to the exact responses of Chasuble and Miss Prism keeps *our* attention, as always, on the language, rather than on the pure comedy of situation. Farce in Wilde is always shaped and controlled by precision of language, and it is this which distinguishes it from farce in general, which is shaped by arbitrariness of event.

The dramatic creation of the dandy, the creation of a world capable of projecting the dandy – we can see the problems involved in these undertakings, and we shall probably be willing to admit that *Earnest* solves them satisfactorily. But a question still remains about the nature of the success, a question which can be brought into sharper focus if we think of Wilde's play in relation to the comedies of other dramatists.

When we finish reading or seeing a play of Shakespeare's we are left thinking of the profound imaginative world which he has created; at the end of a Jonson play we can see how farce can bring to vivid life human vice and folly. But what are we left with at the end of *The Importance of Being Earnest*? There is here no 'perilous stuff that weighs upon the heart', nor 'sport that plays with follies, not with crimes'. Eric Bentley attempts an answer to this question in *The Playwright as Thinker*. [See excerpt in Part Three, above – Ed.] After commenting that nothing is easier than to handle this play without noticing what it contains, he goes on to exhibit its contents:

The margins of an annotated copy of *The Importance of Being Earnest* would show such things as death, money, marriage, the nature of style, ideology and economics, beauty and truth, the psychology of philanthropy, the decline of aristocracy, nineteenth century morals, the class system. What begins as a prank ends as a criticism of life. What begins as intellectual high-kicking ends as intellectual sharp-shooting.

This seems a misleading description because Bentley gives the impression of a play containing serious ideas which have been attractively packaged in wit. The best critic is he who opens the parcel most dextrously. But nothing, surely, is gained by recommending this play as if it were one of Shaw's. Yet again it is possible to see, only too clearly, Mr Bentley's difficulty. Our vocabulary of approval for the drama is dominated by representational considerations like 'truth to character', 'truth to situation', or else by didactic ones like 'social or moral vision'. A dramatist who offers neither character nor social or moral vision would seem to be offering only triviality. What is it, then, which distinguishes *Earnest* from *Charley's Aunt?*

The difference, ultimately, is the same as that which distinguishes Shakespeare and Jonson from countless less successful dramatists, the use of language. But whereas their language was a means to an end, and their end conforms fairly directly with Johnson's definition of the function of literature − 'to enable readers better to enjoy life or better to endure it', Wilde was concerned with the linguistic artifact itself, with a kind of poetry which Auden has described as 'a verbal earthly paradise, a timeless world of pure play, which gives us delight because of its contrast to our historical existence with all its insoluble problems and inescapable suffering'. To think of Wilde's art as merely 'escapist' is to oversimplify the position. What he gives us is a completely realised idyll, offering itself as something irrevocably *other* than life, not a wish-fulfilment of life as it might be lived. Consequently, to think of Wilde's idyll in terms of 'aspiration' or 'rejection' is as idle as the notion of 'accepting' or 'rejecting' Keats's *Ode on a Grecian Urn,* or the urn itself, or Mozart's *Marriage of Figaro.* 'Truth in art is the unity of a thing with itself,' and the truth in Wilde's dictum can be falsified by art too self-consciously pursued, as well as by life. *Salome,* Wilde's last produced play, is a monument to art, not art itself; it is as entangled with an aesthetic commentary on life as *A Woman of No Importance* is with a moral one. *Earnest* is the dramatic expression of a precise aesthetic ideology, where Art is seen as the supreme ordering and perfection of life. In such a play the plot can never be our sort of plot, and so, in Wilde, it is a farce; the characters can never be human, and so, in Wilde, they are pure and simple; the language has to be our language, but if it is the language of paradox it can continually contradict us. Such a play can contain oblique criticism of life, but it will never be a direct imitation of life, since that would imply an intrinsic value in life superior to that of art. Even at its most topical *The Importance of Being Ernest* avoids the didactic and the narrowly satirical, and remains resolutely faithful to its aesthetic aim. It was a success which Wilde achieved only once, and we can feel reasonably certain that the sudden ending of his dramatic career did not deprive us of any better play.

SOURCE: essay in *Sewanee Review*, LXXIV (1966), 501–21.

Arthur Ganz   The Divided Self in the Society Comedies of Oscar Wilde (1960)

It is usually said that Oscar Wilde's society comedies have foolish plots and brilliant dialogue, and as far as it goes this critical commonplace is true. *Lady Windermere's Fan, A Woman of No Importance* and *An Ideal Husband* do in fact have foolish plots and brilliant dialogue. But the foolishness of these plots does not prevent them from expressing Wilde's personal and artistic positions, while the brilliance of this dialogue has often obscured both its value and its meaning. These are the things that I wish to demonstrate here.

This dichotomy between plot and dialogue which mars the society comedies does not appear in Wilde's masterpiece, *The Importance of Being Earnest*. But to achieve the unity of *The Importance* Wilde had to suppress half his nature. That suppression constitutes a kind of deception, for we are given only a part of Wilde's reaction to his world. If we wish to understand fully what Wilde put into *The Importance*, we must also understand what he left out.

But however useful the society comedies are as an explication of *The Importance*, their real significance lies in themselves. Each of these plays contains two worlds, not only contrasting but conflicting. One is the world of the sentimental plots, where ladies with mysterious pasts make passionate speeches and the fates of empires hang on intercepted letters and stolen bracelets. This is the world I will call Philistine. Opposed to it is the dandiacal world, where witty elegants lounge about tossing off Wildean epigrams and rarely condescend to notice, much less take part in, the impassioned actions going on about them. The tension between these two worlds gives to the society comedies their peculiar flavor, their strength, and unfortunately their weakness.

Our first impulse is to admire the charm and wit of Wilde's dandies but to insist that while the shabby mechanisms of his well-made plots might have been suitable for our grandfathers, they will not pass muster with us. In justice to late Victorian literary taste, it should be pointed out that this was precisely the attitude of our grandfathers. William Archer thought he had discerned an English Ibsen in the author of *A Woman of No Importance* and even Bernard Shaw felt that Sir Robert Chiltern of *An Ideal Husband* had struck 'the modern note' in defending his wrongdoing, but these examples are exceptional. Most of the Victorian critics grudgingly admired Wilde's wit and pointed out that his plots were compounds of various well-worn devices.[1] What was said about the society comedies when they first appeared is, for the most part, what is said about them today.

Such judgements are true enough, but to deny the Philistine parts of the society comedies the highest literary merit is not to deny them meaning. If we look closely at these plays, we see that each of them repeats the same pattern of action. A writer of Wilde's obvious gifts is not likely to indulge himself in such a repetition unless it is, for him at least, a meaningful one.

In each play the central character is someone who has in his past a secret sin. Mrs Erlynne, who has alienated herself from good society by running away from her husband, fills that role in *Lady Windermere's Fan*. The motive force in the play is Mrs Erlynne's desire to re-enter that society and be accepted by it. Although she knows the weaknesses of Philistine society, Mrs Erlynne suffers from her ostracism and warns her daughter against a similar fate:

> MRS ERLYNNE You don't know what it is to fall into the pit, to be despised, mocked, abandoned, sneered at − to be an outcast! To find the door shut against one, to have to creep in by hideous byways, afraid every moment lest the mask should be stripped from one's face, and all the while to hear the laughter, the horrible laughter of the world, a thing more tragic than all the tears the world has ever shed. You don't know what it is. One pays for one's sin, and then one pays again, and all one's life one pays. You must never know that.

This speech is, of course, a piece of nineteenth-century stage rhetoric, and if it stood alone in Wilde's work, the reader might safely ignore it. But in every play there are passages, if not as unfortunate in their phraseology, at any rate comparable in their content. The outcast is always repentant and desires forgiveness.

Mrs Erlynne is easily recognisable as that stock figure, the woman-with-a-past, one of the innumerable progeny of Marguerite Gautier,

the lady of the camellias. But Wilde uses this figure for his own purposes. Played off against Mrs Erlynne is a cold and unforgiving
moralist, her daughter, Lady Windermere. The real action of the play
is Lady Windermere's education. She learns that a single act is not a
final indicator of character and that a sinner may be a very noble
person indeed. At the end of the play Lord Windermere tells Lord
Augustus, who is about to marry Mrs Erlynne, that he is getting a
very clever woman. Lady Windermere knows better now. 'Ah', she
says to Lord Augustus, 'you're marrying a very good woman.'

In *A Woman of No Importance* Mrs Arbuthnot is the character who
parallels Mrs Erlynne. Like her predecessor, Mrs Arbuthnot is a
woman with a secret sin in her past. In this case it is the fact that her
son, Gerald, is the product of an illegitimate liaison. Though Mrs
Erlynne has led a life of pleasure and wickedness and Mrs Arbuthnot
has devoted herself to good works, the essential point about each is
that, though a sinner, she has remained pure in heart and therefore,
according to Wilde, deserves to be pardoned. As Mrs Erlynne was
opposed by the inflexible Lady Windermere, so Mrs Arbuthnot is by
the young Puritan, Hester Worsley. Lady Windermere had said that
women who had sinned should never be forgiven. As Mrs Arbuthnot
makes her first entrance, Hester exclaims, 'Let all women who have
sinned be punished.' Hester's conversion is no less complete than
Lady Windermere's. At the end of the play, when Mrs Arbuthnot
points out that she and Gerald are outcasts and that such is God's law,
Hester rebukes her. 'I was wrong', she says, 'God's law is only love'.
Again the sinner has been proved noble at heart, and the Puritan has
been converted.

The woman-with-a-past, in the person of Mrs Cheveley, appears
again in *An Ideal Husband*, but here it suits Wilde's convenience to
make her the villainess. In *An Ideal Husband* the sinner who must be
pardoned is Sir Robert Chiltern, and the Puritan who must be converted is his wife. Chiltern laid the basis of his personal fortune and
thus of his political career by selling a state secret. When he is
blackmailed, he fears not only the ruin of his career but the loss of his
wife, who has always idealised him. Above all, he desires her pardon
and her love. 'It is not the perfect, but the imperfect who have need of
love', he says. 'All sins, except a sin against itself, Love should
forgive.' Even after the threat of blackmail has been removed, Lady
Chiltern demands that her husband retire from public life, but finally
she relents and comes to realise that, as Lord Goring says, 'women are
not meant to judge us, but to forgive us when we need forgiveness.
Pardon, not punishment is their mission.'

It is easy to see the concealed sin and the plea for acceptance and forgiveness as a reflection of the situation forced upon Wilde by his homosexuality. In his journals (29 June 1913) André Gide hints at a concealed meaning in Wilde's plays, presumably along these lines. Robert Merle in his excellent study of Wilde is more specific.[2] He suggests not only that Wilde, in demanding pardon for his sinners, is demanding pardon for himself but that Wilde makes this demand most strongly for Mrs Arbuthnot because her sin, like his, is sexual.

What Merle says is true, but to see in Wilde's plays, or even in the Philistine sections of them, only a reflection of his sexual inversion is to limit them unnecessarily. Wilde, along with many others, had rejected the mores of the ordinary middle-class society of his time, and in his case the isolation of this position was undoubtedly intensified by his sexual eccentricity. But Wilde was far from being the only writer of that period who was torn between a distaste for the values of the society about him and a simultaneous desire to be accepted and praised by it. The exile can never finally free himself of the desire to see his home again.

The Philistine aspects of his plays invariably brought out the worst in Wilde as a stylist, but because the language in which he expresses himself rings false, we cannot assume that the emotion which produces it is also false. Behind the mechanical façades of their well-made plots the society comedies are deeply expressive of the isolation of an artist and an individual man. The Philistine parts of these plays, though of limited aesthetic value, are of the greatest interest, for they reveal that the dandiacal Wilde was not a casual pose nor the easy expression of an amusing impulse but the product of emotional and intellectual conflict.

This conflict is visible not only in the division of his plays but in the opposition of those divided parts. The Philistine and dandiacal points of view are more than different; they are contradictory. The Philistine may insist that his heart has remained pure, but he admits that he has sinned and asks society for pardon. The dandy, however, instead of acknowledging his sin, denies that sin exists and creates a set of dandiacal standards by which he indicts society itself. Where the Philistine is humble, the dandy is belligerent; and where the Philistine's defense is sentimental rhetoric, the dandy's weapon is wit.

But what is loosely called Wilde's wit is not all of a piece. Much, perhaps most, of it is truly dandiacal, and this is what we are concerned with. On the other hand, much of it is simple humor and is to be enjoyed as such. An example is the series of jokes associated with the Duchess of Berwick and her trisyllabic daughter, Agatha, whose lines consist entirely of the phrase 'Yes, mamma', worked into increasingly elaborate and ingenious contexts. Further examples can be adduced indefinitely. Occasionally we find a piece of what may be called capsule wisdom, such as the celebrated remark about the cynic's being one who knows the price of everything and the value of nothing. A more striking example is one of Chiltern's comments in Act II of *An Ideal Husband*. 'When the Gods wish to punish us', he exclaims, 'they answer our prayers.' In addition, Wilde's dialogue often contains touches of genuine satire. When Kelvil of *A Woman of No Importance* remarks that the East End is a very important problem, Lord Illingworth replies, 'Quite so. It is the problem of slavery. And we are trying to solve it by amusing the slaves.' Wilde can be penetrating, but the amount of true satire in his work is slight. The satirist accepts a certain social code and criticizes those who do not follow it, but the dandy is an alien and can never follow ordinary society. All of these elements, humor, wisdom, satire, are present in Wilde's dialogue, but none of them gives it its peculiar flavor; none of them is dandiacal.

Oscar Wilde did not invent dandyism. He inherited a dandiacal tradition in both life and literature, and to this tradition he added certain elements that make Wildean dandyism unique. But to be unique is not necessarily to be isolated. Wilde must have felt himself to be one of the great dandies of the line that included Sheridan, Byron, Brummel, and above all, Benjamin Disraeli.[3] Like Wilde, Disraeli was an artist who had used eccentric clothes and brilliant conversation to seize the attention of Victorian society. But for the true dandy clothes are incidental and wit has a purpose.

The theory of dandyism as a philosophy of life was developed in France by Jules Barbey D'Aurevilly and Charles Baudelaire.[4] In his long essay on Brummell, *Du Dandysme et de Georges Brummell*, Barbey stresses the idea of the dandy as individualist, as the element of caprice in a stratified and symmetrical society. The dandy uses his wit to shock and startle that society while he himself remains impassive. Baudelaire accepts the idea of dandyism as a philosophy. He sees it, in fact, as a kind of religion, a cult of the self. Baudelaire's dandy, like Barbey's, is an individualist in revolt against his society. He is the last burst of heroism in a decadent age.

All of these ideas were intensely sympathetic to Wilde. His dandies, like Baudelaire's and Barbey's, are aristocrats whose elegance is a symbol of the superiority of their spirits. They use their wit to shock the gross Philistines about them. Above all, they are individualists who demand absolute freedom. Wilde insisted on his own individualism and wrote that nothing seemed of any value 'except what one gets out of oneself'.[5] To Wilde anything that interfered with the untrammelled expression of the self was intolerable.

Yet the Wildean dandy, however much he owes to tradition, is not simply a composite of English and French models. Wilde took the figure of the dandy because it embodied much of what he wished to express, but he added to it the elements we recognise as peculiarly Wildean. One of these is the theory of sensation. Wilde was a life-long disciple of Pater's *The Renaissance* with its famous conclusion stressing the desirability of experience itself rather than the fruit of experience. The dandiacal individualist, as Wilde sees him, revels in exquisite sensations. The more of them he can absorb, the richer and more nearly perfect will be his personality.

It is in this reverence for the exquisite that we find the center of the creed of the Wildean dandy. He is a kind of exalted art critic, a savorer of beautiful things. And for Wilde beauty always lay in perfection of form. The content of a work was irrelevant; what was important was 'the satisfying beauty of the design'.[6] Wilde said that an artist 'gains his inspiration from form, and from form purely', and so does the dandy.[7] The essence of the Wildean dandy's code is the substitution of aesthetic values for moral values. The Philistine world is, above all, the world of Victorian morality, but the dandiacal world is the world of pure aestheticism. Dandyism has many aspects and many disguises, but its presence in the society comedies is unmistakable.

A glance at the plays will show how the characteristics I have described appear in Wilde's dialogue. In the opening pages of *Lady Windermere's Fan* we meet Lord Darlington, the first dandy to appear in one of Wilde's comedies. The fact that he is a lord is significant. If the dandy is to dominate his society, he should possess social as well as intellectual superiority, and Wildean dandies tend toward the upper reaches of the peerage. As soon as he enters, Darlington displays his taste by admiring Lady Windermere's roses and then her fan. But more important than his title or his elegance is the fact that he is wicked. 'Dear Lord Darlington', exclaims the Duchess of Berwick, 'how thoroughly depraved you are.' Lord Illingworth, the chief dandy of *A Woman of No Importance*, is introduced in much the same way. Lady Stutfield says of him, 'The world says that Lord Illingworth is very, very wicked.' Even the likable Lord Goring of *An Ideal Husband* boasts of his bad qualities. 'When I think of them at night', he says, 'I go to sleep at once.' The villain in a Wilde comedy is invariably a dandy, for the dandy is inherently anti-social. Breaking a moral convention is, in itself, a pleasure for the dandy. Mrs Allonby of *A Woman of No Importance,* pointing out that women have a better time than men, explains that, 'there are far more things forbidden to us than are forbidden to them.'

The dandy can accept no interference from society. His individualism demands absolute freedom. 'Lord Illingworth says that all influence is bad', reports Mrs Allonby, 'but that a good influence is the worst in the world.' Lord Goring has the same attitude. 'I always pass on good advice. It is the only thing to do with it. It is never of any use to oneself.' A Wildean dandy, in fact, desires to be not only individual, but unique. When Lord Augustus of *Lady Windermere's Fan* ventures to agree with Cecil Graham, the latter answers, 'Sorry to hear it, Tuppy; whenever people agree with me I feel I must be wrong.'

What the dandy seeks from life is a series of exquisite sensations to enjoy. 'Moods don't last', says Mrs Allonby. 'It is their chief charm', Lord Illingworth replies. 'One should always be in love', he explains later. 'That is the reason one should never marry.' Mrs Allonby sums up the dandy's desire for sensation when she remarks, 'Life, Lady Stutfield, is simply a *mauvais quart d'heure* made up of exquisite moments.'

The dandy savors these exquisite moments as he savors any beautiful object, for the rules of aesthetic form are the rules of his life. To the dandy, an aesthetic flaw is a moral flaw. Mrs Cheveley of *An Ideal Husband* explains that 'a woman whose size in gloves is seven and three-quarters never knows much about anything. You know Gertrude has always worn seven and three-quarters? That is one of the reasons why there was never any moral sympathy between us.' From this point of view it is only a step to the assumption that all bourgeois goodness is ugly. 'A woman who moralises', remarks Cecil Graham, 'is invariably plain.' Lady Markby of *An Ideal Husband* dislikes high intellectual pressure because 'it makes the noses of the young girls so particularly large'. She mentions that a friend who had an unhappy life 'went into a convent, or on to the operatic stage, I forget which. No; I think it was decorative art-needlework she took up.' These are phenomena of a very different order, but for the dandy there is no distinction. They are all breaches of form.

The exaltation of the artistic, and thus the artificial, leads to a denigration of the natural. In *Lady Windermere's Fan* Dumby mentions that young Hopper had bad manners. 'Hopper is one of Nature's gentlemen', replies Cecil Graham, 'the worst type of gentleman I know.' In the eyes of the dandy artifice is everything. 'My dear fellow', Graham says to Lord Darlington, 'what on earth should we men do going about with purity and innocence? A carefully thought-out buttonhole is much more effective.'

The essential point of the dandy's creed is always the exaltation of form over content, of externals over internals. 'My dear Windermere, manners before morals', says Mrs Erlynne. In the dandiacal system morals hardly exist. 'It is absurd to divide people into good and bad', Lord Darlington maintains, 'People are either charming or tedious.' (Wilde had used almost exactly these words in the preface to *Dorian Gray:* 'A work of art is neither moral nor immoral, only well or poorly written.') The content of a statement is of no importance if its form is perfect, as Lord Goring implies in his reply to Mabel Chiltern's rebuke. 'That is the first unkind thing you have ever said to me. How charmingly you said it.' Lord Goring is so much a dandy that he even employs a dandiacal butler, and the description of this personage in Act III of *An Ideal Husband* is Wilde's best compact definition of dandyism. *'The distinction of Phipps is his impassivity. . . . The Sphinx is not so incommunicable. He is a mask with a manner. Of his intellectual or emotional life history knows nothing. He represents the dominance of form.'* Here is the key to the dandiacal code. Above all, the Wildean dandy represents the dominance of aesthetic form.

We can see clearly now the nature of the divided self in the society comedies of Oscar Wilde. Speaking in the person of his Philistine self, Wilde, the exile artist, admits that he has sinned in rejecting the mores of society. He insists, however, that he has remained uncorrupted at heart and begs society for pardon and acceptance. Speaking in the person of his dandiacal self, Wilde disdains that society and demands absolute freedom for the expression of the self. He denies the existence of evil and good and maintains that the only realities are ugliness and beauty.

Wilde seems never to have realized the significance of this pattern of division, although it is a persistent one in his work. Only in *The Importance of Being Earnest* did Wilde overcome this pattern and produce a work of pure dandyism and a masterpiece. But *The Importance* does not show the conflict that generated the world of dandyism. We must turn to the society comedies to see that conflict and the nature of the divided self.

SOURCE:essay in *Modern Drama* III (1960), 16–23.

NOTES

1. In this contention they were, of course, entirely correct. Wilde found the plays of Dumas *fils* a particularly useful source-book. Mrs Erlynne's entrance in the second act of *Lady Windermere's Fan* is an adaptation of a scene in *L'Etrangère; Le Fils naturel* provided Wilde with the situation in *A Woman of No Importance*, and the misunderstood letter at the end of *An Ideal Husband* originated in Dumas's *L'Ami des femmes*. It is worth noting, however, that Wilde's borrowings appear in the Philistine parts of his plays but not in the dandiacal.

2. Robert Merle, *Oscar Wilde: Appréciation d'une oeuvre et d'une destinée* (Rennes, 1948), p. 355. [For Gide reference, see p. 22 above – Ed.]

3. For a discussion of Wilde's admiration of Disraeli, see J. Joseph Renaud, 'Oscar Wilde et son oeuvre', *La Grande revue*, XXX–XXXIV (1905), p. 403.

4. See Barbey's *Oeuvres complètes*, XI (Paris, 1927) and Baudelaire's 'Le Dandy', in *L'Art romantique* (Paris, 1931).

5. *De Profundis*, new edn (New York, 1950), p. 79.

6. 'L'Envoi' in Rennell Rodd, *Rose Leaf and Apple Leaf* (Philadephia edn, 1882), p. 12.

7. Oscar Wilde, *Intentions*, new edn (London, 1947), p. 201.

Rodney Shewan   *Lady Windermere's Fan:* The Critic as Dramatist (1977)

Wilde's first comedy has two critical bases: the letter of 1883 in which he spoke of the importance of the 'intellectual idea' upon which 'the health of art' depended,[1] and Meredith's passage on the *aventurière*, 'Muse' of the problem-play. (Wilde may also have responded to Meredith's description of the fan as 'flag and symbol' of the English comedy of manners, although fans were high fashion in the 1890s, and Haddon Chambers' play *The Idler,* which Wilde saw and admired, was quickly cited by reviewers as a probable model for 'the business with the fan'.)[2]

The *aventurière,* or social adventuress, wrote Meredith,

is clever, and a certain division exists in the united scheme for confounding her. The object of this person is to reinstate herself in the decorous world; and either, having accomplished this purpose through deceit, she has a *nostalgie de la boue* that eventually casts her back into it, or she is exposed in her course of deception when she is about to gain her end. A very good, innocent young man is her victim, or a very astute goodish young man obstructs her path. This latter is enabled to be the champion of the decorous world by knowing the indecorous well. He has assisted in the progress of the *aventurières* downwards; he will not help them to ascend. The world is with him; and certainly it is not much of an ascension they aspire to; but what sort of a figure is he? The triumph of a candid realism is to show him no hero. You are to admire him (for it must be supposed that realism pretends to awaken some admiration) as a credibly living young man; no better, only a little firmer and shrewder, than the rest. If however, you think at all, after the curtain has fallen, you are likely to think that the *aventurières* have a case to plead against him. True, and the author has not said anything to the contrary; he has but painted from life, from the specimen he has presented in the bright and narrow circle of a spy-glass.[3]

Wilde makes the *aventurière* in his first comedy a dandy, a figure not merely capable of pleading her cause against convention, but whose life embodies a criticism of convention. He realises Meredith's hint in Act IV, 'to me the psychological act, the act that is newest, most true. For which reason, I suppose, the critics say "There is no necessity for Act IV". But the critics are of no importance.'[4] It is characteristic of Wilde, however, that the moral confrontations and adjustments all take place on a personal rather than a social level. Personality has a fateful quality – is more fateful, ultimately, than fate itself: 'misfortunes one can endure – they come from the outside, they are accidents. But to suffer for one's own faults – ah! – there is the sting of life!' Windermere says this in Act I in defence of Mrs Erlynne, but it applies to all the main characters. The idea of self-responsibility permeates the play.

Wilde found progress at first very slow. Within a few days of his remarks to the *Daily Telegraph* about the costumes for *London Assurance*, he wrote to George Alexander, future producer of *Lady Windermere's Fan*, 'I am not satisfied with myself or with my work. I can't get a grip of the play yet: I can't get my people real.'[5] The revival of *London Assurance* may well have helped to crystallise Wilde's dramatic use of dandyism. Certainly, there is nothing in his later account of the play's genesis to suggest that the impenitent *aventurière* was to become the first comic woman-hero of modern life[6]:

[R.S. quotes 'psychological idea' passage from letter concluding Section 1, Part One, above – Ed.] This is an entirely amoral framework based on purely instinctual egotism. There are no grounds for admiring Mrs Erlynne at all. In the completed play, however, the degree and nature of the admiration accorded her determine the quality of those who accord it.

The three stock situations mentioned by Morse Peckham[7] are the foundation of the dramatic machinery. The threat by the wife to insult the supposed mistress falls flat at the beginning of Act II; the scene of sexual jealousy between the same two characters is defused by Mrs Erlynne's remarkable maternal play-acting in Act III, which she discovers to be, for the moment, wholly true to her own life; and the recognition scene between parent and long-lost child (or rather, as Peckham observes, between child and long-lost parent) is forbidden in Act IV by the apparently selfish parent for wholly unselfish reasons. Wilde adds for good measure an adaptation of the screen scene from Sheridan's *The School for Scandal*. Instead of a lively young wife contemplating a mild flirtation to relieve the dullness of an aging husband, we find a puritan abandoning her husband and child on principle. Instead of Lady Teazle hearing from behind the screen her husband's kindly plans to settle a nice sum on her, and being shamed by it into future continence, Lady Windermere is obliged to listen to the cynical man-of-the-world chatter of Darlington's friends, which, even more perhaps than Mrs Erlynne's warnings, provoke her to exclaim, restored to safety, 'What a lesson!'

The pervasive ironies of the play begin with the first line: 'Is your ladyship at home this afternoon?' The puritan will receive a man capable of wooing her away from her husband, but fights to exclude the woman who turns out to be her own mother. The scene with Lord Darlington, and the introduction of the Duchess of Berwick, define the real nature of the standards that Lady Windermere supposes she ought to uphold, as well as the nature of the standard alternative.

Despite Darlington's partiality, his is the critical voice of the first half of the play. Lady Windermere feels that he is merely 'trivial', and insists that life is 'a sacrament. Its ideal is Love. Its purification is sacrifice.' Darlington's retort – 'Oh, anything is better than being sacrificed!' – is justified by later developments in action and dialogue: specifically, by Lady Windermere's willingness to sacrifice her child and its future; by Mrs Erlynne's socially suicidal sacrifice in Act III; and by Lady Windermere's fear, strange in the mouth of one who called sacrifice 'a purification', that her saviour may think twice about her good action once she calculates how much it has cost her. Ironically, while Darlington appears to be morally slipshod, it is actually the Duchess of Berwick, the Establishment mother, who exemplifies the prevailing *laissez-faire* morality. She tells Darlington that she will not let him know her daughter, because he is 'far too wicked', then promptly introduces him to her: 'Isn't he dreadful? Agatha, this is Lord Darlington. Mind you don't believe a word he says.' She admires Lady Windermere for making a stand about the 'dreadful people' who get asked everywhere, but openly admits their presence in her own house: 'The men get quite furious if one doesn't ask them.' San Juan has noted that Lady Agatha is used as a parody of Lady Windermere's 'pure' and ingenuous standards;[8] but the whole pattern of the Duchess's relationship with her daughter is a comic reflection both on Lady Windermere's treatment of her infant and on Mrs Erlynne's treatment of the infant Lady Windermere years before. Skilled in the wiles of the marriage market, the Duchess remarks (ironically but ingenuously), 'A mother who doesn't part with a daughter every season has no real affection'. (The pair anticipate James's Duchess and her little Aggie in *The Awkward Age* (1899) – aptly enough, one might think, since Lady Windermere, though celebrating her coming-of-age, is still morally and psychologically at the awkward age.) The Duchess of Berwick's success with Lady Agatha completes the parody. The 'little chatterbox' is paired off with Mr Hopper, the rich Australian described by Cecil Graham as 'one of

Nature's gentlemen – the worst sort of gentleman I know'; and this match achieves a symmetry of ingenuousness to which any liaison between Lady Windermere and Darlington could never approximate. Lady Agatha's thirteen yesses, with the last of which she secures her man, may have been suggested by a scene in *The London Cuckolds* (1681) by Edward Ravenscroft. Here a young wife, forbidden by her husband to reply anything but 'No' to strangers who might call, contrives to use the veto to secure the shrewd Towneley, whom she takes to bed. Whether Wilde knew of the parallel or not, his own scene is no less conscious of the rottenness of the respectable norm, whose watchword is 'Somebody should make a stand'.

The traditional opposition between country or pastoral values and town sophistication is also implied by Wilde's reuse of names from 'Lord Arthur Savile's Crime': Lady Windermere, Mrs Erlynne ('a pushing nobody with red hair'), and Lord Arthur were all present. The hint of pastoral Selby at the end of the play recalls the ending of the earlier story, while the choice of so peculiarly Wordsworthian a name as Windermere (in this case, Wilde did not follow his frequent practice of choosing names from the district where he wrote the play) seems studied, especially when Lady Windermere's incompatibility with Darlington – an industrial, though not very urbane, centre near the opposite coast – is one of his most important points.

Having confronted Lady Windermere with the prevailing social values during the firt half of Act I, Wilde puts her values to the test in the second half. When she confronts her husband with his supposed betrayal of their marriage, her 'virtuous' stand betrays itself by a persistent note of vulgarity, repeated in her later soliloquies. In pointed contrast to the discreet circumlocutions or colloquial trivialisations of Darlington and the Duchess, she talks of Windermere's 'mad infatuation' with an 'infamous woman'. She cries that she feels 'stained, utterly stained', and that 'every kiss that you have given me is tainted in my memory'. When Windermere tries to draw from her some objective concern for a woman who has suffered for her mistakes, his wife retorts merely, 'I am not interested in her – and – you should not mention this woman and me in the same breath. It is an error of taste.' Without waiting for any indication that Windermere's explanation might be genuine, she sweeps from the room: 'From this moment my life is separate from yours.'

In Act II the puritan's lack of self-control is contrasted with the dandy's perfect poise. It is, in fact, Mrs Erlynne's air of complete self-confidence, culminating in her conversation with Windermere about his settlement on her prior to her marriage with Lord Augustus, that pushes Lady Windermere off balance and convinces her to fly to the man who has offered her life 'to do with what you will'.

This action is the more perverse since Darlington has already betrayed his own precepts, offering friendship but planning conquest. It is only one of his 'little vanities' to pretend to be worse than other men, he says, adding that his 'modern affectation of weakness', as Lady Windermere calls it, is 'only an affectation'. Darlington thus plays the libertine playing the *honnête homme,* an amusing ultramodern anachronism which counterbalances Lady Windermere's quasi-courtly puritanism. But in Act II Wilde springs a surprise by placing in the mouth of a dandy a speech urging self-fulfilment in outright contradiction of social restraints. The device implies that there is more of the libertine – or the Romantic egotist – in Darlington than meets the eye, and it establishes Wilde's standard of comic self-consistency. In Act I Darlington had found Lady Windermere a 'fascinating puritan'. In Act II it is the woman, not the abstraction, that charms: 'From the moment I met you, I loved you, loved you blindly, adoringly, madly!' He challenges her to defy society and 'be yourself!':

I won't tell you that the world matters nothing, or the world's voice, or the voice of society. They matter a great deal. They matter far too much. But there are moments when one has to choose between living one's own life, fully, entirely, completely – or dragging out some false, shallow, degrading existence that the world in its hypocrisy demands. You have that moment now. Choose! Oh, my love, choose.

When choice proves impossible for her, Darlington increases her confusion by rhetorical sophistries designed to undermine her values: 'Who will blame you? No one. If they did, what matter? Wrong? What is wrong? It's wrong for a man to abandon his wife for a shameless woman. It is wrong for a wife to remain with a man who so dishonours her. You said once that you would make no compromise with things. Make none now.'

Darlington professes the amoral standards of the dandy, but in trying by moral arguments to overbear someone committed to a strict moral standard, he acts not in the interests of comic justice but in his own interests. In *A Woman of No Importance,* Mrs Allonby chaffs Illingworth, 'What a bad man you must be!' He asks, 'What do you call a bad man?' Her reply is, 'A man who admires innocence.' This is what Darlington does. The point emerges during the apparently pointless chatter of Act III, when a dandiacal discussion of what women may reasonably expect from men shows Darlington in his true colours – that anomalous creature, the romantic dandy, who cannot make light of his feelings over cigars.

Darlington's role is to dominate the first half of the play, as Mrs Erlynne's is to dominate the second half. Lady Windermere is first exposed to the influence of a false dandy whom she trusts, then to the influence of a true dandy whom she does not trust. Lady Windermere's flight to Darlington appears the more absurd when we consider that in Restoration comedy he could have played the perfect libertine, mouthing Rochester or one of his imitators: 'Of Nature's freedom we're beguil'd / By laws which man imposes'.[9] In the Victorian context, he sounds like an intruder from Wilde's heroic mode, a disappointed idealist who has fallen back on the dandy's pose without wholly relinquishing his grasp on the romantic's: 'We are all in the gutter, but some of us are looking at the stars.' With such lines as this, he could have made a legitimate hero in *The Duchess of Padua* or *A Florentine Tragedy*. The discrepancy defeats him. 'Nowadays', as he says, 'to be intelligible is to be found out.' Mask and reality are too various. No unity binds external form and inner substance. Darlington, once 'found out', is all too intelligible. Lady Windermere − 'the only good woman I have ever met in my life' − is a paragon that the dandy ought to suspect, not to worship. His exclamation, 'What cynics you fellows are!', sets up his dismissal by Cecil Graham, the perfect type of the trivialised but active intellect. 'What is a cynic?' inquires Graham. Darlington's reply − 'A man who knows the price of everything and the value of nothing' − was to be confirmed in the wholly serious context of *De Profundis*:

Delightful as cynicism is from its intellectual side, now that it has left the Tub for the Club, it can never be more than the perfect philosophy for a man who has no soul. It has its social value, and to an artist all modes of expression are interesting, but in itself it is a poor thing, for to the true cynic nothing is ever revealed.[10]

In comedy, however, Darlington's would-be Romanticism merits a riposte: 'And a sentimentalist, my dear Darlington, is a man who sees an absurd value in everything, and doesn't know the market price of any single thing.' The remainder of the passage from *De Profundis* places Darlington and Graham in their true relations: 'Remember that the sentimentalist is always a cynic at heart. . . . Sentimentality is merely the bank holiday of cynicism.' Darlington's cynicism about the badness of men by comparison with the goodness of women is only a refinement of sentimentality. Indeed, it is hardly less absurd than Lady Windermere's suspicion that all men are bad. In spite of his dandiacal facade, Darlington has too little self-security to qualify for Wilde's critical commonweal. To 'the average suburban playgoer' he may seem to disappear from the plot because of his attempt on the virtuous heroine. To the 'few choice spirits', he is dismissed by his fellow-dandies for having admired her at all.

In Act IV everyone reverts to type, most notably Windermere. Discarding his earlier tolerance, he now judges Mrs Erlynne entirely by appearances, like the rest of society. As soon as the audience has tangible evidence of Mrs Erlynne's true qualities, Windermere resorts to the platitudes of the *status quo*, and is doubly horrified when she assumes the dandy's mask to control her feelings:

I have no ambition to play the part of a mother. Only once in my life have I known a mother's feelings. That was last night. They were terrible – they made me suffer – they made me suffer too much. For twenty years, as you say, I have lived childless – I want to live childless still. (*Hiding her feelings with a trivial laugh.*) Besides, my dear Windermere, how on earth could I pose as a mother with a grown-up daughter? Margaret is twenty-one, and I have never admitted that I am more than twenty-nine, or thirty at most. Twenty-nine when there are pink shades, thirty when there are not. So you see what difficulties it would involve. No, as far as I am concerned, let your wife cherish the memory of this dead, stainless mother. Why should I interfere with her illusions? I find it hard enough to keep my own. I lost one illusion last night. I thought I had no heart. I find I have, and a heart doesn't suit me, Windermere. Somehow it doesn't go with modern dress. It makes one look old. (*Takes up hand mirror from the table and looks into it.*) And it spoils one's career at critical moments.

The subject of dress indicates that the dialogue has reverted to the philosophy of the superficial, 'the great dandiacal joke'[11] which exalts appearances over subjective truth. Mrs Erlynne knows well which role best suits her. She is determined to keep motive and manner in their proper balance – not to play the tragedy queen. Unlike Vera, Beatrice or Salome, she finds self-fulfilment through passionate action too horrifying. For her, 'hearts' belong in costume drama; 'modern dress' requires a different style. Windermere, unable to appreciate these complex reactions, feels outraged by what he thinks her callousness. Being a man of essentially 'natural' tastes, he fails to perceive that even the 'dark hair and innocent expression' of his wife's cherished miniature were 'the fashion' during Mrs Erlynne's youth when the likeness was taken. Like the audience for whom *La Dame aux Camélias* was written, he would have relished a reform. It would have flattered him by confirming the rightness of his values. At the end of *The Man of Mode*, Harriet, young and victorious, reminds Loveit, cast off and embittered and determined to 'lock myself up in my house and never see the world again', that a 'nunnery is the more fashionable place for such a retreat, and has been the fatal consequent of many a *belle passion*'. Mrs Erlynne, who seems almost to echo the speech, allows no one to upstage her – least of all Windermere, who is now firmly back in place as a caryatid of convention after his brief excursion into the world of flesh and blood:

I suppose, Windermere, you would like me to retire into a convent, or become a hospital nurse, or something of that kind, as people do in silly modern novels. That is stupid of you, Arthur; in real life we don't do such things — not as long as we have any good looks left, at any rate. No — what consoles one nowadays is not repentance, but pleasure. Repentance is quite out of date. And besides, if a woman really repents, she has to go to a bad dressmaker, otherwise no one believes in her. And nothing in the world would induce me to do that. No; I am going to pass entirely out of your two lives. My coming into them has been a mistake — I discovered that last night.

By rejecting the moral for the aesthetic posture — society's narrowing alternatives — she may lose much that is valuable, but her position is at least rational, consistent, and free from self-deception or hypocrisy. To Windermere, she has made a 'fatal mistake': she can never 'get back'. Mrs Erlynne calls the error 'almost fatal': she alone knows how near to her daughter the real danger came. Windermere's change of heart emphasises her self-consistency. As San Juan points out, even her lapse into 'sentiment' in Act III corresponds with what Winderemere tells us about her past.[12] The past is laid again, however, and the audience allowed to emerge with the new-found 'shield of intellect' held over 'the new-born babe of pity'.

In a typewritten draft of the play,[13] Wilde made more of the miniature and of Windermere's rudeness, both of them presumably intended to increase Mrs Erlynne's humiliation or discomfiture by the conventional world. He also sketched out an exchange between the pair which would have intensified Windermere's disgust at her behaviour in Act III. Mrs Erlynne comes close to betraying her real motives for going to Darlington's rooms, and thus to revealing her daughter's 'mistake'. Windermere interprets her meaning more grossly, although his answers have, unknown to him, an ironic point. (Brackets indicate the part of the dialogue taken from the typescript.)

MRS ERLYNNE (*shrugging her shoulders*) Don't use ugly words, Windermere. They are vulgar, I saw my chance, it is true, and took it.
WINDERMERE Yes, you took it — and spoiled it all last night by being found out.
MRS ERLYNNE (*with a strange smile*) You are quite right, I spoiled it all last night.
[WINDERMERE I can't imagine what made you do it.
MRS ERLYNNE I wonder myself why I did it now. Suddenly there awoke in one's nature feelings that one thought were dead, or that one thought one never had at all. They wake in one's nature, and then they die.
WINDERMERE Are they dead?
MRS ERLYNNE I think so. I fear so.
WINDERMERE A good thing too.
MRS ERLYNNE Possibly.
     (*Pause*)
WINDERMERE Mrs Erlynne, what are you plotting now? Don't imagine that you can get your reputation whitewashed again. I gave you your opportunity. You threw it away. Your going to Darlington's rooms was monstrous.

MRS ERLYNNE It *was* very foolish of me, wasn't it?
WINDERMERE It was stupid, utterly stupid.
MRS ERLYNNE Yes, I dare say it was.]
WINDERMERE As for your blunder in taking my wife's fan from here and then leaving it about in Darlington's rooms, it is unpardonable.

Mrs Erlynne is still given the chance to rebuke him for his bad grace —
'My dear Windermere, it is a social error to be uncivil, and a social
crime to be candid. To be both uncivil and candid at the same time is
quite unforgivable!' — but the phrase that Wilde finally picked ('My
dear Windermere, manners before morals!') says more in less, and
gives us the motto of Wildean comedy.

The other significant change, made in rehearsal, concerned the
secret of Mrs Erlynne's identity. Wilde had intended that the audience remain ignorant of the mother-daughter relationship until the
last act. [R.S. quotes from letter in Section 1, Part One above, from
'. . . had I intended to let out the secret' to 'her own safety when a
crisis occurs'.] The most remarkable aspect of this argument is its
determined air of self-justification. Several of the points made do not
relate directly to the play even in its draft form, and much of it is self-
contradictory, in effect if not in word. George Alexander, who made
the change during Wilde's temporary absence from rehearsals, seems
to have realised, however, that Wilde's original scheme sacrificed
motive and idea, which he had carefully worked out, to a idea of
dramatic 'suspense' which was largely illusory. An adventuress who
has hitherto shown no interest whatsoever in the fate of the wife
whose husband she has been blackmailing is unlikely to spare a thought
for that wife's social reputation at the expense of her own, particularly
after all the hard work that she has put in to regain it. Wilde feared
that the change would weaken the crucial last act: 'The chief merit of
my last act is to me the fact that it does not contain, as most plays do,
the explanation of what the audience knows already, but that it is the
sudden revelation of what the audience desires to know, followed
immediately by the revelation of a character as yet untouched by
literature.'[1] [From letter cited above.] The play as it stands preserves
the element of revelation, but instead of revealing the mere fact of
blood relationship, it reveals the psychological spring of Wilde's new
character: the *aventurière* as dandy.

It must be admitted that the play does not run as smoothly as my
summary suggests. Many smaller points were overlooked. Sometimes
Lady Windermere fails to function properly even as a type, or times
and other trivia of plot fail to fit. Wilde's main concern, however — a
comic morality based on the idea of self-knowledge and self-consistency — emerges in spite of these imperfections and shapes our

attitudes to all the main characters. Lady Windermere, titular recipient first of the audience's token admiration, then of their tolerant
sympathy, is given her second chance with a well-meaning though
dense husband. Darlington is dismissed by his own confusions, failing
both as dandy and as Romantic lover, though temporarily successful
as a wit. To Mrs Erlynne is left the task of assessing her own merits
and deciding her own future. Her reversion to type is the most
courageous act of the play. Windermere's grudging admiration of that
capacity for explaining things which enables her to retain her hold on
Lord Augustus – her only success in terms of her 'career' – gives
Wilde two critical chances in the play's closing lines. 'Well, you are
certainly marrying a very clever woman', exclaims Windermere, still
resonating with his personal experience of her cleverness. 'Ah,' rejoins
Lady Windermere, 'you're marrying a very good woman.' (Wilde has
in mind the last line of *Le Demi-Monde*:[14] 'You're marrying the
honestest woman I know'.) Windermere's line is the reply of the conventional mind striving to be objective; his wife's is the reply of a woman
eager to give away a flattering phrase that no longer suits her. Lady
Windermere has learned that people cannot 'be divided into good and
bad', but it is too much to expect that she will yet recognise the inept-
ness of bestowing on Mrs Erlynne the very title that Mrs Erlynne has
shown to her to be worthless. This is Wilde's parting gesture to the
double comic standard. For the conventionally minded playgoer, the
'good woman' of the sub-title (in early versions, the title was *A Good
Woman*) starts as Lady Windermere but ends as Mrs Erlynne, and
even so crude a 'critical' reversal has its value. To that part of the
audience alive to the dandy's relative standards, the play contains no
'good woman' at all. Society, in the final analysis, is hardly as sophis-
ticated as Mrs Gamp, and its 'good woman' is a Mrs Harris.

This lightness of touch, unexpected, perhaps, at the end of an
action which somewhat narrowly avoids domestic (if not quite heroic)
tragedy, is matched by Wilde's systematic use of the fan, 'flag and
symbol of our so-called Comedy of Manners, or comedy of South-Sea
islanders under city veneer'. As the fan passes from hand to hand and
from room to room, it seems to define some progression in its owner's
social maturity. It appears at first as Windermere's gift to his wife (an
innocent 'child') on the occasion of her coming of age. Next, it is the
instrument with which she threatens to insult Mrs Erlynne. At the
reception she gives it to Lord Darlington to hold, and it becomes a
physical sign of her need for 'a friend', or husband-substitute, 'tonight'.
When the climax comes, she drops the fan on the floor. It next appears
in Darlington's rooms, where she is almost betrayed by it. Mrs
Erlynne steps in to interpret its presence, and returns it to its owner

next day. By this time, the fan has assumed a definite symbolic significance: it is the attribute and weapon of the competent social adult.
Mrs Erlynne's restoration of the fan to her daughter not only reunites
owner and giver – husband and wife – but also presents Lady
Windermere with a second chance at undergoing the ordeal by society:
that second chance which Mrs Erlynne thereby gives up for herself.
But the fan now bears a social stigma, and it changes hands once
more, becoming a memento for the mother and virtually the staff of
office of the adventuress. Finally entrusted to Lord Augustus, who is
eager to abdicate from society into trouble-free disrepute, it becomes a
symbol of his relationship with Mrs Erlynne: 'you would carry off
anything gracefully, Lord Augustus.' Mrs Erlynne's parting pun is
the biggest hyperbole in the play, and in being so, it defines her part in
their joint future.

Below Wilde's poised estimate of social responsibilities, then, we
can recognise the reservations of his earlier Romantic mode. The
Windermeres retire to their country seat, but will doubtless return in
due course. Darlington and Mrs Erlynne leave England, and on a
much more permanent basis. Their departure is the more significant
in that they are the only characters to whom we are inclined to accord
any critical authority. Admittedly, they do not die, and this is one step
closer to social integration than Vera, Guido, or Beatrice ever
achieved. But there lingers the suggestion that the talented exception – especially the passionate talented exception – needs all his
wits about him and a good deal of luck besides if he is to retain
membership of the club. As Wilde argued in 'The Soul of Man', 'what
the world calls a sin against society' may simply be the fulfilment of a
personality in some way of which society disapproves. Darlington,
indeed, says as much to Lady Windermere. The offence itself, however, is finally of little account. The punishment is for that disregard of
appearances which leads to discovery. In such conditions, private
rather than public estimates of justice are the only humane ones.
Wilde developed this conviction in *An Ideal Husband*, where the
misdemeanour of an ingenuous wife was replaced by the misuse of
privileged information by a public figure. By contrast with *Lady
Windermere's Fan*, the play is optimistic: the comic libertine-Machiavel
is dismissed, the erring hero reprieved, the sympathetic dandy-mediator
integrated by marriage with the conventional part of society. After
that, Wilde moved on, or back, to pastoral farce.

SOURCE: from *Oscar Wilde : Art and Egotism* (London, 1977), pp.
158–68.

NOTES

[Reorganised and renumbered from the original – Ed.]

1. *Letters of Oscar Wilde* (London, 1962).

2. Karl Beckson (ed.), *Oscar Wilde: The Critical Heritage* (London, 1970), pp. 122, 127–8. In fact, Chambers's device involved a bouquet, not a fan, and the resemblances would probably have passed unnoticed if *The Idler* had not been produced so recently at the same theatre, the St James's. Wilde later borrowed various bits and pieces from it for *An Ideal Husband*.

3. George Meredith, *An Essay on Comedy* (1877), new edn, ed. Lane Cooper (London, 1956, 1972), p. 154.

4. *Letters*, p. 332.

5. Ibid., p. 282. [See first extract in section 1, Part One, above. Boucicault's *London Assurance* had been revived by Charles Wyndham at the Criterion on 27 Nov. 1890; Wilde wrote to the *Daily Telegraph* on 2 Feb. 1891, commending the men's fashions: *Letters*, pp. 283–4. – Ed.]

6. Charles Baudelaire, 'De l'Heroisme de la vie moderne': *Oeuvres Complètes*, pp. 949–52.

7. Morse Peckham, 'What Did Lady Windermere Learn?', *College English*, XVIII (1956), pp. 11–14.

8. Epifanio San Juan Jnr, *The Art of Oscar Wilde* (Princeton, N.J., 1967), p. 148.

9. Thomas Shadwell, *The Libertine* (1676), quoted in Dale Underwood (ed.), *Etherege and the Seventeenth-Century Comedy of Manners* (New Haven, Conn., 1957), pp. 13–14.

10. *Letters*, p. 501.

11. Arthur Ganz, 'The Dandiacal Drama', *Dissertation Abstracts*, XVIII (March 1958), p. 1429. [See also preceding study by Ganz in this Casebook – Ed.]

12. San Juan Jnr, op. cit., pp. 141–2.

13. MS Clark W 672, M 2 1 157 [1892], Boxed (2448).

14. A. Dumas *fils*, *Le Demi-Monde* (1855).

Christopher Nassaar On *A Woman of No Importance* (1974)

Wilde was a man who was fascinated by paradox and found it to be his most efficient means of communication. *A Woman of No Importance* exists as a deliberate paradox; it offers a contrast to *Salome* in its comic atmosphere while essentially restating the play's main theme. In *Salome*, Wilde tried to bring the Victorians to a shocking and terrifying confrontation with the evil in human nature, but the play was banned from the English stage by the censors. In *A Woman of No Importance*, he tried again to identify human nature as evil, but this time he chose to take the road of comic subtlety. As Lord Illingworth observes: 'To get into the best society, nowadays, one has either to feed people, amuse people, or shock people.' Wilde was not rich enough to feed people, and his attempt to shock them had been banned from the English stage because of a technicality regarding the use of biblical characters. Wilde must have strongly suspected, though, that it was the overt demonic atmosphere of *Salome* that had led to its censorship. Indeed, *The Times* was typical of the general English reaction to *Salome* when it characterised the play as 'an arrangement in blood and ferocity, morbid, *bizarre*, repulsive, and very offensive in its adaptation of scriptural phraseology to situations the reverse of sacred.'[1] In *A Woman of No Importance*, Wilde attempted to elevate his social position by amusing people.

The main theme of *A Woman of No Importance* is that, despite apparent differences, human beings are basically alike – that is, totally corrupt. This theme is very cleverly camouflaged, though, and the play can be read simply as an amusing and rather touching work of art with no great originality or literary value. Wilde had written of *Salome*: 'Ici et là, il y a des lacunes, mais l'idée du drame est claire' (*Letters*, p. 306). In *A Woman of No Importance*, on the other hand, the main idea is deliberately suppressed and befogged. The essential similarity among human beings is indicated in Act III:

> LADY HUNSTANTON What did Sir John talk to you about, dear Mrs Allonby?
> MRS ALLONBY About Patagonia.
> LADY HUNSTANTON Really? What a remote topic! But very improving, I have no doubt.
> MRS ALLONBY He has been most interesting on the subject of Patagonia. Savages seem to have quite the same views as cultured people on almost all subjects. They are excessively advanced.
> LADY HUNSTANTON What do they do?
> MRS ALLONBY Apparently everything.
> LADY HUNSTANTON Well it is very gratifying, dear Archdeacon, is it not, to find that Human Nature is permanently one – On the whole, the world is the same world, is it not?

The sexual practices of the Patagonian savages were far from what the Victorians would have considered proper. Mrs Allonby – who, at this point, is carrying on a subtle flirtation with Sir John – says they do 'apparently everything', and finds them very close to cultured people. Lady Hunstanton, without understanding her, is gratified 'that Human Nature is permanently one' and amusingly expresses her gratification to none other than the archdeacon. The main theme of *A Woman of No Importance* is that lust, in its hundred different manifestations, is the hallmark of human nature, the one thread that binds human beings together.

The basic split in the play is between those characters who give free expression to their libidinous nature and those who mask it from others and from themselves. The aristocrats of the play wear no

masks. This is made apparent in Act I, which is dominated by the conversation of a group of aristocrats on a garden lawn; but the wit is not
harmless: it is, for the most part, an attack on the Victorian sexual
code, or rather, a careless dismissal of it in favor of sexual looseness.
This is clearly indicated later on:

> LADY HUNSTANTON (*Shakes her fan at him.*) I don't know how it is, dear Lord
> Illingworth, but everything you have said to-day seems to me excesively immoral. It
> has been most interesting, listening to you.

The chief wits of the play are Lord Illingworth and Mrs Allonby, and
Act I ends with a thinly veiled invitation from her to Illingworth to
have an affair:

> LORD ILLINGWORTH Shall we go in to tea?
> MRS ALLONBY Do you like such simple pleasures?
> LORD ILLINGWORTH I adore simple pleasures. They are the last refuge of the com-
> plex. But, if you wish, let us stay here. Yes, let us stay here. The Book of Life begins with
> a man and a woman in a garden.
> MRS ALLONBY It ends with Revelations.
> LORD ILLINGWORTH You fence divinely. But the button has come off your foil.

The curtain drops after two pass up the terrace, smiling at each other.

Much of the wit of *A Woman of No Importance* is borrowed from Lord
Henry Wotton. This is Wilde at his laziest, but the borrowings do
serve an important purpose. Lord Henry was corrupt, and the people
who speak as he spoke identify themselves compactly as being corrupt.
Wotton has been broken up into fragments, as it were, and now
appears diffusely as the entire British aristocracy, though he is at his
most concentrated in Lord Illingworth. The play is a comedy, but the
shadow of Wotton casts its sinister length across it, suggesting dark,
hidden meanings beneath the sparkling surface.

Opposed to the aristocrats in Act I stands Mr Kelvil, a member of
the House of Commons, who is preparing a lecture on his favorite
subject, purity. There is also the American girl, Hester Worsley, one
of the chief characters in the play, whose attitude toward life is unyield-
ingly puritanical. Hester, however, has not yet come of age. Mrs Allonby
remarks: 'She told me yesterday, and in quite a loud voice too, that
she was only eighteen. It was most annoying'. Hester is an innocent,
and she is appropriately in love with another innocent, Gerald
Arbuthnot. 'Mr Arbuthnot', she exclaims enthusiastically, 'has a
beautiful nature! He is so simple, so sincere. He has one of the most
beautiful natures I have ever come across. It is a privilege to meet
him.'

Mrs Arbuthnot is only mentioned in Act I, but in Act II we meet her: 'MRS ARBUTHNOT *enters from terrace behind in a cloak with a lace veil over her head'*. She first appears as a cloaked and veiled woman, but the thrust of the play is to strip away the veils that obscure her corrupt nature. She is a church-going woman, deeply committed to the housing of the poor, and she is introduced to Hester in the following manner:

LADY HUNSTANTON (to *Miss Worsley*) Now, do come, dear, and make friends with Mrs Arbuthnot. She is one of the good, sweet, simple people you told us we never admitted into society. I am sorry to have to say Mrs Arbuthnot comes very rarely to me. But that is not my fault.

As it turns out, however, Mrs Arbuthnot once had an affair with Lord Illingworth when they were both very young, and Gerald is the illegitimate issue of that affair. The theme of the virtuous maiden seduced by the wicked aristocrat was a common one in Victorian literature, and Mrs Arbuthnot sees herself as a poor, abandoned maiden who has had to lead a life of suffering because of Lord Illingworth's wickedness. Her view of her situation is not quite accurate, however:

LORD ILLINGWORTH You forget, Rachel, it was you who left me. It was not I who left you.
MRS ARBUTHNOT I left you because you refused to give the child a name. Before my son was born, I implored you to marry me.
LORD ILLINGWORTH I had no expectations then. And besides, Rachel, I wasn't much older than you were. I was only twenty-two. I was twenty-one, I believe, when the whole thing began in your father's garden.

He continues: 'As for saying I left our child to starve, that, of course, is untrue and silly. My mother offered you six hundred a year. But you wouldn't take anything. You simply disappeared, and carried the child with you.'

Mrs Arbuthnot's behavior is logically inexplicable, but sentiment has a logic of its own and it is tempting to explain her behavior sentimentally. This is not the case, however. Lord Illingworth observes: 'You talk sentimentally, but you are thoroughly selfish the whole time.' As the play unfolds, this view of Mrs Arbuthnot is fully substantiated.

The garden imagery of *A Woman of No Importance* is a crucial key to the play's meaning. 'The Book of Life begins with a man and a woman in a garden', Lord Illingworth observes in Act I, and Mrs Allonby replies that 'it ends with Revelations'. Illingworth's affair with Mrs Arbuthnot had begun in her father's garden, and in Act I Mrs Allonby begins a tentative affair with him in a garden. Gardens and flowers are associated in the play with lust and sin. Mrs Allonby, in Act I, wishes to walk to the conservatory because 'Lord Illingworth told me this morning that there was an orchid there as beautiful as the seven deadly sins'. Given these previous associations, it is disturbing when Mrs Arbuthnot uses garden imagery when referring to her son in Act II:

> MRS ARBUTHNOT George, don't take my son away from me. I have had twenty years of sorrow, and I have only had one thing to love me, only one thing to love. You have had a life of joy, and pleasure, and success. You have been quite happy, you have never thought of us. There was no reason, according to your views of life, why you should have remembered us at all. Your meeting us was a mere accident, a horrible accident. Forget it. Don't come now, and rob me of . . . of all I have in the whole world. You are so rich in other things. Leave me the little vineyard of my life; leave me the walled-in garden and the well of water; the ewe-lamb God sent me, in pity or in wrath, oh! leave me that. George, don't take Gerald from me.

Gerald is compared to a vineyard and a walled-in garden. A faint fragrance of incest begins to fill the air, but the odor remains very faint at this point.

In the clash over Gerald between Lord Illingworth and Mrs Arbuthnot in Act II, Illingworth emerges the victor, and the act ends when he leads Gerald to the terrace. Act III begins with a scene that is highly reminiscent of *The Picture of Dorian Gray*. Illingworth is lecturing Gerald on life in very much the same words that Wotton used to corrupt Dorian:

> GERALD But I am so ignorant of the world, Lord Illingworth.
> LORD ILLINGWORTH Don't be afraid, Gerald. Remember that you've got on your side the most wonderful thing in the world — youth! There is nothing like youth. The middle-aged are mortgaged to Life. the old are in life's lumber-room. But youth is the Lord of Life. Youth has a kingdom waiting for it.

Gerald responds positively to the lecture and takes Illingworth as his spiritual father: 'Lord Illingworth is a successful man. He is a fashionable man. He is a man who lives in the world and for it. Well, I would give anything to be just like Lord Illingworth.' Gerald's true nature is rapidly emerging from the protective shell of innocence, as Dorian's had, and he shows a keen eagerness to embrace Lord Illingworth's dazzling, corrupt world. Mrs Arbuthnot, in an effort to dissuade him, tells him the story of a very young maiden who was ruined by Illingworth; but Gerald places a heavy share of the blame on the young maiden, then lightly dismisses the matter, refusing to believe such stories about Lord Illingworth. Quite rightly, he is unwilling to risk his career because of Illingworth's possible past sexual adventures.

Gerald, however, is in love with Hester Worsley, and Illingworth has made a bet to convert Hester from Puritanism. As Gerald converses with his mother, Illingworth tries to kiss Hester in the garden. She reacts with puritanical terror, and Gerald leaps to her defense, swearing he will kill Lord Illingworth. To stop him, Mrs Arbuthnot reveals that Illingworth is his father. Hester steals quietly off, Mrs Arbuthnot faints, and the act ends with Gerald tenderly leading his mother away. Act II had ended with Gerald squarely in his father's camp, but Act III ends with him moving back into that of mother. Indeed, the mother's revelation effectively isolates him in a separate world with her.

Act IV is the most interesting act of the play, for in it Mrs Arbuthnot shows herself − to the perceptive reader or viewer − as a true daughter of Herodias, a cultured Victorian version of Salome. In this act, she reveals the true reasons why she abandoned Illingworth as soon as their child was born. One reason is that the child displaced the father as the object of her affection and she wanted him entirely for herself: she took the male child for her lover and ran away with him. In a gush of emotion, Mrs Arbuthnot explains herself to Gerald:

MRS ARBUTHNOT No office is too mean, no care too lowly for the thing we women love − and oh! how I loved *you*. Not Hannah, Samuel more. And you needed love, for you were weakly, and only love could have kept you alive. Only love can keep any one alive. . . .

You thought I spent too much of my time in going to Church, and in Church duties. But where else could I turn? God's house is the only house where sinners are made welcome, and you were always in my heart, Gerald, too much in my heart. For, though day after day, at morn or evensong, I have knelt in God's house, I have never repented of my sin. How could I repent of my sin when you, my love, were its fruit! Even now that you are bitter to me I cannot repent. I do not. You are more to me than innocence. I would rather be your mother − oh! much rather! − than have always been pure. . . . Oh, don't you see? don't you understand?

The fruit of Mrs Arbuthnot's adventure in her father's garden was Gerald, and she has been feasting on that fruit ever since. The fragrance of incest is no longer faint but very strong. Mrs Arbuthnot's name − Rachel − also indicates her incestuous character, for the biblical Rachel was both Jacob's cousin and, along with her sister Leah, his wife. Jacob, moreover, was a younger brother who cheated his elder brother Esau of the rights and privileges of seniority. Wilde is very clever, though, for it is possible to see Mrs Arbuthnot as a sentimental, tender-hearted mother. The mask is lifted only for the very perceptive. Mrs Arbuthnot herself seems quite blind to her incestuous feelings. She has placed upon her eyes, not the covering of him who would see his God, but simply the covering of excessive sentimentality.

Ironically, Hester overhears Mrs Arbuthnot, rushes to her, and embraces her. Hester had earlier declared that a man and a woman who have sinned should both be punished, but now she rejects her harsh Puritan attitude and insists that God's law is love. What she means, though, is that God's law is love for Gerald, since she shows no inclination whatsoever to forgive Lord Illingworth. The reason she forgives Mrs Arbuthnot is because she recognises a deep kinship with her: 'In her all womanhood is martyred. Not she alone, but all of us are stricken in her house.' Gerald had been insisting that his mother and Lord Illingworth marry, if only formally, for duty's sake.

Marriage, however, places the male in a dominant position, and what both Hester and Mrs Arbuthnot seem to want is the opposite of this. In the parent-child relationship, the parent controls the child, and this is one reason Mrs Arbuthnot had preferred Gerald to Illingworth. 'You were weakly', she says to her son. Gerald, it seems, is destined to remain controlled. When he approaches Hester, she waves him back for having dared to insist that his mother marry Illingworth: 'You cannot love me at all, unless you love her also. You cannot honour me, unless she's holier to you.' The result is that Gerald withdraws his request, kneels before his mother, kisses her hands, and says: 'You are my mother and my father all in one. I need no second parent.'

It is only after Gerald has been literally brought to his knees that the two women are satisfied. Hester, moreover, has identified herself so thoroughly with Mrs Arbuthnot that the latter now considers her an appropriate wife for Gerald:

MRS ARBUTHNOT (*Rises, and taking Hester by the hand, goes slowly over to where Gerald is lying on the sofa with his head buried in his hands. She touches him and he looks up.*) Gerald, I cannot give you a father, but I have brought you a wife.

GERALD Mother, I am not worthy either of her or you.

MRS ARBUTHNOT So she comes first, you are worthy. And when you are away, Gerald ... with ... her – oh, think of me sometimes. Don't forget me.

Mrs Arbuthnot had said earlier that she could not repent of her sin, and she does not repent now. She brings Gerald a girl in her own image and practically instructs the boy to think of his mother when he is making love to his wife. Vicariously, Mrs Arbuthnot will remain Gerald's lover.

This incestuous marriage is given a final dramatic twist at the end of the play. Gerald and Hester are in the garden together, but the mother does not follow them, so they return to fetch her. Gerald kneels down beside his mother:

MRS ARBUTHNOT My boy! My boy! My boy! (*Running her fingers through his hair.*)
HESTER (*Coming over.*) But you have two children now. You'll let me be your daughter?
MRS ARBUTHNOT (*Looking up.*) Would you choose me for a mother?
HESTER You of all women I have ever known.

To the Victorians, this must have been a charming and tender scene. What has happened, though, is that Hester, by embracing Mrs Arbuthnot as her mother, has symbolically made herself Gerald's sister. Her marriage to Gerald, then, is the marriage of a brother and sister.

It is a marriage, moreover, that will be dominated by Rachel Arbuthnot, who seems an inseparable part of it. Like the biblical Jacob, Gerald will have two wives, both incestuously related to him. Appropriately, the play ends with the three, intertwined like a spider web, withdrawing into the ubiquitous garden, the symbol of lust and sin. Mrs Arbuthnot began her adult life in her father's garden with Lord Illingworth. Spiritually, she has never developed beyond that garden. Human nature being what it is, all human beings − Puritans included − enter the garden or Eros as soon as they emerge from the shell of innocence, and they remain there the rest of their lives. Mrs Arbuthnot is a woman of no importance because she is like everybody else in this respect.[2]. . .

A Woman of No Importance is a unique play; it is the only comedy the decadent movement ever produced. The funniest joke of the play, however, is one that only Oscar Wilde and his closest friends must have enjoyed at the time: Wilde had given the Victorians *Salome* once again, this time in the guise of a comedy with a large sentimental streak. The Victorians, failing to penetrate the façade and recognise the play's demonic content, applauded, and Wilde found himself a famous playwright. And not unjustly so. The play is a good and a challenging one, with definite Freudian overtones. A stage production that brings out its demonic content − perhaps by providing it with a heavily suggestive garden setting − may prove very interesting indeed.

SOURCE: extracts from *Into the Demon Universe* (New Haven, Conn. and London, 1974), pp. 109–22.

NOTES

[Reorganised and renumbered from the original − Ed.]

1. Quoted in *Letters of Oscar Wilde* (London, 1962), p. 335, note 4.
2. The purity-obsessed Mr Kelvil gives vent to his lust within the framework of marriage and is the father of eight children. Lady Caroline, who invariably calls him

Mr Kettle, is not much mistaken, if we regard the kettle as a phallic symbol. Her mistake is double-edged, however, for it also reveals the reason for her interest in him – an interest that fades as soon as she discovers he is married and has a family. Even the archdeacon is a married man, though the state of his sexual impulse is indicated by the lamentable and deteriorating physical condition of his wife.

Otto Reinert   Satiric Strategy in *The Importance of Being Earnest* (1956)

Almost everyone agrees that *The Importance of Being Earnest* is good fun, but few have tried to show that it is also a good play. To say that Wilde has written a brilliant farce is not to say why it seems both funnier and more significant than other superior farces, and to say that the farce satirises Victorianism is not, at this late date, to tell us why it amuses at all. From some of the incidental comments one gets the impression that the play in untouchable, so exquisite that criticism would be fatal – stupid abuse of something bright and fragile. A few critics, who take their business more seriously, refuse even to be charmed. The play 'never transcends . . . the incomplete or the trivial', Edouard Roditi writes in his generally perceptive book on Wilde (1947). 'Its tone is that of satire, but of a satire which, for lack of a moral point of view, has lost its sting and degenerated into the almost approving banter of a P.G. Wodehouse.'

But only a curious form of critical blindness can dismiss *Earnest* as a trifle of dialogues. It merits attention both as satire and as drama. The farce is meaningful. Tone and plot have been successfully integrated, and the whole is more truly comic – because normative – than a well-made play to end all well-made plays, a vehicle for the utterance of witty nonsense. Awareness of its satirical strategy precludes the criticism that it is elusive of reasoned analysis for lack of any kind of rationale.

Wilde first employed a pattern of ironic inversion in *An Ideal Husband,* the play immediately preceding *Earnest.* Its hero, Lord Goring, is not the irresponsible dandy he seems to be, the surface frivolity is not the real man, and his flippant paradoxes emphasise the irony of his moral position relative to that of [Sir Robert] Chiltern, the pretended pillar of society. For the first time in his plays Wilde puts the fine art of epigram to serious purposes: it participates in the total meaning of the play.

Lord Goring's wit expresses that ironic attitude to life that guarantees moral salvation in Wilde's world. But though the brand of wit is similar in *Earnest*, such an attitude cannot be attributed to any one or several of the characters in the later play, simply because it has no hero (or heroine) in the sense in which Lord Goring is the hero of *An Ideal Husband*. The characters in *Earnest* never stop being flippant; their flippancy is their whole nature and not, like Lord Goring's, the mocking mask of enlightened irony in a pompous society. The only ironist in *Earnest* is Wilde himself, who not only has abandoned the simple ethics of thesis melodrama but also has deliberately sacrificed the illusionistic conventions of naturalism in order to gain what Francis Fergusson calls (in *The Idea of a Theater*, 1949) a 'limited perspective, shared with the audience, as the basis of the fun', showing 'human life *as* comic . . . because . . . consistent according to some narrowly defined, and hence unreal, basis.'

That is why there is no reason to be embarrassed by the farce label. The play's merit is that it is *all* farce, capable of serving as a lucid image of the non-farcical reality that is kept strictly outside the play. Wilde has respected his paradoxes. He is no longer putting them to menial service as bright spots in sentimental thesis plays or as devices of crude melodramatic irony. *The Importance of Being Earnest* is one sustained metaphor, and aesthetic detachment is the only mood in which it can be intelligently enjoyed. It insists on being acted straight, for if we should feel, even for a moment, that the characters are aware of what absurdities they are saying, the whole thing vanishes. Once object and image are confused there is a blurring of vision. No one in his right mind gets emotionally involved with the destinies of Algernon and Cecily, Gwendolen and Jack. But it is precisely their emotive neutrality as figures of farce that allows Wilde's characters to establish his 'limited perspective': Wilde's basic formula for satire is their assumption of a code of behavior that represents the reality that Victorian convention pretends to ignore.

Algernon is explaining his reluctance to attend Lady Bracknell's dinner party: 'She will place me next Mary Farquhar, who always flirts with her own husband across the dinner table. That is not very pleasant. Indeed, it is not even decent . . . and that sort of thing is enormously on the increase. The amount of women in London who flirt with their own husbands is perfectly scandalous. It looks so bad. It is simply washing one's clean linen in public.' To say that Algernon's tone here is consciously flippant is to miss the joke altogether. The quip is not a quip; it means what is says. Algernon is indignant with a woman who spoils the fun of extra-marital flirtation and who parades her virtue. He is shocked at convention. And his tone implies that he is elevating break of convention into a moral norm. He is not the first figure in English satire to do so; among his ancestors are Martin Scriblerus, other assumed identities in Pope and Swift (including Gulliver), and the apologist for Jonathan Wild. What they all have in common is that they derive their ideals for conduct from the actual practice of their societies, their standards are the standards of common corruption, they are literal-minded victims of their environments, realists with a vengeance.

Here is Algernon on conventional love institutions: 'I really don't see anything romantic in proposing. It is very romantic to be in love. But there is nothing romantic about a definite proposal. Why, one may be accepted. One usually is, I believe. Then the excitement is all over.' And here is his vision of the post honeymoon tea table:

> ALGERNON Have some bread and butter. The bread and butter is for Gwendolen. Gwendolen is devoted to bread and butter.
> JACK And very good bread and butter it is too.
> ALGERNON Well, my dear fellow, you need not eat as if you were going to eat it all. You behave as if you were married to her already. . . .

The girls, too, implicitly accept this inverted code. In the proposal scene between Jack and Gwendolen the latter acts out reality: girls about to be proposed to quite realise the situation and are annoyed by their suitors' conventionally bungling approach. In the second act Gwendolen explains to Cecily that she always travels with her diary in order to 'have something sensational to read in the train'. One of Cecily's first speeches expresses her concern for 'dear Uncle Jack' who is so 'very serious' that 'I think he cannot be quite well'. When Algernon, at their first meeting, begs her not to think him wicked, she sternly replies: 'If you are not, then you have certainly been deceiving us all in a very inexcusable manner. I hope you have not been leading a double life, pretending to be wicked and being really good all the time. That would be hypocrisy'. Paradoxical morality cannot be argued much further than this, and the speech upsets even Algernon. In context it cuts down to the very core of the problem of manners with which Wilde is concerned. It epitomises the central irony of the play, for the Bunburying Algernon, in escaping the hypocrisy of convention, becomes a hypocrite himself by pretending to be somebody he is not. (Even Miss Prism participates. She is telling Cecily about her youthful novel: 'The good ended happily, and the bad unhappily. That is what Fiction means.')

Only Jack and Lady Bracknell seem at first glance to be outside the pattern of inversion, expressing shock when confronted with the code of cynical realism. But their conventionality is not genuine. Jack is a confirmed Bunburyist long before Algernon explains the term to him, and Bunburyism is most simply defined as a means of escape from convention. He occasionally acts the role of naive elicitor of Algernon's discourses on Bunburyism and is not such a consistent theorist of the realist code, but his behavior is certainly not conventional.

One of Lady Bracknell's main plot functions is to be an obstacle to Jack's romance with Gwendolen, but a systematic analysis of her speeches will show, I think, that she has no illusions about the reality her professed convention is supposed to conceal: '. . . I do not approve of mercenary marriages. When I married Lord Bracknell I had no fortune of any kind.' To her the speech is neither cynical nor funny. It represents that compromise between practical hardheadedness and conventional morality that she has worked out to her own satisfaction and behind which she has retired in dignified immunity. In other speeches she advocates Algernon's code with as much sanctimoniousness as he: 'Well, I must say, Algernon, that I think it is high time that Mr Bunbury made up his mind whether he was going to live or to die. This shilly-shallying with the question is absurd. Nor do I in any way approve of the modern sympathy with invalids. I consider it morbid.' She moralises on behalf of people who take it for granted that illness in others is always faked and that consequently sympathy with invalids is faked also, a concession to an artificial and – literally – morbid code. The frivolous banter accomplishes something serious. It exposes the polite cynicism that negates all values save personal convenience and salon decorum. Life and death have become matters of *savoir-vivre*.

The following speech presents a somewhat more complex case, because Lady Bracknell is here simultaneously deferring to convention and exposing its sham: 'French songs I cannot possibly allow. People always seem to think that they are improper, and either look shocked, which is vulgar, or laugh, which is worse. But German sounds a thoroughly respectable language, and indeed, I believe is so.' To laugh at presumably improper songs is to fly in the face of convention and break the delicate fabric of social decorum. But the opposite reaction is hardly less reprehensible. To register shock at indecency is indecently to call attention to something people realise the existence of but refuse to recognise. In her last sentence she quietly gives away the polite fiction that people in society know foreign languages.

When the pattern of inversion operates the characters either express or assume a morality that is deduced from the actual behavior of high society, though the existence of conventional morality is sometimes recognised as a fact to come to terms with. What the accumulation of paradox adds up to is an exposure both of hypocrisy and of the unnatural convention that necessitates hypocrisy. In elegant accents of pompous bigotry Wilde's puppets turn moral values upside down. 'Good heavens', Algernon exclaims when Lane tells him that married households rarely serve first-rate champagne. 'Is marriage so demoralising as that?' We are made to share Wilde's view of the ludicrous and sinister realities behind the fashionable façade of an over-civilised society where nothing serious is considered serious and nothing trivial trivial.

But *Earnest* is, before anything else, a play, an imitation of *action*, and no discussion of tone apart from its dramatic setting can account for the extraordinary impact of the play as play. It is rather odd, therefore, to notice that even critics who have been aware of serious satiric implications in the dialogue have been prone to dismiss the plot as negligible, as, at best, 'inspired nonsense'. 'The plot', writes Eric Bentley, in *The Playwright as Thinker* (1946), 'is one of those Gilbertian absurdities of lost infants and recovered brothers which can only be thought of to be laughed at', and he defines the function of 'the ridiculous action' as constantly preventing the play from 'breaking into bitter criticism'. [See Bentley's excerpt in Part Three, above – Ed.] There is truth in that, but the action has another and far more important function as well: it informs the satiric dialogue with coherent meaning.

The action of *The Importance of Being Earnest* is about just that – the importance of being earnest. The title is as straightforward a statement of theme as any literalist could ask for. Specifically, the play deals with the consequences of that way of not being earnest that Algernon calls Bunburying, and it is Bunburying that gives the plot moral significance. The key speech in the play is Algernon's little lecture to Jack: 'Well, one must be serious about something, if one wants to have any amusement if life. I happen to be serious about Bunburying. What on earth you are serious about I haven't got the remotest idea. About everything, I should fancy. You have an absolutely trivial nature.' Bunburying means to invent a fictitious character, who can serve as a pretext for escaping a frustrating social routine, regulated by a repressive convention. The pretended reason for getting away is perfectly respectable, even commendable, according to convention: to comfort a dying friend, to rescue a fallen brother. Thus defined, Bunburying is simply the mechanism that sets in motion the preposterously elaborate plot of mistaken identities. But the word has also a wider meaning. Significantly, Algernon *happens* to be serious about Bunburying – that is, it is not the subterfuge itself that is important, but the commitment to a course of action that will provide fun. The Bunburyist in the wider sense is serious about not being serious, and

Bunburyism is the alternative to a convention that fails to reckon with the facts of human nature. It stands for behavior that will give experience the shading and perspective that convention denies it. To be serious about everything is to be serious about nothing; that is, to trifle. Algernon charges Jack (unfairly, as it happens) with a failure to discriminate among life values, to see that monotone of attitude blunts the spirit and deadens joy. And this is precisely Wilde's charge against Victorianism.

The Bunburyist lives in a world of irresponsibility, freed from the enslavement of a hypocritical convention. He enjoys himself. But life beyond hypocrisy is life in a dangerous climate of moral anarchy, and, like most states of revolt, Bunburyism is not ideal. The escape from convention is itself a flagrant instance of hypocrisy: pretense is the price the Bunburyist pays for freedom from the pretense of convention. In his title pun Wilde catches the moral failure of dandyism. Just as the conformist pretends to be, but is not, earnest, so Algernon and Jack pretend to be, but are not, Ernest.

What Wilde is saying, then, is that all normal Victorians who want to retain the respect of their conventional society are, perforce, Bunburyists, leading double lives, one respectable, one frivolous, neither earnest. Bunburyism, as Algernon confesses in the opening of the play, is the application of science to life, to the exclusion of sentiment. Sentiment properly belongs to art. The science is the science of having a good time. These are obviously false distinctions, and all that can be said for Bunburyism as a way of life is that it offers relief from a social round where, in Lady Bracknell's words, good behavior and well being 'rarely go together', and where, according to Jack, 'a high moral tone can hardly be said to conduce very much to either one's health or one's happiness'. Bunburyism marks one of the extreme points in the swing of the pendulum, Victorianism the other.

Neither of the two Bunburyists is either earnest or Ernest – before the very end.[1] It is only then that they become, and in more than a single sense, themselves. When the action begins they have already escaped the mortifying seriousness of convention, but it takes them three acts and the movement from town to country – the movement has symbolic relevance as a return to 'naturalness' – to regain their balance and become earnest, that is, neither conventionally nor frivolously hypocritical. At the end of the play the respectable (though amorous) Miss Prism (her name suggests 'prim prison') has been unmasked, the four young people are romantically engaged, Jack has discovered his Bunburying identity to be his true self, and Lady Bracknell must recognise the contemptible orphan of Act I, 'born, or at any rate, bred in a handbag', as her own sister's son. The plot, as it were, makes a fool of respectability and proves the two Bunburyists 'right' in their escapade. But it also repudiates Bunburyism. Algernon, who as a Bunburyist spoke cynically about proposals and matrimony in Act I, is happily proposing marriage to Cecily in Act II, and at the end his initial false dichotomies between life and art, science and sentiment, have been resolved in romance. The radical remedy of Bunburying has effected a cure, the pendulum rests in the perpendicular, and we share Jack's final conviction of 'the vital Importance of Being Earnest'. The two adjectives have not been chosen lightly.

SOURCE: essay in *College English*, XVIII (Oct. 1956), 14–18.

NOTE

[1] It is the one flaw in a superbly constructed play that Algernon remains Algernon at the end and thus ineligible as a husband for Cecily. To say that she does not seem to mind at that point or that Dr Chasuble is quite ready for the christening cannot conceal the flaw. It staggers the imagination to try to think of any way in which Wilde could have turned Algernon into a second Ernest, but, given the plot, he ought to have done so.

Richard Foster   Wilde as Parodist: A Second Look at *The Importance of Being Earnest* (1956)

The Importance of Being Earnest is apt to be a stumbling block both to the detractors and admirers of Oscar Wilde as a man of letters. Those who want to dismiss him as the greatest ass of aestheticism may be troubled to find themselves, in this play, laughing with rather than at Wilde. Those few, on the other hand, who see in the whole of Wilde's work the same revolutionary quest for new means and materials of literary expression which characterised the poetic innovators of nineteenth-century France sometimes find it hard to laugh at all. Meanwhile, the play continues to flourish as one of the world's most robust stage classics. Part of the critics' difficulty – an inadequacy frequently experienced by critics, never by audiences – is that they cannot accurately name its type. The terms 'farce' and 'comedy of manners', the labels most frequently applied to *Earnest*, are neither of them adequate designations of the especially subtle and complicated artistic 'being' that the play has.

I

Farce, first of all, depends for its effects upon extremely simplified characters tangling themselves up in incongruous situations, and upon a knowing audience gleefully anticipating their falling victim, in their ignorance, to some enormous but harmless confusion of fact or identity. We think of *The Comedy of Errors,* of *She Stoops to Conquer,* of Uncle Toby about to show 'the very place' to the breathless Widow Wadman. Wilde's characters are certainly uncomplicated, and he makes use of some farce situations, such as Jack's mourning scene and his recognition scene at the end of the play. But the comedy of *Earnest* subsists, for the most part, not in action or situation but in dialogue. The dialogue, furthermore, is everywhere an exercise of wit – a subtler comic effect than farce can comfortably take very much time for. This is only a tentative claim, to be expanded on later, that the play is a very intellectual kind of comedy, too intellectual, certainly, to be described simply as a farce.

The Importance of Being Earnest is more often, and perhaps somewhat more accurately, regarded as a comedy of manners. Ridicule and exposure of the vanities, the hypocrisies, and the idleness of the upper classes is, to be sure, the main function of its verbal wit. Moreover, the stock patterns of Restoration and eighteenth-century manners comedy are evident in various characters: Jack and Algernon, though in quest of love rather than riches or intrigue, are unmistakably brothers to the opportunistic young wits that hunted in pairs through the social jungles of earlier comedy; Cecily and Gwendolen are their quarry; Lady Bracknell's is the dowager role, though she is more dominant and more shrewdly financial than her shrill, physical Restoration forebears; but perhaps Miss Prism's middle-aged sexuality, only just contained by the strictures of Victorian propriety, makes her, after all, a more direct descendant of Lady Wishfort.

But *Earnest*, in spite of these qualities, is not a true comedy of manners either. It is not even nearly one. A comedy of manners is fundamentally realistic: it requires the audience to accept the world presented on the stage as a real world, a possible world; and its human foibles, even if heightened and exaggerated in the play's satirical exposure of them, are nevertheless laughed at as representations of real excesses. A clear sign of the realism of manners comedy is the fact that there are characters in it that can always recognise a fool. The laughter that the witty young bucks of the older comedy share with the audience at the expense of a fool or fop unites the 'real' world and the world of the play by showing that the same criteria for reason and unreason are valid in both. But Jack and Algernon are strangely respect-

ful of Prism and Chasuble − two clear fools − because fools must be
taken seriously in the extra-rational world of Wilde's play. When we
recognise this extra-rational quality of Wilde's play, we begin to see
that its satirical effects are less close to *The Way of the World* and *The
Rivals* than to 'The Rape of the Lock' and *Patience*. Where Congreve
and Sheridan created a pretty close, if heightened, imitation of that
world, Wilde and Gilbert and Pope performed an alchemic *reductio ad
absurdum* of it. Folly is *represented* in the comedy of manners, *essentialised*
in Pope's mock epic, Gilbert's operettas and Wilde's play.

Wilde accomplishes this essentialisation of folly by creating an 'as
if' world in which 'real' values are inverted, reason and unreason
interchanged, and the probable defined by improbability. The structure and materials of this 'as if' world become especially interesting
when we remember that the English theatre was, at this time, just
beginning to get over a century-long siege of melodrama and sentimen-
talism. Gwendolen's observation, for example, that 'in matters of
grave importance, style, not sincerity, is the vital thing' has the effect
of ridiculing the 'poetic' manner of contemporary melodrama, which
Robertson and Jones had already rebelled against. Early in Act I just
after Jack has confessed 'the whole truth pure and simple' about
Cecily and his fictional brother Ernest, Algernon delivers an even
more direct and sweeping critical dictum: 'The truth', says Algy, 'is
rarely pure and never simple. Modern life would be very tedious if it
were either, and modern literature a complete impossibility.' From
this point on, Wilde's play is to be a satiric demonstration of how art
can lie romantically about human beings and distort the simple laws
of real life with melodramatic complications and improbably easy
escapes from them. Wilde has accomplished this by purloining from
the hallowed edifice of romantic literature certain standard characters, themes and plot situations in order to build out of them a comedy
that fuses contemporary social satire with a straight-faced taking-off
of the usages of the popular fiction and drama of Wilde's time, and,
inevitably, of other times as well.

II

Wilde's first technique is to spoof the timeless romantic fictions of
love's inception. The myth of love at first sight undergoes a kind of
superparody in the scene where Cecily does Algernon's punctual love-
making one better by recounting from her 'diary' the story of their
engagement, his love letters (which she has written), the breaking of
their engagement according to the demands of romantic love ritual,
and their re-engagement, in its casually incongruous juxtaposition of

values, is reminiscent of Pope's satiric method in 'The Rape of the Lock', where the deaths of lap-dogs and of husbands are of equal consequence: 'Today I broke off my engagement with Ernest. I feel it is better to do so. The weather still continues charming.' Gwendolen's love for Jack is sympathy itself; it is the old romantic idea of spiritual love based on simplicity and Platonic sensibility: 'The story of your romantic origin, as related to me by mamma, with unpleasing comments, has naturally stirred the deeper fibres of my nature. Your Christian name has an irresistible fascination. The simplicity of your character makes you exquisitely incomprehensible to me.' In a more sacred context, Desdemona, who saw her lover's visage 'in his mind' just as Gwendolen sees Jack's in his name, fell in love with Othello for somewhat similar reasons. 'My story being done', says Othello, 'she gave me for my pains a world of sighs./ She swore, in faith, 'twas strange, 'twas passing strange,/'Twas pitiful, 'twas wondrous pitiful.' Othello sums up the nature of her love, and of Gwendolen's, when he says, 'She loved me for the dangers I had passed. . . .'

Wilde reinforces his parody of the beautiful innocence of love at first sight and the spiritual impregnability of Platonic love by short-circuiting what our expectations would be if this were either the usual romantic melodrama or a real comedy of manners. Lady Bracknell's cupidity has arisen suddenly as an impediment to both marriages. But while the two young men – who ought to bounce away with a witticism or else do something dashing – are prostrate with devotion, the two young ladies are already making other plans. Gwendolen, the exponent of ideals and ideal love culled from 'the more expensive monthly magazines', promises Jack, with superbly hardheaded double vision, that 'although [Lady Bracknell] may prevent us from becoming man and wife, and I may marry someone else, and marry often, nothing can alter my eternal devotion to you'. And though Algernon, the true voice of cynicism, is preposterously ready to wait seventeen years until his beloved legally comes of age at thirty-five, Cecily, the unspoiled country lass, belies her simple kind by declining his devotion: 'I couldn't wait all that time. I hate waiting even five minutes for anybody. It makes me rather cross.'

A standard complication of the literature of love that is parodied here is the love breach or 'misunderstanding' – the lie, the secret sin out of the past, the error in judgement, the buried flaw of character that rises unbidden to the surface – which threatens to destroy love's ideality. But as the cases of Red Crosse and Una, Tom Jones and Sophia, Elizabeth and Darcy, and dozens of others have demonstrated, the breach can usually be healed if the offending party undergoes some penance or performs some act of selfless generosity or courage, whether psychological or material, in order to prove himself. In *Earnest* the love breach occurs when Gwendolen and Cecily discover that their Ernests are impostors named, respectively, Jack and Algernon; and the restoration of love is made possible when Jack and Algernon declare themselves ready to face the horrors of a christening. The situation at this point is so patently ludicrous, and the sentiments expressed by the two girls are at once so absurdly didactic and so resounding with the bathos of melodramatic reconciliation that we can hardly miss, amid the satire of manners, Wilde's strong undercurrent of literary satire.

But perhaps the most impressive evidence that Wilde's play is, in part at least, an elaborate literary lampoon, lies in the circumstances of the two pairs of lovers. The relationship of Algernon to Cecily, first of all, is essentially that of Rochester to Jane Eyre, of Mr B. to Pamela. It is the situation of the jaded, world-weary, cynical, and preferably dissolute male being reformed, regenerated, and resentimentalised by the fresh, innocent, and feeling girl reared in isolation from the 'world', preferably in the country. Algernon's cynicism is obvious enough in his nastily witty observations on life, and in his boredom with all amusements. The sign of his dissoluteness, one of Wilde's most brilliant comic strokes, is his constant hunger, his entire inability to resist stuffing himself at every opportunity. By this means Wilde has reduced the roué figure to a man of straw – or muffins. And he thrusts him through in the bit of dialogue where Algernon-as-Ernest learns from Cecily that Jack is going to banish him, and that he will have to choose between Australia and 'the next world'. Cecily questions whether he is good enough even for 'this world', and Algy admits that he isn't: '. . . I want you to reform me. You might make that your mission, if you don't mind.' 'I'm afraid I haven't time, this afternoon', Cecily responds unfeelingly. In a line or two it turns out predictably, that Algernon is hungry. 'How thoughtless of me', says Cecily. 'I should have remembered that when one is going to lead an entirely new life, one requires regular and wholesome meals.'

The point of Wilde's satire is found in the nature of Algernon's reformation. Before his first interview with Cecily is over, Algernon is engaged to be married and reconciled to getting christened. But he had already been exploded in his very first exchange with Cecily, when his supposedly irretrievable sophistication is bested by the supposedly artless and sheltered country girl's supersophistication: 'I hope you have not been leading a double life, pretending to be wicked and being really good all the time. That would be hypocrisy.' With this the wit has passed from Algernon to Cecily, and he never regains it at any time when she is on the scene. The moral of Wilde's parody:

the rake is a fake, girlish innocence is the bait of a monstrous mantrap, the wages of sin is matrimony.

Jack's troubled pursuit of Gwendolen embodies still another stock situation of romantic love fiction. As classic as *The Winter's Tale,* as old-fashioned as *Caste,* and as modern as last night's television play or last week's movie, it is the problem situation of two lovers separated by a barrier of class difference. Sometimes it is a matter of money, sometimes of blood. But in the majority of cases true love is saved by some last minute miracle, usually a surprising revelation of someone's real identity. The most impressive exercise of this kind is probably in *The Conscious Lovers,* where Steele relieves the long-suffering young Bevil by allowing his indigent sweetheart to prove to be the long lost daughter of Mr Sealand, the fabulously wealthy parent of the girl Bevil had been unhappily scheduled to couple with in a purely business marriage. The enormity of Steele's resolution is only a little less notable than Wilde's parody of the type. After herding all his characters down to Shropshire to witness the marvels of his *deus ex machina,* Wilde parades before their eyes an extraordinary succession of coincidental revelations culminating in Jack's discovery not only that he is Algernon's brother but that his name really *is* Ernest.

Wilde delicately frames his recognition scene as a theatrical take-off by making Lady Bracknell say, with lofty aesthetic dread, 'In families of high position strange coincidences are not supposed to occur. It is hardly considered the thing.' Gwendolen, however, is having a splendid time: 'The suspense is terrible. I hope it will last.'

III

In Edouard Roditi's book *Oscar Wilde* (1947) we read this astonishing statement about *The Importance of Being Earnest* and its stupendous finale:

> . . . its plot is at times too heavily contrived, especially in the last act: the sudden revelation of Miss Prism's past solves too conveniently the problems of the hero's origin, and too many of the embarrassing lies of the play are too neatly resolved into truth. Such reliance on the whimsies of chance weakens the satire of a comedy of manners; its plot should seem to grow more directly out of the follies of its characters, mirroring the irrationality of an absurd society of human beings responsible for their own predicaments rather than the irresponsible tricks of a contemptibly frivolous destiny. (p. 138)

Mr Roditi, a critic who takes Wilde very seriously, has mistaken his most celebrated work for an inchoate comedy of manners and has therefore drawn the unfortunately academic conclusion that it is formally imperfect and artistically trivial. The play's 'flaws' – the contrivances of plot, the convenience of its coincidences, and the neatness of its resolution – are, of course, its whole point. The subtlety of Wilde's art is such that it is easy to mistake *Earnest* for something it isn't, or else to dismiss it as a charming but inconsequential frill. But if intelligent laughter is better than mere laughter, it is worth understanding what kind of comedy Wilde has achieved by wedding social satire with literary burlesque.

Nothing in the play, first of all, is quite what it seems. The characters seem to wear badges of their natures; yet their sentiments and actions continually revoke and deny them. Jack and Algernon, tagged as clever young worldlings, are readily sentimentalists and fussbudgets at heart. Algernon, it has already been pointed out, is quite fully exposed early in Act II. And Jack, though he waves once or twice the flag of cynical wit or clever pretense, worries and perspires through most of the play, muttering pettishly against Algernon's 'nonsense' and appetite. He is a fuddled incompetent from the moment, early in Act I, when Algernon first challenges him on the matter of Cecily; and Gwendolen's wooing, only a little later, very nearly shatters him.

This same phenomenon in reverse is true of the two girls. Both of them bear the marks of the romantic Female. Both are pleased, first of all, to represent themselves as 'better' than their world: Cecily because she has been preserved, unspoiled, in countrified isolation, and Gwendolen because she is, in Jack's phrase, 'a sensible intellectual girl' whose nature has been enriched by heavy reading and brave thinking. But both also deport themselves as proper young ladies who appear to submit to the wishes of their parents and guardians when the plot requires them to; this is because the true romantic Female is never a stickler for rebellion. Yet these rarefied and genteel girls are the worldliest of schemers. They manipulate their lovers like men on a chess board, and one cannot escape the feeling, furthermore, that even Lady Bracknell prevails ultimately because they permit her to.

The dramatic effect of the comedy, then, is not of foolish but real people flaunting the real world's laws of reason, but of archetypal roles being gravely travestied. The characters know they are in a play, and they know what kind of play it is. Cecily and Gwendolen 'do' parodies of themselves as they assist their lovers in their own self-ridiculing transformation from cynical wits to true men of feeling. The same is true of Prism and Chasuble, even of Lane, who knows perfectly well that he is the type of the wry butler-confidant who is smarter than his employer. Lady Bracknell is the only exception: her mind's eye, steadily on the funds, sees other matters – love, literature, virtue – exactly for what they are. She is a kind of choric ballast that weights the satire's indirection with direct scorn.

Wilde's society dramas, which try to come to grips realistically with real problems, are very nearly ruined by the fact that so many of the characters 'talk like Oscar Wilde'. But Wilde's specialty, the squinting epigram that is at once murderous and suicidal, is perfectly at home in *Earnest*. It is the verbal function of that queer double consciousness that permeates the whole play and transforms it into a kind of parody. It is quite right that Cecily, who manoeuvres under the aegis of wide-eyed innocence, should say of her own journal of unspoiled reactions, 'It is simply a very young girl's record of her own thoughts and impressions, and consequently meant for publication.' Here burlesque of the Miranda character fuses with exposure of a grotesque type of littérateuse. A similar satiric fusion takes place when Cecily discovers that her innocent 'nanny', Miss Prism, is, surprisingly, one of the three-volume ladies of Richardsonian sentiment and sensation. Cecily hopes that her novel did not end happily. 'The good', answers prim Miss Prism, with shrewd business prowess, 'ended happily, and the bad unhappily. That is what fiction means.'

Such passages, deftly worked into the total fabric of the comedy, hold the key to Wilde's methods and purposes. By exposing and burlesquing the vacuities of a moribund literature Wilde satirises, too, the society that sustains and produces it; he has given us an oblique perspective on a society's shallowness through direct ridicule of the shallow art in which it sees its reflection. It is this subtle merging of matter and form that helps to make *The Importance of Being Earnest* an intellectual tour de force of the first order as well as one of the great comic masterpieces of the theatre.

SOURCE: essay in *College English*, XVIII (Oct. 1956), 18–23.

David Parker   Oscar Wilde's Great Farce
(1974)

It is generally agreed that *The Importance of Being Earnest* is Oscar Wilde's masterpiece, but there is little agreement on why it should be thought so or on how it works as a play. Though we can sense a solid substance beneath the frothy surface, the nature of that substance remains an enigma. Surprisingly little real criticism has been written about the play, and much of that which has is sketchy or tedious. One of the few critics whose mind seems to have been genuinely engaged by the play is Mary McCarthy, but she has written about it only briefly, and despite her admiration clearly finds it repugnant. 'It has the character of a ferocious idyll', she says, and complains that 'Selfishness and servility are the moral alternatives presented'.[1] Most of what she says about the play cannot be denied, yet there is a wrong note somewhere. Though it is almost always feeble to complain about critics using the wrong standards, I think we have to do so here. *The Importance of Being Earnest* does not tackle problems of moral conduct in the way that most plays do. In it, Wilde expresses a comic vision of the human condition by deliberately distorting actuality and having most of the characters behave as if that vision were all but universal. It is fair enough to complain about the vision entire, but to complain simply about the selfishness, without asking what it suggests, is on a par with complaining about the immorality of *Tom Jones*.

Though McCarthy uses the wrong standards, and therefore sees the play through a distorting lens, what she sees is there and needs to be studied. Her notion about the play's advocacy of selfishness may be got into better focus if we compare it with what William Empson says about the heroes of Restoration comedy: 'There is an obscure paradox that the selfish man *is* the generous one, because he is not repressed, has "good nature", and so on.'[2] This seems to represent more accurately what goes on in Wilde's play, if only because it resembles Wilde's own way of thinking. Moreover, the play clearly owes something to the Restoration comic tradition. 'My duty as a gentleman', says Algy, 'has never interfered with my pleasures in the smallest degree', thus neatly summing up the principles by which the young bloods of Restoration comedy lived. They were understood to be gentlemen because they were Natural Men, responsive to impulse, capable of falling in love, and so on, in contrast to the inhibited, conventional, rule-obeying, theory-loving tradesmen, Puritans and pedants whom they despised. The heroes of Restoration comedy have been criticised too, often with justice, but one thing should be clear by now: their roguishness, their carelessness about money and sexual behavior, was presented not simply to be admired as such. These things had symbolic value as well. The suggestion was that aristocratic young men needed to abandon conventional morality and get back to basic impulse, if the values they represented (moral independence, for example) were not to be annihilated by commercialism and Puritanism. Their roguishness was a proof of freedom, as well as an excuse for scourging the bourgeoisie. Algy's selfishness, and that of the other characters, demands a similar interpretation. It has a satirical force, of course: the manners of the upper classes are being laughed at; but there is more to it than that. In Wilde's vision, a sort of honorable selfishness becomes not merely a virtue, but a moral *sine qua non*.

Wilde's play, it seems to me, is more successful than most Restoration comedies because it is more pure – more purely absurd, if you like. The process of distorting actuality for expressive purposes is carried out more thoroughly, and the play's moral and aesthetic integrity is better maintained. In the dialogue alone, there is a more consistent heightening, amounting to a transfiguration of everyday conversation. The trouble with many Restoration comedies is that they express values only half-believed in by the audience for which they were intended. The characters praise aristocratic recklessness and sneer at commerce, yet the original courtly audience was committed to, and dependent on, commerce for at least a large part of its wealth.[3] As a result, because of a secret uncertainty in the playwrights, there is often a confusion between symbolic action and action seriously recommended to the audience for imitation. We are presented with hyperbolic actions and sentiments, which we find not entirely convincing and perhaps a shade hysterical. There is the standard paradox of Restoration comedy, for instance: all moralists are hypocrites; only libertines can see the truth and maintain a fundamental decency. The confusion carried over into real life. Many of the court wits and gallants tried to live out such paradoxes, not always with happy results. Wilde too tried to live out his own paradoxes, with decidedly unhappy results, but in his greatest play artifice and advice do not get mixed up. 'I don't quite like women who are interested in philanthropic work', says Cecily. "I think it is so forward of them." This is funnier, and more percipient, than jokes about hypocritical Puritan tradesmen. Wilde's symbol for sensual vitality and obedience to impulse is itself more wisely chosen than that of the Restoration playwrights: instead of using sexual behavior, he uses eating, something much more easily distanced. Contrary to what McCarthy says, *The Importance of Being Earnest* rarely slips over into recommending attitudes that are morally repellent – relative to Restoration comedy, at any rate. You have to stand a long way off from the play to be able to think so. It is difficult to get indignant with the characters.

The farcical structure helps distance what we see, and Wilde exploits it in other ways too. Farce is not necessarily trivial, and even when it is, through its very nature it usually makes assertions and raises questions about human identify; that is what makes the same situations enduringly popular. The hero of farce is usually a cunning rogue who, in order to gratify some impulse, spins an elaborate deception, which his victims seem constantly on the verge of exposing, so that he is constantly threatened with defeat, punishment or humiliation. We admire the hero because he has the courage to obey his impulses and because his tricks render him protean – free from imposed identity. We despise his victims because they are prisoners of manners, which repress impulse and forbid deception. They seem narrow and timid. A more highly wrought and expressive sort of farce is that in which all (or most) of the protagonists are rogues, who compete to satisfy their impulses. The moral independence of the most versatile, the most protean, is endorsed by success. *The Importance of Being Earnest* belongs to that sort.

Moreover, Wilde consciously exploits the concern of farce with human identity. The joke in the title is often thought of as a mock-pompous piece of frivolity, but it is more than that. The play might as justly be named 'The Importance of Being'. The whole thing is comically addressed to the problem of recognising and defining human identity; we are made to see wide significance in Jack's polite request, 'Lady Bracknell, I hate to seem inquisitive, but would you kindly inform me who I am?'. The pun on *earnest* and *Ernest* merely makes the title more suitably comic. Neither being earnest nor being Ernest is of much help when confidence is lost in the substantiality of human identity. The concern with identity is repeatedly underlined in the text of the play, where statements that seem superficially only to poke fun at upper-class frivolity continually edge the mind toward a contemplation of the insubstantiality of identity. 'It isn't easy to be anything nowadays', complains Algy in the first act. 'There's such a lot of beastly competition about.' And only a few lines later, Gwendolen feels obliged to deny that she is perfect: 'It would leave no room for developments, and I intend to develop in many directions.'

More than most writers of farce, Wilde was conscious of this concern with identity, so natural to the form, and he uses it to express a preoccupation which the nineteenth century gave birth to, and the twentieth century cherishes. Lurking always in the depths of the play is a steady contemplation of Nothingness, of *le néant*, which is all the more effective for its being, in contrast to most of its manifestations, comic in mode. Instead of making Nothingness a pretext for despair, Wilde finds in it a challenge to the imagination. For him, Nothingness in human identity, in human claims to knowledge, in the organisation of society, becomes a field to be tilled by the artist – by the artist in each of us.

In many ways a writer owing more to French than to English traditions, in this respect too Wilde shares a quality of vision with Flaubert, Villiers, Zola, Barbey d'Aurevilly and Mallarmé. They differ from each other, of course, as Wilde differs from them, but in the vision of each, as Robert Martin Adams says, 'The shell of personal identity collapses, the yolk of individuality is split. Even grossness is a form of transparency, even knowledge is a form of complicated and difficult ignorance (Flaubert).'[4] Yet for Wilde this brings liberation, not despair. Though he has Algy complain about what we might call the epistemological complacency of the English, he has him do it gaily: 'That is the worst of the English. They are always degrading truths into facts, and when a truth becomes a fact, it loses all its intellectual value.'

If *The Importance of Being Earnest* looks back to the French nineteenth century it also looks forward to the twentieth century and the drama of the absurd. The plot is absurd, in an obvious sense, and many critics have argued that it should be dismissed as a Gilbertian fantasy. It seems to me, however, that it is important, in the negative way that plots are, in the drama of the absurd. Everyone responds to preposterous situations in a way that is crazily systematic, defending his responses with absurdly sententious generalisations. Besides being used as a symbol for sensual vitality, eating becomes a subject for absurd imperatives. Algy, for instance, declares that 'One should always eat muffins quite calmly. It is the only way to eat them.' People's behavior and sentiments act as a parody of the real world; such, it is suggested, is the nature of all action, all moralising. But Wilde carries off this parody better than most of the playwrights whom we now describe as dramatists of the absurd. He is never obvious. His parody always works at two levels, which enrich each other: it pokes fun at the manners of a particular class, and it satirises the human condition. To my knowledge, only Pinter and Albee do anything at all like this, with comparative success.

Nothingness is repeatedly evoked in the verbal texture of the play in a way that prefigures techniques of the drama of the absurd. Characters are always using words like *serious* and *nonsense* in a manner that sends out little ripples of significance. 'If you don't take care', Jack warns Algy,

your friend Bunbury will get you into a serious scrape some day.'
   ALGERNON I love scrapes. They are the only things that are never serious.
   JACK Oh, that's nonsense, Algy. You never talk anything but nonsense.
   ALGERNON Nobody ever does.

Serious was recognised as a canting expression in the nineteenth century. 'No one knows the power', wrote 'F. Anstey' in 1885, 'that a single serious hairdresser might effect with worldly customers' (*OED*). Algy's quasi pun works as a protest against the importance attached by the Victorians to the very business of attaching importance (parodied more broadly in Miss Prism); for them, it is often apparent, this was a means of imposing form and stability on a world whose evanescence they half-suspected, a procedure of course unacceptable to Wilde. The joke is parallel to the one about *earnest*.

The play on the word *nonsense* expresses a sensibility that is recognisably modern, though it lacks the anguish that is now usually part of it. The sense of futility that arises out of the contemplation of Nothingness is felt only by those whose belief in human dignity requires support from a religious mythology, or a quasi-religious mythology, such as that subscribed to by many humanists. When his mind was at its most creative, Wilde felt no such need, willingly abandoning intellectual comfort and security for intellectual adventurousness in the unknown and unknowable. Algy's perception of universal nonsense is cheerful; it has the gusto of quick intelligence; and because it also works as a gibe at Algy's class, it has a quality of immediate practical shrewdness that makes it the more acceptable.

In the middle of the play, *absurd* itself is used repeatedly to evoke a sense of immanent Nothingness. Jack cannot understand how he should have a brother in the dining-room: 'I don't know what it all means. I think it is perfectly absurd.' Algy will not deny that he is Jack's brother: 'It would be absurd.' Jack says the same about the notion that Algy should lunch twice, and he thinks Algy's presence in the garden at Woolton 'utterly absurd'. Algy disagrees with the contention that he has no right to 'Bunbury' at Woolton: 'That is absurd. One has a right to Bunbury anywhere one chooses.' Gwendolen and Cecily agree that it is 'absurd to talk of the equality of the sexes'.

These words are used in jokes and casual comments that do not stand out in the text and are likely to be delivered in a carelessly cynical manner, as bits of flimflam designed simply to gain the speaker a tactical advantage in the argument; but they crop up repeatedly and affect the whole flavor of the play.

The use of paradox performs the same function much more obviously. Each paradox is a sort of miniature stylistic enactment of the notion expressed in one of the boldest: 'In matters of grave importance style, not sincerity, is the vital thing.' This pokes fun at the beau monde, of course, but it also hints at an answer to the problems raised in the jokes about *earnest* and *serious*. Once belief in epistemological certainty is abandoned, style, liberally interpreted, is more important than sincerity. By imposing a consciously provisional order onto evanescent reality, it makes practical decisions possible. Paradox imposes this order in a particularly striking way. It confounds conventional notions about order, identity and dissimilarity, synthesising new orders out of the confusion it exposes. Far from concealing chaos and disharmony, it rejoices in them, embraces them courageously, and takes them as a challenge to human wit and ingenuity. Wilde's rapid sequences of paradox after paradox picture for us a world in which men make, undo and remake reality with almost every sentence they utter.

Of course, not all the paradoxes in *The Importance of Being Earnest* are purely verbal or confined to one remark. There is a sustained effort in the play to dissolve conventional notions of order in fields where they tend to hypertrophy. Wilde depicts a world in which the socially endorsed certainties are continually evaporating; values respecting social class, education, the Church, money, love and the family undergo constant metamorphosis. Attitudes toward the family, in particular, are grotesquely transformed. Algy cheerfully dismisses the sentiments associated with kinship: 'Relations are simply a tedious pack of tedious people, who haven't got the remotest knowledge of how to live, nor the smallest instinct about when to die.' Others invert the normal sentiments. Lady Bracknell speaks of an acquaintance whose husband has died: 'I never saw a woman so altered, she looks quite twenty years younger.' Gwendolen complains about her lack of influence over her mother: 'Few parents nowadays pay any regard to what their children say to them! The old-fashioned respect for the young is rapidly dying out.' She approves of her father's domestication, however: 'The home seems to me to be the proper sphere for the man. And certainly once a man begins to neglect his domestic duties he becomes painfully effeminate, does he not?'.

In plot and action, too, conventional notions about family life are broken down. The handbag in Jack's family history excites Lady Bracknell's famous protest: 'To be born, or at any rate bred in a hand-bag, whether it had handles or not, seems to me to display a contempt for the ordinary decencies of family life that reminds one of the worst excesses of the French Revolution. . . .' The comedy is enhanced, of course, by the oddity of Lady Bracknell's own notions (or at least her way of expressing them). She seems to conceive family as something subject to human volition, and can advise Jack 'to make a definite effort to produce, at any rate, one parent, of either sex, before the season is quite over'. Though we may see parody of upper-class snobbery here, others do will relations into – and out of – existence, without there being any feeling of parody. Jack invents a brother; the girls invent ideal husbands. (Algy's Bunbury is only a friend, but the effect is much the same.) At the other extreme, the characters accept the family relationships revealed at the end of the play, with an absurd eagerness that is just as effective in ridiculing conventional notions. This is particularly evident in Jack's outburst, when he mistakenly assumes

Miss Prism to be his mother. She indignantly reminds him that she is unmarried. 'Cannot repentance wipe out an act of folly?' he cries. 'Why should there be one law for men and another for women? Mother! I forgive you.' The family is a category of everyday understanding that is one of the first to crumble before the vision of Nothingness. That is what enables Wilde's characters to adopt such a variety of postures with respect to it.

Individual identity, too, dissolves before the vision of Nothingness. That is why farce, and its traditional concern with human identity, was so useful to Wilde. Each character in *The Importance of Being Earnest* is a sort of vacuum that attains to individual identity only through an effort of the creative imagination. They are like Sartre's famous waiter in *L'Être et le Néant*, except that they make their decisions consciously, and that we are pleased rather than nauseated by the process. Each attains to identity in the mode of *being what he is not*.[5]

It is a sense of the insubstantiality of human identity which causes Wilde to place such emphasis on impulse (on selfishness, if you like). Admit all the problems of epistemology and impulse still remains. Obedience to impulse is a defiant way of asserting some sort of basic identity. Algy's obsession with food is an example. 'I hate people who are not serious about meals', he complains. 'It is so shallow of them.' Beneath the parody of manners, we can detect in this a perception, truthful within the terms of reference the play allows. Algy is prepared to use the word *serious* here because there is something fundamental to relate it to. When appetites are all that is substantial in human identity, all else must seem shallow. The two girls place a similar reliance on impulse. Both have faith in first impressions, and both are surprisingly candid about their sexual appetites. Cecily tells Algy, 'I don't think you should tell me that you love me wildly, passionately, devotedly, hopelessly. Hopelessly doesn't seem to make much sense, does it?.'

They are quick to change, though. When, after mutual declarations of devotion, Algy tells Cecily he will wait seventeen years for her hand, she replies, 'Yes, I felt it instinctively. And I am so sorry for you, Algy. Because I couldn't wait all that time. I hate waiting even five minutes for anybody. It always makes me rather cross. I am not punctual myself, I know, but I do like punctuality in others, and waiting even to be married is quite out of the question.' Changeability, in fact, is a corollary of obedience to impulse. As impulses vary, so must the attitudes of the individual. The protagonists of Wilde's play recognise this, particularly the girls. 'I never change, except in my affections', Gwendolen announces. Their changeability is most amusingly demonstrated in the first meeting of Gwendolen and Cecily, when, in the course of a single scene, they proceed from mutual suspicion to mutual affection, thence to mutual detestation, and finally to mutual affection again, all the time firmly maintaining that they are consistent. The audience is likely to laugh at this sort of thing because it realises that literary and social conventions are being ridiculed, but there is more to the comedy than that. There is a core of truth in what we are presented with: human beings do change. The joke lies in the way the characters are neither distressed nor surprised at their own changeability. In Wilde's world nothing else is expected.

Love might seem a surprising ingredient in such a world, but it is a play of courtship, and love does have importance in it. Love is based on impulse, after all, and for Wilde it is action, not object; a courageous creative effort of the will, not a substantial inner something; the free play of the imagination, not a faculty. The characters of the play constantly deny the substantiality of love, in speech and action. Their courtships consist in patterns of interlocking fantasy and wit; they woo through imposture and fancy; they pursue and fly; they test and torment each other. Never is there anything static or certain about their relationships. 'The very essence of romance is uncertainty', says Algy. 'If ever I get married, I'll certainly try to forget the fact.' Wilde is following Restoration comedy again, here. 'Uncertainty and Expectation are the Joys of Life', says Congreve's Angelica. 'Security is an insipid thing, and the overtaking and possessing of a Wish, discovers the Folly of the Chase.'[6] And as with Restoration comedy, we admire the lovers for their courage and their wit. We feel that they are absurd too (all action in the play is absurd; the secret is not minding), but at the same time we are made to feel that they are somehow right as well. The theme of sentimental education, normally found in romantic comedy, is parodied by inversion. Fantasies the lovers have about each other are confirmed rather than cured, almost as if wit, the creative imagination (call it what you will), were able magically to force the world into the shapes it suggests to itself. We feel, at any rate, that the lovers earn their partners by growing toward them, through wit.

Because the characters live in a world in which order is constantly vanishing, they scorn theory, consistency and the appearance of simplicity. 'The truth', as Algy says, 'is rarely pure and never simple.' Certainly, in matters of identity, seeming intelligibility is to be distrusted. 'The simplicity of your nature', Gwendolen tells Jack, 'makes you exquisitely incomprehensible to me.' The characters are alert, not to a harmonious universal nature, but to a proliferation of separate, deceptive and contradictory sense-impressions. Knowledge comes only through the imagination. Gwendolen laughs at Jack's misgivings over her delight in his being called (as she thinks) Ernest. He cautiously inquires how she might feel were his name not Ernest, but she will not listen. 'Ah, that is clearly a metaphysical speculation', she says, 'and like all metaphysical speculation, has very little reference at all to the actual facts of real life, as we know them.' This is an ironic node. The observation by itself fits in with the general theme of the play, but in the immediate context the joke is against Gwendolen (and Jack, when we think how he must feel). He has only assumed the name of Ernest; her notions are just as 'metaphysical'; and what seem to be the actual facts of real life thoroughly justify such a speculation. Yet at the end of the play, Gwendolen's faith in the name, her conviction that she will marry an Ernest, and her insistence that her lover conform to her ideal are all justified; we learn that Jack's true name is Ernest. One effect of all this is to satirise faith in ideals by having it vindicated absurdly, but there is more to it than that. We feel delighted at the outcome, not like the recipients of a warning. We are made to feel that confident fantasies justify themselves, that a bold imagination is more useful than plodding attention to apparent facts.

In Wilde's world truth itself dwindles into insignificance. The characters have a strictly practical attitude to the relationship between statements and actuality, the latter being so elusive. Charged with being named John, Jack declares, 'I could deny it if I liked. I could deny anything if I liked.' And he is embarrassed when required to utter things in strict correspondence with what seem to be facts: 'it is very painful for me to be forced to speak the truth. It is the first time in my life that I have ever been reduced to such a painful position, and I am really quite inexperienced in doing anything of the kind, so you must excuse me if I stammer in my tale.' He goes on to say that he has never had a brother, which turns out to be untrue; Algy is his brother. Once again the inference is that truth cannot be discovered through the senses and the intellect alone. Jack's witty lies are more percipient. The comic inversion of truth and untruth is maintained in Jack's dismay, when he learns that what he had thought to be lies are true. 'Gwendolen', he says, 'it is a terrible thing for a man to find out suddenly that all his life he has been speaking nothing but the truth. Can you forgive me?' She can. 'There is always hope', she says, 'even for those who are most accurate in their statements.' Even when it is the art of living, we are tempted to gloss, 'Lying, the telling of beautiful untrue things, is the proper aim of Art'.[7]

Jack and Algy certainly attain their ends through lying. They are true rogues, impulsive, lovers of deception and imposture. They fulfil themselves in the way of all rogues: by discovering human freedom in protean identity. Doubtless what they do permits us to laugh at the mad antics young gentlemen get up to, even to disapprove mildly, but

the candid spectator will admit that their tricks inspire above all else a
feeling of moral liberation. Jack's double life may be exposed, Algy's
Bunbury may be deprived of his existence, but these deceptions serve
their purpose, and part of us at least is glad.

Gwendolen and Cecily rely on beautiful untrue things as much as
their suitors do, but instead of deceiving the world through imposture,
they demand that the world accept the pleasing fantasies they choose
to project onto it. The heroes adopt identities to suit the occasion; the
heroines imagine identities to suit the persons with whom they choose
to associate. Gwendolen explains her principles in love: 'We live, as I
hope you know, Mr Worthing, in an age of ideals. The fact is constantly mentioned in the more expensive monthly magazines, and has
reached the provincial pulpits, I am told. And my ideal has always
been to love someone of the name of Ernest. There is something in that
name that inspires absolute confidence.' She is very firm about this,
and Cecily, whose words on the subject are almost identical, is nearly
as firm. The comic parallel generates a certain irony against the girls;
we are tempted to laugh at them for sharing a folly, yet we cannot help
admiring the strength of their resolution, absurd though it is. Though
idealism is burlesqued, we are made to admire the wit and courage
required to impose a pattern on the world, even such a one as this.

The women in the play are generally stronger and more resourceful
than the men. The latter are forced to prevaricate in a way that at
times seems shuffling, even abject, whereas the former are always perfectly poised and move with imperturbable grace from one contradictory posture to another. I suspect that this has something to do with
Wilde's own personality and personal history, but the pattern makes
sense on its own terms. The play may be seen as a disquisition in favor
of a set of attitudes more normally associated with women than with
men. It commends the sort of character that accepts experience, with
all its confusions, and accommodates itself through provisional
opportunist adjustments – through style, in short. It pokes fun at
hard and fast ideas about reality, at that aggressive kind of intelligence which seeks to control reality through theory. Rightly or wrongly,
women are thought of as conforming more often to the subtle
stereotype; men are thought of as conforming more often to the
aggressive stereotype. Wilde was not simplistic about this. The
embodiment of aggressive masculine intelligence in the play is
Miss Prism, but that is part of the joke against her. The other women
are naturally more at home in Wilde's world than the men.

Lady Bracknell, of course, is the character that most thoroughly
exemplifies feminine strength. Delightful though she is, she is likely at
first to baffle the audience's expectations because she is cast in the role

of obstructionist to the lovers; in a conventional romantic comedy she would have to be defeated and humiliated. Yet that is not what happens to her, and it is difficult even to imagine it happening. The critics have recognised that she rises above this role; she has even been called a goddess. Satisfaction is what Lady Bracknell requires, not defeat, because, irrespective of her role, she is the character that embodies most forcibly Wilde's notions about the creative power of the imagination. Out of the nebulous material of society fashion, she wills into being a world of rock-hard solidity, obedient to her dispensation, before which all other worlds, real and imagined, fade into ghostly insubstantiality. The audience may laugh at the burlesque of a fashionable hostess, but there is reverence in the laughter. Her directives on the acceptable and the proper are not empirical observations on the state of fashion; they are the utterances of a lawgiver, endowed with all but divine afflatus. Her response to Jack's Belgrave Square address is typical:

> LADY BRACKNELL The unfashionable side. However, that could easily be altered.
> JACK Do you mean the fashion or the side, Lady Bracknell?
> LADY BRACKNELL Both if necessary, I presume.

In contrast to the characters of farce who are imprisoned by manners, Lady Bracknell makes manners, and all the trivia of fashion, the building material of a world in which her will is law. She obtains freedom through manners, and she is powerful because she can impose her world on others.

Miss Prism and Dr Chasuble are funny because they fail to impose their worlds on others, and in failing weakly parody the central characters. Their trouble is that they do not realise what they are doing and think that their rules and theories represent a real, substantial, unchanging world. Dr Chasuble calls Miss Prism Egeria (an appellation much better suited to Lady Bracknell), but though she enunciates laws and definitions, they are tamely borrowed, not her own. Her paradoxes are amusing, not because they represent an attempt through wit to impose order on confusion, contradiction and human folly, but because they indicate an unawareness of these things. Indeed, she does not realise that they are paradoxes. The audience laughs at her, not with her, when she describes her novel thus: 'The good ended happily, and the bad unhappily. That is what Fiction means.' Clearly she is a fit partner for Dr Chasuble, who is thoroughly insensitive to the present moment (he is always misinterpreting the situation) and given to forcing an all-purpose moral onto any situation. His famous sermon is an example: 'My sermon on the meaning of the manna in the wilderness can be adapted to almost any occasion, joyful, or, as in the present case, distressing. I have preached it at harvest celebrations, christenings, confirmations, on days of humiliation and festal days.' Both Miss Prism's novel and Dr Chasuble's sermon, it is clear, recommend an ordered picture of the world, which excludes the sense of absurdity behind order, central to Wilde's vision: a sense that *The Importance of Being Earnest*, in its entirety, practically demonstrates.

It is beyond the scope of this essay to fit the suggested interpretation of the play into the general scheme of Wilde's ideas, but it is not difficult to see how it may be reconciled with Wilde's views on art, individuality, morality, crime, politics, and so on. What I have tried to do is to provide an interpretation fitting in with notions concerning farce, the drama of the absurd, and existentialist theories of identity, all of which have been fashionable in recent years. This can certainly help us like and understand the play, but I do not wish it to be thought that I am suggesting it be admired because it is 'relevant' (whatever that word might mean nowadays). It seems to me that it should be admired, not simply because it expresses a characteristically modern sensibility, nor even because it does so before its time, prophetically, but because it does so supremely well. It is possible to dislike the play, on grounds similar to those set out by Mary McCarthy, if only because it is possible to dislike the sort of sensibility it expresses. Its vehicle, the literary tradition to which I suggest the play belongs, is one that readily allows the writer to sink into self-indulgence. Some feel it permits little else nowadays. But I think that if we are prepared to accept the sensibility and the tradition as capable of producing excellence (if, in other words, we are prepared to adopt appropriate standards in judging the play), we are compelled to recognise the excellence of Wilde's play. To the contemplation of Nothingness, of the absurd, Wilde brings qualities of wit, intelligence and (not least) appetite for life, rarely found so abundantly in such a context. *The Importance of Being Earnest* is a great farce because it transcends the normal limitations of the form. Wilde used the form to make a play that is sparkling, but profound as well.

SOURCE: essay in *Modern Language Quarterly*, XXXV (1974), 173–86.

NOTES

[Reorganised and renumbered from the original – Ed.]

1. Mary McCarthy, *Sights and Spectacles, 1937–1958* (London, 1959), pp. 105–6.

2. William Empson, *The Structure of Complex Words* (London, 1951), p. 192.

3. See H.R. Trevor–Roper, *The Gentry, 1540–1640, Economic History Review Supplements*, 1 (London, 1953), pp. 52–3.

4. Gustave Flaubert, *Nil,* English trans. (London, 1966), p. 244.

5. Jean-Paul Sartre, *Being and Nothingness,* trans. Hazel E. Barnes (London, 1957), pp. 59–60.

6. *Love for Love*, in *Comedies by William Congreve*, ed. Bonamy Dobrée (London, 1925), pp. 310–11.

7. Oscar Wilde, 'The Decay of Lying'.

SELECT BIBLIOGRAPHY

EDITIONS

The standard edition of Wilde's complete works remains the 14–volume sequence edited by Robert Ross, published by Methuen in 1908. The fullest popular edition is: *The Works of Oscar Wilde,* edited by G.F. Maine (London, 1948), re-edited as *The Complete Works of Oscar Wilde* (1966), with an introduction by Vyvyan Holland (Wilde's younger son).

The most useful one-volume edition of the principal plays is in the Penguin collection (1954, with reprintings). The New Mermaid series now includes first-rate annotated editions of *Lady Windermere's Fan* and *The Importance of Being Earnest,* edited by Ian Small and by Russell Jackson respectively.

BIBLIOGRAPHIES and BIOGRAPHICAL MATERIAL

'Stuart Mason' (C.S. Millard), *Bibliography of Oscar Wilde* (London, [1914]); reprinted edition (London, 1967).
E.H. Mikhail, *Oscar Wilde: An Annotated Bibliography of Criticism* (London, 1978).

Rupert Hart-Davis (ed.), *The Letters of Oscar Wilde* (London, 1962).
H. Montgomery Hyde, *Oscar Wilde* (London, 1976).
E.H. Mikhail (ed.), *Oscar Wilde: Interviews and Recollections,* 2 vols (London, 1979).
Hesketh Pearson, *The Life of Oscar Wilde* (London, 1946); revised edition (London, 1954).

CRITICISM

In addition to the works excerpted in this Casebook, the following are recommended for further study:

(a) *Books*

Karl Beckson (ed.), *Oscar Wilde: The Critical Heritage* (London, 1970). Covers the period 1881–1927.
Alan Bird, *The Plays of Oscar Wilde* (London, 1977).
Philip K. Cohen, *The Moral Vision of Oscar Wilde* (Cranberry, N.J., 1979).
Richard Ellmann (ed.), *Oscar Wilde: A Collection of Critical Essays* (Englewood Cliffs, N.J., 1969).
St John Ervine, *Oscar Wilde: A Present Time Appraisal* (London, 1951).
Erika Meier, *Realism and Reality* (Bern, 1967), esp. pp. 158–95.
Edouard Roditi, *Oscar Wilde* (Norfolk, Conn., 1947).
Epifanio San Juan Jnr, *The Art of Oscar Wilde* (Princeton, N.J., 1967), esp. pp. 196–204.
Kevin Sullivan, *Oscar Wilde* (New York, 1972).
George Woodcock, *The Paradox of Oscar Wilde* (London and New York, 1949).

(b) *Articles and Essays*

W.H. Auden, 'An Improbable Life', *New Yorker* (9 March 1963), pp. 155–71.

James Agate, 'Wilde and the Theatre', *Masque*, 3 (1947), pp. 5–23.

Joseph W. Donohue Jnr, 'The First Production of *The Importance of Being Earnest*', in Kenneth Richards and Peter Thomson (eds), *Essays on Nineteenth-Century British Theatre* (London, 1971), pp. 125–43.

Richard Ellmann, 'Romantic Pantomime in Wilde', *Partisan Review*, XXX (1963), pp. 342–55.

B.H. Fussell, 'The Masks of Oscar Wilde', *Sewanee Review*, LXXX (1972), pp. 124–39.

Arthur Ganz, 'The Meaning of *The Importance of Being Earnest*', *Modern Drama*, VI (1963–64), pp. 42–52.

Alan Harris, 'Oscar Wilde as Playwright: A Centenary View', *Adelphi*, XXX (1954), pp. 212–40.

Robert J. Jordan, 'Satire and Fantasy in Wilde's *The Importance of Being Earnest*', *Ariel, I: 3 (1970), pp. 101–9.*

E.H. Mikhail, 'French Influences on Oscar Wilde's Comedies', Revue de Littérature Comparée, XLII (1968), pp. 220–33.

E.H. Mikhail, 'Self-Revelation in *An Ideal Husband*', *Modern Drama*, XI (1968–69), pp. 180–6.

Arthur H. Nethercot, 'Oscar Wilde and the Devil's Advocate', *PMLA*, LIX (1944), pp. 833–50.

Arthur H. Nethercot, 'Prunes and Miss Prism', *Modern Drama*, VI (1963–64), pp. 112–16.

E.B. Partridge, The Importance of Not Being Earnest', *Bucknell Review*, IX (1960–61), pp. 143–58.

Morse Peckham, 'What Did Lady Windermere Learn?', *College English*, XVIII (1956), pp. 11–14.

L.A. Poague, *'The Importance of Being Earnest:* The Texture of Wilde's Irony', *Modern Drama*, XVI (1973), pp. 251–7.

Otto Reinert, 'The Courtship Dance in *The Importance of Being Earnest*', *Modern Drama*, I (1958–59), pp. 256–7.

Dennis J. Spininger, 'Profiles and Principles: The Sense of the Absurd in *The Importance of Being Earnest*', *Papers on Language and Literature*, XII (1976), pp. 49–72.

Geoffrey Stone, 'Serious Bunburyism: The Logic of *The Importance of Being Earnest*', *Essays in Criticism*, XXVI (1976), pp. 28–41.

Harold E. Toliver, 'Wilde and the Importance of "Sincere and Studied Triviality"', *Modern Drama*, 5 (1963), pp. 389–99.

Paul Wadleigh, 'Earnest at the St James's Theatre', *Quarterly Journal of Speech*, LIII (1966), pp. 58–62.

James M. Ware, 'Algernon's Appetite: Oscar Wilde's Hero as Restoration Dandy', *English Literature in Transition*, XIII (1970), pp. 17–26.

A.G. Woodward, 'Oscar Wilde', *English Studies in Africa*, II (1959), pp. 218–31.

NOTES ON CONTRIBUTORS

MAX BEERBOHM (1872–1956): dandy, wit and caricaturist; his original works include *Zuleika Dobson* (1911) and *Seven Men* (1919). He was dramatic critic of the *Saturday Review* from 1899 to 1910.

ERIC BENTLEY (b. 1916): Cornell Professor of Theatre in the State University of New York at Buffalo, and previously (1954–69) Brander Matthews Professor of Dramatic Literature in Columbia University. His books include *What is Theatre?* (1956) and *The Life of the Drama* (1964); he is also a celebrated translator and theatre director.

JOHN DRINKWATER (1882–1937): poet and playwright, he was for many years associated with the Birmingham Repertory Theatre. Among his plays are *Abraham Lincoln* (1918), *Oliver Cromwell* (1921) and *Bird in Hand* (1927).

ASHLEY DUKES (1885–1959): critic and playwright, best known for his management of the Mercury Theatre, London in the 1930s, where many foreign and *avant-garde* plays were presented. His own best play is *The Man with a Load of Mischief* (1924).

A.E. DYSON: Reader in English in the University of East Anglia, and co-editor of the *Critical Quarterly*. His publications include *The Crazy Fabric* (1965), *The Inimitable Dickens* (1970), *Between Two Worlds* (1972), *Masterful Images*, with Julian Lovelock (1976) and *Yeats, Eliot and R.S. Thomas* (1981). He has also contributed volumes to the Casebook series of which he is the General Editor.

RICHARD FOSTER: Professor of English at Macalaster College, St Paul, Minnesota since 1968. His publications include *The New Romantics* (1962).

ARTHUR GANZ: Associate Professor of English, City College, New York; author of articles on Pinter, Shaw and Giraudoux, editor of a volume of studies on Pinter, and co-editor of *A Dictionary of Literary Terms* (1975).

IAN GREGOR: Professor of Modern English Literature in the University of Kent at Canterbury. His publications include *The Moral and the Story*, with Brian Nicholas (1962) and *The Great Web* (1974), a study of Thomas Hardy's novels.

J.T. GREIN (1862–1935): Dutch in origin, he took British nationality; founding the Independent Theatre Club in London in 1891 in order to stage performances of uncommercial plays of artistic merit, his productions included Shaw's *Widowers' Houses* (1892). He reviewed for a number of the leading journals of his day.

ST JOHN HANKIN (1869–1909): a prominent Edwardian playwright influenced by both Wilde and Shaw; his best-known plays are *The Return of the Prodigal* (1905) and *The Cassilis Engagement* (1907).

ARCHIBALD HENDERSON (1877–1963): American professor of mathematics whose principal leisure interest was drama; he wrote the authorised life of Bernard Shaw and enjoyed an extensive correspondence with him.

P.P. HOWE (1886–1944): publisher and writer, he was the author of books on the repertory theatre movement and on J.M. Synge. He wrote the standard life of William Hazlitt (1922) and edited his collected writings.

'LEONARD CRESSWELL INGLEBY': pseudonym of Cyril Arthur Edward Ranger Gull (1876–1923), a journalist and prolific author of adventure and mystery novels under such pen-names as 'Guy Thorne'. His *Oscar Wilde: Some Reminiscences* appeared in 1912.

C.E. MONTAGUE (1867–1928): essayist, literary critic and reviewer on *The Manchester Guardian* for most of his working life. His *Disenchantment* (1922) describes his experiences serving in the First World War; he also published short stories, essays and *Rough Justice* (1923), a novel.

CHRISTOPHER NASSAAR: awarded his doctorate at the University of Wisconsin, he currently lectures in English in the University of Beirut, Lebanon.

VINCENT O'SULLIVAN (1868–1940): Irish-American writer spending most of his life in France. In 1897 he befriended Wilde and paid for his visit to Naples; his *Aspects of Wilde* (1936) contains many fascinating sidelights on its subject.

DAVID PARKER: after university studies at Nottingham and Sheffield, he lectured for some years in the University of Malaya; he is now Curator of the Dickens House Museum, Doughty Street, London.

ARTHUR RANSOME (1884–1967): though now known almost exclusively for his children's books – notably the series begun with *Swallows and Amazons* (1930) – he was earlier noted for his political journalism and books of travel, especially in Russia, and for his literary criticism.

OTTO REINERT: Professor of Drama and Comparative Literature in the University of Washington, Seattle, since 1972; his publications include articles on Restoration and eighteenth-century drama and on plays of the modern period, and an edited collection of essays on Strindberg.

RODNEY SHEWAN: published his *Oscar Wilde: Art and Egotism* in 1977.

JOHN RUSSELL TAYLOR: author and journalist; his work includes books on the cinema, the post-war British theatre, and Art Nouveau. His *Anger and After* was published in 1962. For several years the film critic of *The Times*, he now contributes frequently to it reviews of art exhibitions and commentary on the visual arts.

A.B. WALKLEY (1855–1926): drama critic for a number of journals, including the *Speaker*, the *National Observer*, the *Star* and (1900–26) *The Times*; he published many of his reviews in volume form. Shaw dedicated *Man and Superman* to him, and he appears as Mr Trotter in *Fanny's First Play*.

INDEX

Figures in **bold type** refer to main entries in the Selection. Wilde's plays are listed separately; for his non-dramatic works, see under 'Wilde, Oscar'.